WHAT'S FAITH GOT TO DO WITH IT?

WHAT'S FAITH GOT TO DO WITH IT?

Black Bodies/Christian Souls

Kelly Brown Douglas

ORBIS BOOKS

Maryknoll, New York 10545

Founded in 1970, Orbis Books endeavors to publish works that enlighten the mind, nourish the spirit, and challenge the conscience. The publishing arm of the Maryknoll Fathers and Brothers, Orbis seeks to explore the global dimensions of the Christian faith and mission, to invite dialogue with diverse cultures and religious traditions, and to serve the cause of reconciliation and peace. The books published reflect the views of their authors and do not represent the official position of the Maryknoll Society. To learn more about Maryknoll and Orbis Books, please visit our website at www.maryknoll.org.

Published by Orbis Books, Maryknoll, NY 10545-0308.

Manufactured in the United States of America

Library of Congress Cataloging-in-Publication Data

Douglas, Kelly Brown.
    What's faith got to do with it? : Black bodies / Christian souls / Kelly Brown Douglas.
        p. cm.
    Includes bibliographical references (p.   ) and index.
    ISBN 13 : 978-1-57075-609-2 (pbk.)
    1. African Americans—Religion.   2. Racism—Religions aspects—Christianity—History.   3. Body, Human—Religious aspects—Christianity—History of doctrines.   4. Platonists.   I. Title.
    BR563.N4D68 2005
    270'.089'96—dc22   2005009223

To James H. Cone and David O. Woodyard,
true mentors and friends
who have never let me settle for anything
less than my own theological voice

Contents

Part I
What Is It about Christianity?

Part II
What Is It about Black Faith?

Acknowledgments

EVEN THOUGH WRITING is a solitary task, it cannot be done without the encouragement and support of others. There are many persons, far too numerous to mention individually, who did or said just the right thing at just the right time to inspire and sustain me during this writing project. To each and every one of them I am most grateful. There are those, however, who gave to me in ways that deserve special mention.

This project would not have come to fruition without the support of Orbis Books. I especially thank Robert Ellsberg, who not only shepherded this project through but also helped me to strengthen my theological arguments.

I am thankful for the dialogues with students and faculty at Goucher College. These dialogues helped me to clarify my own thinking. I am particularly grateful to two former students, Gabrielle Rivera and Isaac Lawson, whose compelling questions and perceptive insights presented me with enriching theological challenges.

I am most appreciative of those who not only inspired this work through their own theological witness and commitment, but also provided me with the forums to share my ideas and took the time to thoughtfully engage my work. I especially thank Marvin Ellison, Dwight Hopkins, Mary Hunt, Letty Russell, Linda Thomas, and Emilie Townes.

There are no two persons who have been more supportive of and giving to this project than my colleagues and brothers Angelo Robinson and Ronald Hopson. Words are not enough to express my gratitude to them for painstakingly reading through several drafts of this work and most of all for always being there with whatever it was I needed when this journey got particularly tough. Thanks guys!

Above all, I thank my life partner, Lamont, and my son, Desmond. They make each and every day a joyous and loving day. Without their patience, love, and understanding I could have not completed this work.

Introduction

THIS BOOK BEGAN with the dogged questioning of one particularly gifted student, Gabrielle. Gabrielle was raised in a profoundly religious Latino household. Her parents were devout evangelical Christians. She had attended Catholic schools. Yet, when she came to college she was still searching for her own religious voice. She was looking for a way to express her spirituality that embraced who she was: a young woman discovering the richness of her culture and passionately committed to human justice. In her search she took several of my religion classes, in which we often discussed the role of religion in the struggle for justice. One day, as Gabrielle reflected on Christianity's relationship to issues of race, gender, and sexual justice, she very pointedly asked me why I am a Christian. "How could you, a black woman, possibly be Christian," she asked, "when Christianity so often contributes to your oppression as a black and as a female?" Gabrielle's question immediately reminded me of Malcolm X's sharp attack on black Christians decades before. He too wanted to know how black people could be Christian when Christianity had been used to keep them enslaved. Malcolm X did not understand the logic of a people adopting the religion of their oppressors, and neither did Gabrielle. She was as impatient for an answer as Malcolm X no doubt was. And so, I answered her.

I replied that I am a Christian because my grandmothers were, and it was their Christian faith that helped them to survive the harsh realities of what it meant for them to be poor black women in America. I went on to tell Gabrielle that my grandmothers were Christian because their mothers and grandmothers were Christian. Indeed, it was a Christian faith that allowed their mothers and grandmothers to survive the brutality of the slavery into which they were born. I am Christian, I elaborated, because it was the

God of Jesus Christ that my enslaved forebears witnessed to. It was this God about whom they testified as being with them in their suffering, providing for them in their need, affirming their humanity, and eventually setting them free. I am Christian because my grandmothers, who knew not the slavery of their mothers and grandmothers, were certain that it was the God of Jesus Christ who had "brought them a mighty long way" into freedom.

My response, however, was not enough for Gabrielle. While she appreciated the power of black faith and the tenacity of the faith tradition, she remained unsatisfied. Eventually she, like Malcolm X surely would have done, pressed her question further. "Regardless," she said, "of the persistence of black faith, how come black people adopted the religion of their oppressors? That doesn't make sense to me." I answered this question by beginning with the keen observations of Gayraud Wilmore: "From the beginning the religion of the descendants of the Africans who were brought to the Western world as slaves has been something less and something more than what is generally regarded as Christianity."[1] I went on to explain that the Christianity of the enslaved was quite different from that of their enslavers, and indeed served as a critique of slaveholding Christianity. Perhaps given their African religious heritage, along with their oppressed reality, the enslaved—I said—were able to discern that the God of Jesus Christ was a God of justice, freedom, and love. In fact, I concluded, black Christianity was a witness to the hypocrisy of white Christianity.

But still Gabrielle persisted. She pronounced at one time, "Isn't there something wrong with a religion that can be continually used to oppress people?" It was at this point that I heard the depth of her question. It would not be enough for me to tell her that many religions have been used to oppress people, especially when those religions fall into the wrong hands. For me to make a distinction between a particular religion and the people who practice it would not have addressed the complexity of her concern. She wanted to know something more fundamental about Christianity itself. She wanted to know if there was an inherent theological flaw in Christianity that made it vulnerable to cruel manipulation. This was the very question asked by post-Christian feminist Mary Daly decades before as she made her journey beyond Christianity. Daly rhetorically queried that, if Christianity has been used this way (i.e., to oppress women) and has had a long history of being used this way, is there not something wrong with Christianity itself.[2] Was there something wrong with Christianity itself?

Gabrielle's question coincided with my own concern to better understand the injustice perpetuated within the black church community, particularly in regard to gay and lesbian persons. Beyond understanding the historical-cultural context that helps to create black church homophobia, perhaps there is something endemic to Christianity itself that is inclined toward inequity and the disregard for certain human bodies. To reiterate, what is it about Christianity that lends itself to being used in oppressive ways? This is what Gabrielle wanted to know and it was this question that prompted this book. Gabrielle's question in fact compelled me to assess theologically the feasibility of the black Christian tradition.

What is it about Christianity that has allowed it to be both a bane and a blessing for black people? Clearly it has played a significant sanctioning role in the white assault on the black body. Christianity has conspired with white supremacy not simply in the horror of enslaving black people but also in the odious deed of lynching them. It has provided theological legitimation for the overall dehumanizing denigration of black bodies. Yet it has also sustained black people in their struggle against white dehumanization. It has provided them with the strength and courage to resist white assaults on their bodies. Paradoxically then, Christianity has both fueled white racist fury and nurtured black faith. How is this possible? Is there something inherently theologically problematic about Christianity that makes it vulnerable to being used in deleterious ways and thus lethal in conjunction with whiteness? At the same time, is there something theologically constitutive of Christianity that critiques such evil use, thus making it appealing to oppressed peoples and thereby empowering in relation to blackness? Specifically, what is it about Christianity that allows it to conspire with white racism and at the same time to affirm black people? Furthermore, is there something about Christianity when in conjunction with blackness that foments a black faith tradition that disrespects certain black bodies? This book represents my efforts to respond to these questions in both a general and a more personal way.

This book has several interrelated objectives: (1) to examine the theological impulses inherent to Christianity that make it compatible with white supremacist ideology and practices; (2) to discern the theological disposition of Christianity that has generated a potent black faith tradition; (3) to explore the implications of this investigation for the black faith community in its responses to particular black bodies; (4) to provide the theological tools for black church people to affirm their Christian identity without adopting the theological paradigms that have supported the white attack on their black bodies and other bodies; (5) and to answer Gabrielle's initial question to me, "how can I, a black female, be a Christian." In this book I do not aim to provide conclusive answers to the complicated issues surrounding Christianity in general, and the black faith tradition in particular, when it comes to either's complicity in human oppression. Rather, it is my intention to provoke more thorough critical theological discourse on the efficacy of a black Christian tradition as well as the black faith community's role in the demoralizing treatment of certain human bodies within the black church community itself. Let us now look at how this book will proceed.

Part 1: What Is It about Christianity?

In an effort to appreciate the complexity of Christianity's role in the white attack on the black body as well as its continued role in issues of racial, gender, and sexual injustice, this book begins with an exploration of problematic alliances made during Christianity's theologically formative years. Part 1 builds on the familiar claims that it has been Christianity's alliance with Platonic dualism and power that has created an oppressive Christian tradition. While affirming the correctness of these claims, this part further suggests what it is about Christianity that makes such alliances problematic. The premise of part 1 is that these alliances exploit various aspects of Christianity's theological core in such a way as to allow for Christianity's compatibility with white supremacists' notions and activity. Part 1 provides the theologically conceptual foundation for understanding both Christianity's compatibility with white ideology and its allure to black people.

While lynching is not the focus of this study, throughout this book the white lynching of black bodies provides the historical-cultural paradigm for accessing the complexity of Christianity's complicity in attacking black bodies. Part 1 consists of three chapters.

Chapter 1: A Platonized Tradition

The premise of chapter 1 is that Christianity's alliance with Platonic/Stoic thought was the primary troubling alliance that laid the foundation for a terrorizing Christian legacy in relation to black bodies. The early Christian apologetic tradition is highlighted as signaling the fusion made between Christian thought and Platonic/Stoic philosophy. Chapter 1 identifies a *closed monotheism* and *christological paradox* as two problematic aspects of Christianity's theological core that made both Platonic and Stoic thought appealing. The underside of these theological characteristics is examined as they come into contact with Platonic/Stoic thought. This chapter expressly argues that Platonic and Stoic thought coalesced with Christianity's theological core to establish an influential Christian tradition, identified as *platonized* Christianity, which advanced antagonistic dualistic paradigms and a demonization of the flesh/body. Platonized Christianity is implicated in the attack against the black body.

Chapter 2: Christianity and Power

The premise of chapter 2 is that Christianity's alliance with social/political power is the crucial theologically corruptive alliance. This chapter suggests that Christianity's link with power had a theologically transformative impact upon an influential Christian tradition—namely, platonized Christianity—thus making Christianity's complicity in acts such as lynching not only possible but also theologically sustainable. Particular and focused attention is given to the problematic of Christianity's central symbol, the cross, when invested with social/political power. René Girard's theory of sacrifice is utilized to discern the implications of the Christian cross in the white attack on the black body. In the end, this chapter maintains that given Christianity's theological core—that is, closed monotheism, christological paradox, and crucifying cross—an alliance with social/political power invariably sets in motion a legacy of Christian tyranny in relation to certain human bodies.

Chapter 3: A Heretical Tradition

Chapter 3 identifies the platonized Christian tradition as heretical and Christianity's investment with social/political power as anti-Christ. While reiterating those aspects inherent to Christianity that make the connection with Platonic/Stoic thought and power both possible and problematic, this chapter also specifies those theological characteristics of Christianity that defy such connections. Focused attention is given to the incarnation and the crucifixion/resurrection event. This chapter argues that these two defining aspects of Christianity contest the inclination toward dominating power and body devaluation characteristic of a platonized Christian tradition. Special attention is given to the implications of the "classical" atonement tradition within the black faith tradition. This chapter ultimately clarifies that the influential Christian tradition that has sustained terror against black bodies is grounded in a theological heresy and a christological anathema.

Part 2: What Is It about Black Faith?

Part 2 moves us from a theologically conceptual analysis of Christianity's complicity in the white attack of the black body to a more theologically concrete exploration of its participation in this attack. This part looks specifically at the complex role that platonized Christianity plays in the black faith tradition. In so doing, it moves beyond the obvious ways in which Christianity has sanctioned or justified the attack on the black body—that is, slavery—to the more dubious ways in which it has infected both the black psyche and spirituality, thus shaping black people's responses to their black bodies and the bodies of others. This section provides a theological alternative to the platonized view of the body in an effort to move the black church community beyond a theology that denigrates blackness. Part 2 consists of three chapters.

Chapter 4: Christian Theology and White Ideology

Chapter 4 explores the inevitable collusion between platonized Christianity and white cultural ideology. The Enlightenment metanarrative serves as the backdrop for understanding the development of platonized Christianity in relation to white culture. This chapter initially specifies the compatibility between the theological foundation of platonized Christianity and the ideological basis for white supremacy. It next argues that this inherent compatibility made the advent of religious racism in eighteenth- and nineteenth-century America almost certain. This chapter further explores how evangelical Protestantism provided ample apologia for the white racist treatment of black people by "everyday" white Christians. The Great Awakenings provide the historical-theological prism through which evangelical Protestantism is examined. In the end, chapter 4 maintains that "whiteness" and platonized Christianity create an unholy alliance for black people, thus calling into question the feasibility of a platonized black faith tradition.

Chapter 5: Black Bodies/White Souls

Chapter 5 examines the lethal interaction between white culture and platonized Christianity when it comes into contact with blackness. This chapter specifically explores, from the vantage point of the black faith tradition, both the positive and the negative impact that platonized Christianity has had on black lives.

The chapter first reveals how this tradition, again as it has been primarily transmitted through evangelical Protestantism, has affirmed black people in their blackness, nurtured a sense of divine worth and equality, and even saved black lives. It further shows, however, that this platonized tradition has also alienated black people from their very blackness and own black bodies. One of the central arguments of this chapter is that platonized Christianity in conjunction with white cultural ideology has compelled black women and men to adopt a *hyper-proper sexuality* to secure a "white" soul, thereby redeeming their black body. This chapter also examines how a platonized black faith tradition has interacted with patriarchal and heterosexist discourse to suborn denigrating disregard for the bodies of black women and dehumanizing treatment of nonheterosexuals (especially gay black men) within the black church community. James Baldwin's novel *Go Tell It on the Mountain* provides the primary resource for the arguments made throughout this chapter. Chapter 5 ultimately suggests the need to reevaluate the viability of a platonized faith for black men and women.

Chapter 6: Black Faith Reexamined

Chapter 6 provides a theological alternative to a platonized black faith tradition, one that is more compatible with blackness. The premise of this chapter is that with a firm appreciation for blackness, as expressed in the black faith tradition, the "true" nature of Christianity can flourish. This chapter specifically argues that even though a platonized theological tradition has had positive value for black people, it essentially defies the blackness of the black faith tradition. This chapter offers a twofold definition of blackness, derived from the black faith tradition, which entails both a particular historical-cultural identity and a moral commitment. Chapter 6 thus proposes that it is crucial for the black church community to reconnect to the blackness of its faith tradition. In making this claim chapter 6 identifies certain core theological themes of black faith that connote its blackness. The concluding portion of this chapter argues that it is in reclaiming its own nonplatonized black religious heritage, a heritage that precipitated the critique of whiteness, that the black church community will be able to truly free itself from a platonized Christian tradition that compels attacks against the black body. A womanist perspective provides the theological foundation for this critical assessment of the black faith tradition.

A Womanist's Postscript:
How Can I Be a Christian?

This concluding section finally answers the initial question put to me by Gabrielle, "How can I, a black woman, be a Christian?" My answer reflects the journey made throughout this book as well as the journey I have made over the last ten years in my efforts to better understand the faith of my grandmothers. In the end, it is that faith to which I hold myself accountable, for it is that faith that reflects the "truth" of Christianity.

Part I
What Is It about Christianity?

1

A Platonized Tradition

ON DECEMBER 7, 1899, the *New York World* newspaper described the crowd gathered for the lynching of twenty-year-old Richard Coleman this way:

Not one person in the crowd wore a mask. The leaders of the mob disdained the semblance of any disguise. Every act was done in the open. There was no secrecy. The population of the whole city and country for miles around, *church men and church women,* professional and business men of eminence, people of distinguished ancestry, formed the mob, and not a single regret for the horrible tragedy can be heard to-night from one end of the town to the other.[1]

On June 24, 1903, the *Chicago Record-Herald* reported:

The Rev. Robert A. Elwood, pastor of the Olivet Presbyterian church, preached a sensational sermon on the probable lynching of [George] White last Sunday evening. The text of the sermon was widely distributed and this was believed today to have had much influence in the lynching of White which followed.

Rev. Elwood took his text from Corinthians V., 13: "Therefore put way from among ourselves that wicked person. . . ."

"And honorable judges, if you do not hear and heed these appeals, and that prisoner should be taken out and lynched, then let me say to you with a full realization of the responsibility of my words, even as Nathan said to King David of old,

Mark - dmoniac
scapegoating

3

after his soldiers had killed Uriah, 'Thou art the man,' so I would say to you. The responsibility for lynching would be yours for delaying the execution of the law.[2]

Lynching reflects the unmitigated evil of white racist terror perpetrated on black bodies. It was one of the most violently gruesome weapons used by white society to maintain power over black men and women, particularly during the Reconstruction and post-Reconstruction South. Despite the fact that lynching was primarily a Southern phenomenon, its message was universal: no longer the property of white people, black life had little or no value in white society, apart from providing "strange fruit to swing from Southern trees." Lynchings, especially spectacle lynching, made clear that there was no "protected space" for black people in a white racist society.

While the lynchers were most often protected from prosecution for their vile assaults by being regarded as "persons unknown," such anonymity was only a legal ruse. The lynchers—those who had an actual hand in the crime and those who were a part of the mob of spectators—were known, if not specifically, at least in the main. W. E. B. Du Bois observed that lynchings were often initiated by a "nucleus of ordinary men."[3] To be sure, the lynch crowds were made up of "good" men and women of white society, including "good" Christian men and women. As it happens, most of the lynchings took place in one of the most Christianized parts of the United States, the South (more will be made of this connection later). Struck by this fact, one 1899 editorialist urged the community to be "aghast," as he was especially appalled that a bastion of Christianity, a small Georgian town, was the scene of the particularly horrid lynching of Sam Hose.[4] He wrote:

The nation and the whole civilized world must stand aghast at the revelation. A civilized community numbering thousands, at the drop of a hat, throws off the restraints and effects of many centuries of progress and stands forth in naked savagery of the primitive man. Men and women cheer and express feelings of triumph and joy as the victim is hurried on to the stake to make a Sunday holiday in one of the most orthodox religious communities in the United States. They cut off his ears, his fingers and other members of the body, and strip him and pour oil upon him while the spectators crowd desperately for positions of advantage in the great work of torture and death.[5]

Further indication of the Christian involvement in lynchings was the fact, as reflected in the Hose lynching, that many of these violent spectacles of murderous rampage on black bodies took place on Sunday afternoons—as if to have a picnic of black flesh after church.[6] Indeed, the Hose lynching took place after church. The reality of significant Christian participation in, if not instigation and sanction of, a crime as odious as lynching brings us to the point of this chapter.

Lynching in and of itself is not the focus of this chapter or book. Lynching is a complex phenomenon of racial hatred that demands its own intense research. However, inasmuch as lynching reveals the utter evil of white terror against black bodies, it also reflects the magnitude and complexity of the problem when considering the Christian tradition in relation to black men and women. Lynching brings the gravity of Christianity's connection to black oppression into sharp focus. If Christianity can be mixed up in a deed as base as lynching, then what does that suggest about the Christian religion in general?

Is there something about Christianity itself that permits "church men and church women" to participate in wicked attacks against black bodies with relative religious impunity? Is there something in Christian theology that provides a pastor with the temerity to initiate the extralegal slaughter of a black man? How is it that Christianity has indeed forged a legacy that tolerates acts as depraved as lynching? Why is Christianity so often implicated in vicious crimes of racial, gender, and sexual hatred? Is there something intrinsic to Christianity that makes its complicity in assailing certain human bodies not simply possible but perhaps highly probable?

These questions do not represent new challenges to Christianity. Given the history of Christian involvement in various forms of human oppression, many persons have pondered the essential character of the Christian faith. They have searched for ways to explain Christianity's ignoble tradition, a tradition not reserved for just black bodies. Again, from its earliest beginnings Christianity has been involved in vile attacks against various human bodies, its earliest victims being perhaps the Jewish community. The challenge is to understand the reasons for Christianity's dishonorable history. Some have blamed the apostle Paul for perverting Jesus' message to such an extent that it could be so easily used for inhumane purposes. Sociologist Orlando Patterson goes so far as to call Paul's interpretation of Christianity "hegemonic religious minstrelsy" because of the way Pauline texts have been used to support white oppression of black bodies. He notes, as pointed out above, that the lynching phenomenon was most prevalent in an area of the United States highly influenced by Pauline religiosity.[7]

Other critics of Christian history have viewed Constantine's conversion as a critical foreboding twist in the Christian story. In his award-winning book *Constantine's Sword*, James Carroll comments that after Constantine's conversion "the [Christian] Church became an entity so different from what had preceded it as to be almost unrecognizable."[8] He specifically argues that Christians were no longer the powerless persecuted ones, but now with the empire on their side, they were able to become powerful persecutors—especially of Jews.

Still others have identified Christianity's christological center as the source of its complicity in systems and structures of oppression. Feminist theologian Carter Heyward indicts the conceptualization of Jesus as Christ as being pivotal in the production of "wrong" relationality. No matter how one interprets the relationship between Jesus' divinity and Jesus' humanity, Heyward argues that humanity and divinity are inevitably construed in oppositional relationality. The classical christological confession established at Chalcedon in 451 that confirmed Jesus as at once perfectly human and perfectly divine invariably projects, Heyward claims, a "dualistic epistemology." This dualistic way of knowing subsequently lends itself to "wrong relations" between "ourselves, the world, or God."[9]

That Christianity has a dubious history in regard to matters of human oppression is undisputed. That it has often supported the violent denigration of human bodies, especially black bodies, is also evident. Not as clear, however, are the reasons for Christianity's historical "underside." Multiple social, cultural, and theological factors have all contributed to this disreputable history. Essentially, Christianity's complicity in human oppression *is* a complicated matter.

Yet, even while appreciating these complexities, certain theological claims and philosophical influences can be isolated as playing a substantial role in producing an oppressive Christian legacy. This chapter will attempt to specify the theological/ideological foundation of Christianity's unjust legacy. Before doing so, however, certain underlying assumptions must be recognized. The first has to do with the comprehensive nature of Christianity's involvement in acts such as lynching.

The depth of Christianity's involvement in human oppression is not measured simply by direct Christian participation in injustice. To be sure, particular Christians' actions may have little or nothing to do with their Christian faith. Their crimes against certain human beings may reflect their peculiar appetite for human brutality along with other social and political factors. The fact that they are Christian may be only incidental to their involvement in barbarism. Even with that said, however, the preponderance of Christian involvement in human oppression raises the question of how Christianity itself contributes to such a tradition of inhumane terror.

A significant assumption of this book is that Christianity's involvement in human injustice is not always as obvious as Christians directly calling on their faith to support their crimes against humanity. Christianity's collusion with injustice is more insidious. In order to grasp the subtle nature of Christianity's complicity with human oppression one must have an understanding of discursive power. The late French philosopher Michel Foucault is helpful in this regard.[10]

Foucault argues that unjust social relationality is not effectively sustained solely, if at all, through the use of brutal force. He stresses that power, specifically inequitable power, is not coercive or repressive. Rather, it is disciplinary and productive. Power's disciplinary character exercises certain constraints over the body and the collective consciences of individuals. It compels people to behave in certain ways in relation to themselves and others. Power's disciplinary aspect obliges persons to adhere to certain societal and personal standards particularly as it regards people's views of their own status and role in society as well as their interactions with and treatment of others.

In order for power's disciplinary character to be actualized, however, people must be made aware of the rules and regulations of society. At the same time, they have to believe that such rules and regulations make sense. That is, they must have some "legitimate" reasons for behaving in a certain manner in regard to both themselves and others. Essential to power's actualization, therefore, is its productive character.

Power's productive character begins with a "will to knowledge." That is, power itself generates the kind of knowledge it needs to be sustained. It enlists various communities of intelligence, such as the scientific community, to provide the knowledge base to legitimize the social, political, and institutional constructions of power. For instance, in order to support claims of black inferiority, white racist power relied on the scientific community. This community provided evidence of presumably innate black inferiority through specious fields of study such as phrenology and physiognomy. Such scientific research was the foundation for eighteenth-century scientific racism, which will be discussed later in this book. Essentially, the scientific community provided the "objective" knowledge needed to support white racist power. The knowledge "willed" by power is then carefully disseminated through public discourse through schools, media, and various social institutions. Discourse is therefore critical to the actualization of power. In other words, discursive power fuels and sustains social, political, and even ecclesiastical power. It is through discourse that people not only learn to behave in a certain manner but are also socialized into supporting the reality of unjust power. Foucault puts it simply, "Discourse transmits and produces power. It reinforces it."[11]

It is in understanding the nature and function of discursive power that we can begin to understand Christianity's profound involvement in human oppression. Christian theology is an essential component of discursive power. It can provide, and has in fact provided, religious legitimation for inequitable social relationships. Essentially, Christianity has provided a "sacred canopy" for certain inequitable power relations. It has done this both explicitly and implicitly. Christianity's explicit involvement is seen, for instance, with the advent of religious racism in the eighteenth century when various Christian "scholars" provided biblical and theological knowledge to support black people's nonhuman or inferior status.[12] In this regard, Christian thinkers provided the knowledge "willed" by white racist power.

But perhaps Christianity's more dangerous involvement in human oppression is implicit. That is, the Christian theological tradition has contributed to a certain *collective theological consciousness* that allows for, if not sanctions, unrelenting oppression of various human beings. What the most notable and influential Christian theological tradition both emphasizes and does not emphasize provides a theological framework for Christian men and women to participate in attacks as vile as lynching. This theological tradition is disseminated most prominently in Christian institutions through the hymns people sing, the creeds they recite, and/or the sermons they hear. Thus, the prevailing premise of this book is that an influential Christian theological tradition plays a significant role in sustaining unjust power especially as it provides the theological dimension of discursive power. This leads us to the primary assumption of this particular chapter.

The underlying assumption of chapter 1 is that the theological groundwork for a "terrorizing" Christian tradition, one that would permit if not support lynching, was established during Christianity's formative years. This chapter expressly argues that various elements of Platonic and Stoic thought coalesced with significant aspects of Christianity's theological core to provide a theoretical basis for Christian participation in human oppression, particularly black oppression. The chapter will proceed by identifying both the essential theological affirmations and the philo-

sophical ideas that interacted to create a troubling theo-ideological foundation. The chapter will conclude by looking at the unsettling Christian tradition—one that explicitly and implicitly
supports human oppression—invariably set into motion by this
troubling foundation. Chapter 1 thus provides the essential conceptual framework for discerning the viability of Christianity itself
for black women and men. In so doing, it is the first step toward
answering the driving question, "How am I, a black female, a
Christian?" Let us now turn to Christianity's potentially "problematic" theological core.

A Problematic Theological Core

A Closed Monotheism

Christianity was cultivated in a first-century Greco-Roman world.
This world was filled with religious and philosophical movements
attempting to discern the nature of the universe and humanity's
place within it. Many of these movements assumed a multiplicity
of divine beings and/or forces beyond the human realm. These
forces were thought to be responsible for the providence and
machinations of earthly existence. There was, for instance, the
Egyptian "mystery" religion of the mother goddess Isis and her
consort Osiris that attempted to explain—among other things—
fertility. The Isis cult was one of many "mystery" religions—such
as Serapis, Cybele, and Mithras—that existed in the first-century
world. A good number of these religions were syncretistic and
thereby borrowed liberally from one another.

There were also various philosophical schools of thought, such
as the popular Platonism. Platonism suggested a world of forms
independent of the "sensible" world. Platonists argued that this
world of forms could not be apprehended by the sense perceptions
but could only be accessed by reason (more will be said about this
later). While popular, Platonism was again just one of the many
philosophical schools of thought present in Greco-Roman society.

Although these various religions and philosophies were typically
polytheistic, they had monistic impulses. One supreme source was

often considered behind the many gods of the various mystery religions. [These religions usually admitted a divine unity behind the practical plurality of divine beings.] Such was also the case for Plato's world of forms. Thus, while the society into which Christianity entered was polytheistic—that is one that embraced a variety of gods—the culture of which Christianity was a part was inclined toward monism. The people of that time were becoming more and more attracted to monistic interpretations of reality, at least on a conceptual, if not practical, level.[13] That is, they affirmed that in supernatural reality there was perhaps one supreme unifying being, even as they continued to recognize the workings of various divine beings within the earthly realm. Historian Henry Chadwick speculates that this early "striving toward monotheism"[14] perhaps signaled a need for unity, especially religious unity, in the Greco-Roman empire. Whatever the case may be, because of the monistic sentiments present within the culture, the emergence of a monotheistic religion like Christianity was not alarming or immediately seen as threatening to the Greco-Roman polytheistic world. What caused the civil authorities to view Christianity with suspicion was the manner in which Christianity defined its monotheism and hence the way in which Christians related to the rest of the polytheistic world. It is here that we begin to see the potential for problems.

Christianity, reflective of its roots as a Jewish sect, is grounded in a strict monotheism. This particular type of monotheism is grounded in the Jewish concept of election. Jewish faith begins with the belief that the one God, through the covenant made with Abraham, elected Israel to be a great nation and to show forth the promises of God throughout the world.[15] This covenant was reinforced when God freed the Israelites from Egyptian bondage. The people of Israel henceforth considered themselves God's "chosen people." As such they were obligated to be loyal only to the God of Abraham and not to consort with any other people and their gods. The Mosaic commandment made it clear: "I am the Lord your God, who brought you out of Egypt, out of the land of slavery. You shall have no other gods before me" (Gen. 20:2-3).[16] Also made clear in the election of Israel was the fact that the God of

Abraham was the one true God. All other gods were considered "false" and reflections of evil realities. Such a claim was presumably consistent with the prophet Isaiah's report of God saying, "I am the first and I am the last; apart from me there is no God" (Isa. 44:6). Furthermore, as other gods were considered evil, so too were the followers of those gods. Thus, Israelites considered themselves an elect people blessed by the one true God; they considered all other peoples—that is, foreigners—the nonelect.

When Christianity emerged as a sect within this Jewish faith tradition, it did not abandon the notions of God's elect and of there being only one true God. Rather, it redefined who the elect were and reidentified the true God. For Christians, the elect were those who were devoted to the God of Jesus Christ. Christians began to see themselves as the "new Israel," if not the "true Israel."[17] Christians considered their God to be the "most true God."[18] Support for this claim could ostensibly be found in the words of Jesus such as those reported in the Gospel of John, "I am the way and the truth and the life. No one comes to the Father except through me" (John 14:6). In this regard Christianity went beyond the strict monotheism of its Jewish heritage and projected a *closed* monotheism. Consistent with its Jewish heritage, Christianity demanded total devotion to its God. No other gods were to be tolerated, let alone worshiped by its devotees. But perhaps more unrelenting than their Jewish forebears, Christian thinkers argued that it was through *their* religion that "every *tongue* believing in God *was brought together*."[19] In the Christian mind, non-Christians were at best godless and at worst evil. Essentially, the Christian faith was not open to the notion that there was any avenue apart from Christianity for accessing divine truth. In fact, as we will soon see, Christianity's closed monotheism projected a closed universe. That is to say, it was believed that no other gods were tolerated within the universe itself. What this resulted in within the Christian tradition, again unlike the Jewish tradition from which Christianity emerged, was a zeal for evangelism. It was not enough for Christians to cling adamantly to their God. Instead, Christians also disavowed the gods of others.

Thus, one of Christianity's essential theological claims left it virtually unprepared to coexist peaceably with other religions. Christianity was fundamentally intolerant of them. It dismissed other gods as evil pagan realities and the followers of those gods as agents of evil. The closed monotheism of Christianity invariably projected a *sanctified polarization* of historical-cultural reality. Once more, to be Christian was to be of God, to be non-Christian was to be against God. As mentioned above, this sanctified polarization was based upon a corresponding polarization of the cosmos. Much of mainstream Christian thinking posited a worldview that presented the Christian God as one good, powerful, supernatural force opposed by numerous other evil supernatural forces. (Ironically, Christianity's closed monotheism virtually necessitated other divine beings as a way of explaining the presence of adherents to other beliefs, as well as the reality of evil.)[20] Needless to say, Christianity was unsuited for the polytheistic Greco-Roman world. It is not surprising, then, that Christians would soon be regarded as a menace to society and as enemies of the Roman government. The Christian refusal to acknowledge and pledge allegiance to the gods of the empire invited a stern governmental response, albeit the harsh persecution that Christians received albeit unwarranted. More to the point, however, the foundation for Christian persecution of others was established with this rigid type of monotheism.

To recapitulate, Christianity moved beyond a strict monotheism (one which demands that its adherents show strict allegiance to a particular God) and demanded a *closed* monotheism. This was a monotheism based on a "jealous" God—one who refuses to share its glory, its people, or its world with other gods. In this respect, Christianity can be interpreted as a religion closed to the possibility that there are other gods or forces that might reveal some measure of truth or goodness about the world to other peoples, namely, non-Christians. Christian monotheism is not a monism that allows for the possibility that "everything in the world might be known by somebody, yet not everything by the same knower . . . [or that] the wisest knower that exists may yet remain ignorant of much that is known to others."[21] Proponents of a closed monotheism insist that all that is to be known (that which is true and good) is reflected in their God, and only those who follow their God can possibly attain that knowledge (i.e., truth). Again, none except Christians are given any credit for possessing knowledge or truth, since other gods are considered "false" or evil beings. This type of monotheistic understanding has encouraged Christians not to be content simply with the worshiping of their one God, but also to denigrate the gods of others, thus attempting to persuade others to follow the Christian God or, worse yet, to torment non-Christians.

Early Christian literature often reflects the dangerous "religio-cultural" bias fostered by Christian monotheism. For instance, Gregory of Nyssa wrote that the gods of the "pagans" were born of "narrow intelligence" because the pagans mistook the wonders of nature as divine. He explained, "They did not bring their conception of the Deity to halt at any single one of the things they beheld, but deemed each thing they looked on in creation to be divine."[22] Pagan gods were also regularly portrayed in Christian literature as idols reflective of "idol mania." One early Christian letter put it sharply, "[Your idols] are without life or feeling or power of movement, all rotting away and decaying. These are the things you call gods, the things you serve."[23]

So, a closed monotheism is inherently antagonistic. It projects a polarized society and cosmos. In so doing, it fosters divisions between Christians and just about everybody else. It creates oppositional, *us versus them* relationships. Non-Christians are seen as outside of the truth. At best they are treated as unenlightened or misguided pagans in need of conversion; at worst they are thought of as stubbornly non-Christian and therefore witting enemies not only of Christianity but also of the truth. For again, the gods non-Christians espouse are considered false *daimones* (demons), and hence, cosmic adversaries to the "most true God."[24]

Essentially, the closed nature of Christian monotheism precludes an appreciation for religio-cultural difference. To be religiously different is to be wrong and misguided if not inhabited by evil beings. Religious scholar Elaine Pagels makes the point when she says of early Christianity:

Although many pagans had come to believe that all the powers of the universe are ultimately one, only Jews and Christians worshiped a single god and denounced all others as evil demons. Only Christians divided the supernatural world into two opposing camps, the one true God against swarms of demons; and none but Christians preached—and practiced—division on earth. By refusing to worship the gods, Christians were driving a wedge between themselves and all pagans.[25] *Essence of Qanon*

Pagels points to this divisive attitude in the writings of early Christian apologists such as Justin Martyr. Even though his writings on the "logos" might suggest a more open attitude toward other gods, Justin also succumbed to the bias of Christianity's closed monotheism.[26] In speaking of Christians who once followed other gods, Justin writes:

> out of every race we who once worshipped Dionysus the son of Semele and Apollo the son of Leto, who in their passion for men did things which it is disgraceful even to speak of, or who worshiped Persephone and Aphrodite . . . or Asclepius or some other of those who are called gods, now through Jesus Christ despise them, even at the cost of death. . . . We pity those who believe [such stories], for which we know the demons are responsible.[27]

The antagonistic/oppositional propensity that is natural to a closed monotheism portends a troubling reality. One can already begin to see from this single theological claim of Christianity the underpinnings of a terrorizing Christian tradition. While the strict monotheism of early Judaism initially led the Israelites to act aggressively against non-Israelite nations, characterizing these nations as evil, other factors were able to mitigate its responses to other faith traditions. Practically speaking, when Israel itself was politically weakened, its aggression toward other nations was abated. Though still strident about its strict monotheism, thus demanding of Jewish people utter loyalty to the God of Abraham,

a weakened Israel was not able practically to oppose other religious cultures. Perhaps more significantly, there was a strand of
Jewish thinking that perceived it as "wrong to insult the religious
feelings of others," and thereby proclaimed the necessity to be
kind to strangers.[28] Finally, as Jews began to incur social and political suffering, Jewish leaders became more invested in protecting
the rights of fellow Jews to practice their traditions than they were
concerned with repudiating the god of non-Jews.[29] In general, the
strict monotheism of Judaism has seemed more concerned with
the devotion of Jewish people to their religion than with the people of other faith traditions, unless those people impinged on Jewish faith. In this sense a strict monotheism does not necessarily
project intolerant behaviors toward other faith traditions as seems
natural to a closed monotheism. However, even though a closed
monotheism is likely to foster religio-cultural bias, it is not the
only contributing factor to Christianity's legacy of oppression. In
order, therefore, to understand Christianity's complex troubling
legacy one must also appreciate how other theological and philosophical factors coalesced with Christian monotheism. Let us
explore another pivotal theological factor.

A Christological Paradox

Christianity's distinctive claim is that Jesus, a first-century Jew
from Nazareth, is the Messiah. This claim was the basis for the first
Christians' break with Judaism. Non-Christian Jews did not
believe that Jesus was their nation's long-awaited Davidic Messiah.
This Christian messianic claim was a key factor in Christianity not
simply remaining a Jewish sect, but becoming an independent religious movement. The way in which Christianity has defined the
Messiah has played a significant role in Christianity's dubious history.

The Christian understanding of the Messiah is grounded in a
definite christological paradox that characterizes both Jesus' ontological (i.e., his being) and existential (i.e., his ministry) reality. To
confess Jesus as Christ/Messiah is to proclaim that he is God

incarnate—a perfect, embodied revelation of God. In Jesus, God is *en sarki*, that is, enfleshed. Ultimately, for Christians to confess that Jesus is Christ is for them to proclaim that two distinct natures come together in him: the divine and the human. The essence of Jesus' ontological reality is thus a dual nature.

The long early church debate spawned by the confession of Jesus as Christ is well documented. One significant issue of debate was concerned with how precisely two disparate natures could come together in one being. The fourth ecumenical council held at Chalcedon in 451 eventually resolved this issue by affirming that Jesus was both *fully human* and *fully divine*.[30] This council defended the reality of the incarnation as established at the first ecumenical council of Nicaea and clarified that neither incarnational nature corrupted the integrity of the other. The Chalcedonian definition explained:

> our Lord Jesus Christ is . . . truly God and truly man . . . made known in two natures without confusion, without change, without division, without separation, the difference of the natures being by no means removed because of the union, but the property of each being preserved.[31]

Important for our discussion are not the details of the protracted christological debate that led to Chalcedon, but rather the confessed messianic paradox that, in part, precipitated the debate: the paradox between divinity and humanity.[32] In the debate there was general consensus, as evident in the Chalcedon settlement, that divinity and humanity represented two different natures, regardless of whether nature was construed as a "collection of qualities," as the "concrete character of a thing," or in some other way.[33] That divinity reflected the nature of God was also generally affirmed. God, in fact, was considered the only being that could be "perfectly" divine. Therefore, to be divine was to be "uncreated and immortal," without beginning and without end.[34] Divinity meant being unrestrained by mundane *human* characteristics. The implications of the distinction between what it meant to be human and what it meant to be divine will be discussed later in this chapter. For now, it is important to recognize that the Christian understanding of what it means ontologically for Jesus to be Christ rests on a christological paradox.

To reiterate, Jesus' essence is distinguished by two different natures coming together. The classical Western christological tradition says that he is Christ because he is constitutively both divine *and* human. Thus, as Christ, he embodies an ontological paradox, the paradox of divinity and humanity. A similar paradox shapes Jesus' existential reality, that is, his ministry.

That Jesus was the Messiah meant not only that he was God incarnate but also that he was "the bearer of God's rule."[35] Jesus' very earthly presence signaled the imminent arrival of God's kingdom. That the Messiah was present, as Christians believed, indicated that the kingdom of God was at hand. At the same time, according to gospel accounts, Jesus understood his ministry as one of preparing people for God's impending kingdom. In announcing his own ministry, Jesus said, "The time has come. . . . The kingdom of God is near. Repent and believe the good news!" (Mark 1:14). The New Testament gospellers thus present his words and deeds as shaped by an acute attentiveness to the approaching kingdom of God. In this way they often suggested a profound difference between the practices of God's kingdom and those of the human world. For instance, Jesus reportedly explained to his disciples that in God's kingdom, "many who are first will be last, and many who are last will be first" (Matt. 19:30). In effect, Jesus informed his followers that the kingdom of God would mean a revolutionary change in the way things were; it would disrupt the status quo. Throughout his ministry Jesus attempted to clarify the kind of life required on earth in light of the divine revolutionary change that was about to occur.[36]

To understand Jesus' ministry as focused on God's kingdom again bespeaks a paradox. Just as two distinct natures come together in Jesus' very being, two different realms of existence come together in his ministry. In him, two worlds effectively collide, that of God and that of humankind. Although completely present in the human realm, Jesus' earthly existence is thoroughly oriented toward the divine realm.

What we find, then, is that Christianity's christological core is fundamentally a twofold paradox. Jesus is at once human and divine in both his being (ontologically) and in his ministry (existentially). This twofold divine/human paradox is decisive in who he is as Messiah. Hence, the defining character of Christianity depends on a definite "paradox."

This identification of Christianity's christological center as a paradox is deliberate in an effort to make a subtle, yet important distinction. This distinction is crucial to appreciating the complexity of the theo-ideological foundation that informs Christian participation in dehumanizing acts. It will also be important for answering the ultimate question concerning Christianity's viability for black people. Specifically, identifying Christianity's christological core as a paradox differentiates it from being an inherent dualism, thereby allowing for a more precise understanding of Christianity's collusion with dualistic perspectives that invariably give rise to a troubling Christian tradition. Before turning to this collusion let us first explain the distinction.

A paradox points to difference. It suggests two apparently contrasting or even self-contradictory things coming together to express a possible truth. It may also point to a person who exhibits contrasting natures.[37] It is with this two-part definition in mind that the Christian Messiah can be viewed as a paradox. In the Messiah, two contrasting natures (divinity and humanity) come together in the one person of Jesus presumably to express a truth about reality.

It is also significant to note that a paradox implies a relationship by virtue of the fact that two elements do come together. The nature of a paradoxical relationship, however, is not specified. It is because of this lack of specificity that a paradox is not intrinsically a dualism.

In theological understanding, dualism connotes a particular kind of relationship. It commonly refers to an oppositional/antagonistic way of relating. In a dualistic relationship mutuality of difference is precluded. Dualistic paradigms place contrasting objects or elements into hostile and/or hierarchical interactions. One element of a dualistic relationship is typically overpowered, dominated, or not respected by the other. One element is typically revered while the other is vilified; one is considered good and the other evil.

What a paradox and a dualism hold in common is the acknowledgment of difference entering into relationship. Where they diverge is in how that relationship of difference is construed. A paradox does not dictate the terms of the relationship; a dualism does. Hence, a paradoxical relationship can be mutual or reciprocal. A dualistic relationship, by definition, does not exhibit such complementary qualities. It is for this reason that Christianity's christological core should be principally regarded as a paradox, not a dualism. Indeed, the Chalcedon settlement strongly insinuates a nondualistic model of relating. It stipulates that in Jesus neither divinity nor humanity is overpowered or diminished by the other, but that the integrity of each is maintained. It suggests an equal, mutual relationship at the incarnational heart of Christianity's christological core.

Yet, regardless of how Christianity's christological center might theoretically resist dualistic perspectives, there definitely has been an influential, oppressive Christian tradition that has generated "dualistic epistemologies" and ways of relating. Christian participation in vicious attacks on the black body reflects this tradition. Carter Heyward is thus correct in her indictment of Christianity for nurturing systems and structures epitomized by "wrong relationality." She is also right to point out that Christianity's complicity with dualism is a chief factor in its malevolent tradition.[38] What must be stressed, however, is that there is no simple explanation for Christianity's collusion with dualism and its harmful effects. While, for instance, its christological center contributes to its alliance with dualistic perspectives, and thus "wrong relationality," it does so only inasmuch as it is a part of Christianity's wider theological core. Any insight, therefore, into Christianity's vulnerability to dualistic schemas requires an awareness of the way in which Christianity's closed monotheism and christological paradox interact to form a profoundly problematic theological core especially as this core engages certain philosophical perspectives. The precipitating factors of Christianity's collusion with dualistic paradigms are important to discern because it is this collusion, as will be later demonstrated, that generates an oppressive tradition and thus portends trouble for the black body. At the same time, it is just as imperative to determine those aspects of Christianity that might act against this collusion. These aspects suggest Christianity's suitability for black people. Let us for now examine what makes Christianity susceptible to dualistic perspectives.

The Problem of Difference

Christianity's theological core is characterized by difference. Both its monotheistic starting point and christological center engage difference, though the way in which they do so varies. The closed monotheism in which Christianity is grounded rejects difference. Although, as pointed out earlier, monistic perspectives in general do not by necessity generate hostility with diverse viewpoints, closed monotheism typically does. Closed monotheism rejects other gods, and hence other religions. Closed monotheism strongly resonates with dualistic patterns of thinking about the universe and relationships with people seen as different. Again, it places different realities into polarized relationships. It does this in both the cosmic and human realms. Thus, a closed monotheism, if not tempered by other principles, will invariably foster dualistic epistemologies and consequently "wrong relationality."

In the case of Christianity, however, a closed monotheism does not exist in isolation. Dualistic perspectives are therefore not an inexorable fact of Christian theology. Specifically, Christianity's closed monotheism theologically coexists with a twofold christological paradox. As will become evident in chapter 3, this christological paradox is one of the theological principles that can mitigate the dualistic proclivities of a closed monotheism.

Nevertheless, while Christianity's christological paradox does not necessitate, and may even resist, dualistic notions, it is vulnerable to them. What it shares with a closed monotheism is the need to determine the parameters of an identified difference. That is, both the christological and monotheistic natures of Christianity demand standards by which to distinguish the difference between two disparate realities. Closed monotheism demands these standards in terms of the Christian and non-Christian realities, again both cosmically and historically. The christological paradox requires similar standards in terms of the divine and human ways of being.

What, for instance, is it that distinguishes Christians from non-Christians? What is it that distinguishes divinity from humanity, God's ways from human ways, or God's ways from evil ways? These questions imply a certain set of identifiable behavioral and conceptual standards that must be established. These are the standards by which Christians will be identified and which they will be compelled to follow. These are the standards that suggest the *ways*, if not the *being*, of God.

Of course, it must be kept in mind that given the closed monotheistic nature of Christianity, to be a Christian was considered, especially by early Christians, to be among the people of God. The standards by which Christians were defined were thought to be compatible, if not synonymous, with the ways of God. In this regard, for all practical purposes the only standards that needed to be established were those that differentiated between God's ways and the ways of those forces that opposed God, especially as both were manifest in people. It is in the establishing of these standards of difference that Greek philosophy began to significantly influence Christian thought. In addition, this Greek philosophical influence ensured the development of a Christian tradition that was virtually inextricably bound to dualistic contrivances.

In effect, Christianity's theological core compels the need to define difference, be it the difference between Christians and non-Christians or divinity and humanity. While these expressed differences do not necessitate dualistic patterns of explication, they certainly lend themselves to such. It is in this way that Christianity's closed monotheism and christological paradox form a problematic (though not inherently so) theological core. These two elements are problematic inasmuch as they invite troubling dualistic perspectives on the world and humanity. To reiterate, it is

Christianity's link with dualistic perspectives that provides for its unsettling relationship to the black body, not necessarily the monotheistic or paradoxical nature of Christian theology itself. Let us now turn to how this link was forged.

Influential Philosophical Perspectives

A hellenized Jewish tradition gave birth to Christianity. Even before the Christian sect emerged, Jewish scholars wrestled with the impact of Greek culture on Hebrew religion. There were those, of which the Pharisees are an example, who did not view Hellenistic culture positively. For these anti-Hellenistic Jews, any compromise or dalliance with Hellenistic thought was considered an offense against the Hebrew God, who demanded complete loyalty. This segment of the Jewish community was stubbornly faithful to religious traditions as expressed in Jewish law.

There were others in the early Jewish community who viewed Hellenistic thought and Hebrew faith as compatible. These Jews tended to be of the Diaspora, meaning that they lived away from Palestine. Signaling its accommodation to Greek culture, Diaspora Judaism produced the Septuagint, a Greek translation of the Hebrew scripture. Philo, an Alexandrian contemporary of Jesus and one of the most influential Jewish thinkers of his time, epitomized hellenized Judaism. He argued that Greek philosophy and Hebrew scripture pointed to the same God. He further asserted that Greek philosophers actually drew upon Hebrew thought in constructing their beliefs. That which Greek philosophers tried to speak of literally, Philo maintained, Hebrew scripture spoke of allegorically. Relying on the Platonic distinction between the true and the material realms, he reasoned that the scriptures' "true" meaning was revealed through an allegorical reading, as opposed to a literal one.[39] Christianity was born from a more hellenized Jewish tradition such as the one that which Philo represented.

Another significant Greek thinker was Seneca, a leading Stoic philosopher and contemporary of Jesus. Both Seneca and Philo no doubt impacted Jesus' teachings, if not directly at least indirectly, as they helped to shape the intellectual climate of which Jesus was a part. To be sure they had a bearing on the thinking of the apostle Paul.

Paul was a Diaspora Jew whose early years were spent in the hellenized city of Tarsus. Though he later became a part of the Pharisaic community, Paul was very much influenced by Greek thought and culture. Thus, after his conversion to Christianity, Paul often noted the continuity between Greek and Christian thought. Similar to Philo, he argued in his sermon on the Aeropagus that Christianity resonates with certain Stoic beliefs. Again reminiscent of Philo, he suggested that what the Greek philosophers considered to be unknown in terms of divine reality was made known to Christians through Christ. Paul proclaimed, "I have even found an altar with this inscription: *To An Unknown God*. Now what you worship as something unknown I am going to proclaim to you" (Acts 17:23). Yet, regardless of how significant Christian leaders like Paul stressed the compatibility between Christian faith and Greek philosophy, early Christian communities continued to disagree over the relationship Christians were to have with Greek culture. The "apostolic assembly" depicted in Acts 6 refers to this conflict.[40] This conflict was precipitated by the fact that the more Christianity spread among the Gentiles (non-Jews), the more hellenized it tended to become. The point is that, given the Greco-Roman world of which Christianity was a part, a Hellenistic philosophical influence was practically unavoidable. To suggest, therefore, that it was the Hellenistic influence itself that corrupted Christianity is to oversimplify the matter. For Christianity is manifestly a hellenized religion. As we will see, it is not the fact of a hellenized influence that augurs trouble for the Christian tradition; rather, it is the way in which Christian thinkers combined certain Hellenistic philosophy with Christian theology. The coalescing of Platonic and Stoic thought with Christianity's problematic theological core (that is, its closed monotheism and christological paradox) was instrumental in the formation of a questionable, yet influential, Christian tradition. It would provide the necessary theo-ideological foundation for Christianity's explicit and implicit complicity with black dehumanization. Let us look to see how this was the case.

The Platonic/Stoic Influence

As mentioned earlier in this chapter, Platonism theorized that there were two different spheres of existence. This notion was rooted in Plato's own quest for what was unchangeable or permanent even in the midst of a changing, transitory world. Plato eventually conceived that there was a realm of the unchangeable. This was the "world of forms." This world was transcendent, immaterial, and "non-sensible." It was the world of true knowledge—a world that could be penetrated only by reason. Corresponding to this world of forms was the changeable world of "particulars." This was the mundane, material, sensible world in which humans lived. It was the world of sense perceptions and "opinions." In Platonic thought these two worlds were not of equal value. For Plato, that which was permanent and unchanging was superior to that which was transitory and changeable. Hence, what was superior could be apprehended only by the "esteemed" intellect and was off-limits to sense perceptions. Plato speaks of these two worlds, and hence ways of knowing, in a dialogue from *Timaeus*:

> First then, in my judgment, we must make a distinction and ask, What is that which always is and has no becoming, and what is that which is always becoming and never is? That which is apprehended by intelligence and reason is always in the same state, but that which is conceived by opinion with the help of sensation and without reason is always in the process of becoming and perishing and never really is.[41]

This Platonist privileging of one reality over the other is what has come to be known as "Platonic dualism." This dualism is characterized by two separate entities maintaining their distinctiveness even as they are related to each other. This relationship, however, is antagonistic since one entity is more valued than the other.

Platonic dualism readily translated into a corresponding theology. Specifically, Plato argued that prior to its existence in the body, the soul belonged to the "non-sensible" world of forms.

The body, however, was a part of the world of senses. Thus, the soul represented the permanent and more valued part of the human person. Plato put it plainly: "The body of heaven is visible, but the soul is invisible and partakes of reason and harmony, and, being made by the best of intellectual and everlasting natures, is the best of things created."[42] Consistent with its dualistic nature, Platonism further contended that the duty of the human being, especially of the philosopher, was to attain true knowledge by focusing on the unchanging world of forms, and thus overcoming the trap of the body. Essentially, the human goal was to free one-self from the body in order to achieve the true knowledge.

It is also important to recognize that Plato believed in one universal form that was perfectly good and behind the many forms of the non-sensible world. All forms were thought to have derived from this universal form. This idea of a universal form led many to consider Platonism a monistic philosophy. It was perhaps this monistic bent that initially attracted Christians to Platonic thought. As Platonism developed and gave way to "Neoplatonic" expressions, the idea of the one transcendent being became more pronounced as did the dualism.[43]

Stoic thought existed alongside Platonism. Stoicism emerged around 300 B.C.E. One of its most influential proponents was Seneca, as mentioned earlier, a contemporary of Jesus. Stoic thought, similar to Platonism, presented both a metaphysical and ethical system. Also like Platonism, it projected a monistic view of reality. Stoicism, however, rejected the Platonic disregard for the material world. It denied the split between a transcendent and material reality, denying—at least metaphysically—the Platonic dualism. For Stoics there was only one realm of existence, the material realm. Accordingly, Stoics argued that God was immanently present throughout the material/earthly world. Stoicism posited what has been described as a "pantheistic monotheism" in that God was a pervasive part of the material realm. Again, Christians were undoubtedly attracted to the monistic nature of Sto-icism, even though they rejected its pantheistic claims.

More significant to understanding the Platonic/Stoic influence on Christianity is the recognition of what the two philosophies held in common, namely, a high regard for reason. Stoics believed that the proper goal of the human being was to live in accordance with the rational principle present in the one material world. This belief was the foundation for their rigid ethic. This ethic described the ideal state of living as *apatheia*. *Apatheia* was not a passive state. Rather, it was a "spiritually active" life to be lived independently of passion and thereby governed by reason. This Stoic understanding of *apatheia* corresponds to Platonic dualism. Just as Platonist thought devalues the body and passion, so does Stoic thought. Again, for Stoics, the highest state of living is one epitomized by reason and released from bodily desires.

Essentially, both Platonic and Stoic philosophies project a dualistic paradigm. Platonism proposes a dualistic worldview that exalts transcendent/divine reality and disparages mundane/human reality. This worldview accompanies a Platonic theology that reveres the human soul and dismisses the body. Stoicism shares the Platonic approach to the human person, as it too devalues the body for its "innate" extravagances, namely, passion. Stoicism thus proposes a dualistic ethic for life. It is important to note that passion in both philosophies is equated to lust and sexual pleasure. Thus, both Stoic and Platonic thought thereby argued that sexual pleasure must be controlled, if not eliminated, in order for a person to ascend to the highest level of human living, one that approximated the transcendent/divine realm. Both philosophies held antisexual/antibody attitudes.

The integration of these two philosophies into Christian thought produced a tradition driven by dualistic thinking and ascetic sentiments. Platonism's dualistic metaphysic helped Christian thinkers to enunciate the differences compelled by Christianity's theological core. The Platonist perspective sharpened the distinctions between divine and human realities. Divinity was characterized by reason, while humanity was identified with passion. Divinity reflected that which was invisible and eternal. Humanity reflected that which was visible and temporal. Divinity was esteemed and humanity was devalued. The assimilation of Platonic thought into early Christian thinking essentially amplified the difference endemic to the christological paradox. In so doing, it cre-

ated such a profound distinction between the two realities per-
sonified by Jesus' ontological and existential existence as to make
a dualistic christological tradition, that is, one in which divinity
and humanity are construed in oppositional ways, virtually
inevitable. (In this regard, the nondualistic impulse of the Chalcedon settlement becomes even more remarkable.[44])

Furthermore, the incorporation of the stoic state of *apatheia*
suggested a standard for distinguishing Christians from non-
Christians, God's way from human ways. Christians were marked
by a lifestyle not given to sexual pleasure or excesses. Asceticism
and celibacy were considered the earthly way of life most compatible to divine ways and reflective of the kingdom of God. Pagans
were thereby characterized as people driven by passion with ram-
pant sexual appetites. This lustful pagan behavior was thought to
reflect the ways of their gods.

Overall, Platonic and Stoic thought joined together in Christian thinking in such a way as to exploit the dualistic vulnerability
of Christianity's theological core. The Platonic belief in the world
of forms (that is, the immaterial/true world) as being different
and superior to the world of senses (that is, the material/earthly
world) combined in Christian thought with the Stoic ethic defined
by *apatheia*. In this way, a significant strand of Christian thought
adopted a theology that esteemed the immaterial, or divine, world
(what came to be viewed as the world of reason, spirit, and soul)
while it renounced the material, or human, world (considered the
world of passion, flesh, and body). This particular Christian tradition routinely *divinized* the soul and *demonized* the body. The
soul was identified as the key to salvation, while the body was
viewed as a salvific impediment. The body was essentially condemned for being the source of the very sexual desires that ostensibly tainted humanity and thus separated humans from God. This
dualistic approach to distinguishing divinity from humanity and
the soul from the body is the mark of a prominent Christian tradition that resulted from the integration of Platonic/Stoic thought
with Christian theology. This tradition is best described as *platonized* Christianity.

Platonized Christianity characteristically fosters dualistic ways of perceiving the world as well as relating to the non-Christian world. It utilizes a dichotomous sexualized ethic to discern the acceptability/holiness of various people. It essentially dehumanizes people based on a sexualized characterization of them. This platonized tradition invariably belies the nondualistic quality of Christianity's theological core as again suggested by the "classical" christological settlement. Practically speaking, as will be seen later, it predictably leads to Christian actions that betray the ways in which Jesus' ministry signified the kingdom of God; that is, it leads to oppressive responses to particular peoples. Most importantly, this is the tradition that has been most troubling for black men and women. Let us now look more closely at platonized Christianity by first answering the question: Why a *platonized* tradition?

A Platonized Christian Tradition

Without doubt, there were other dualistic influences on early Christianity besides Platonism; Manichaeism and Gnosticism are two notable examples. Both popular religions harbored radically dualistic perspectives on the world. Manichaeism taught that the universe contained two great opposing forces, good and evil. Evil was identified with the earthly, material, or bodily realm. The Manichaean goal was to free oneself from matters of the body so as to be free from evil. *Budhism*

Although there were many different Gnostic schools of thought, Gnosticism generally argued, like Manichaeism, that there was a great divide between the spiritual world and the material world. The material world was likewise regarded as evil. Gnostics believed that the acquisition of a special gnosis or wisdom led to a person's redemption from the material world.[45] Various strains of Christianity reflected Gnostic and Manichaean influences—even though both schools of thought were eventually rejected by mainstream Christian thinkers for being nonmonotheistic and/or too disparaging of the material world.[46] More to the point, neither Gnosticism, Manichaeism, nor any other perspective

had the pervasive impact on Christian thought and Western society that Platonism did. Platonism provided the definitive dualistic
paradigm that is built into the very fiber of Western worldviews,
including that of Christianity. The Platonist metaphysic set in
motion the dualistic perspectives that place different things into
relationships of opposition. Platonism is most often considered
responsible for the dualistic paradigm that privileges the soul over
the body. Finally, the Platonic influences on Christianity were early
and extensive. These are the reasons that the dualistically oriented
tradition of Christianity is identified in this book as a *platonized*
tradition.

The apostle Paul is perhaps the earliest and certainly most influential representative of this platonized tradition. Though no
doubt informed by Jesus' teachings on sexuality and the body,
Paul goes beyond Jesus in developing a sexual ethic that in effect
disavows "passion" and places the body and soul in a relationship
of duality. These Pauline attitudes toward the flesh provide the
biblical foundation for platonized Christianity. That this tradition
seems biblically based contributes to both its allure and danger for
the black community. The overall problem, however, is that platonized Christianity is supported by Pauline attitudes that secrete
dualistic perspectives on the world and humanity. Moreover, these
attitudes are not necessarily compatible with Jesus' teachings and
therefore perhaps betray the integrity of Jesus' ontological nature
of being at once *fully* human and *fully* divine. Before looking more
closely at Paul's views, let us first consider Jesus' teachings on the
body sexual to better appreciate Paul's role in the development of
platonized Christianity as well as the way in which the reality of
Jesus contests this form of Christianity.

Religious scholars have convincingly pointed out that while
Jesus was no doubt influenced by Platonic and Stoic thought, he
did not possess an irrevocable disdain for the body and sexuality.
Rather, as he admonished people to prepare for the arriving kingdom, he urged them to refrain from sexual activity. He counseled
that fulfilling the needs of passion was not prudent, given what
was about to take place. He put forth a code of sexual behavior
that was driven by his belief in the imminent arrival of God's king-

dom. While this code rebuked those who were consumed with fulfilling bodily needs, it did not label those persons irredeemable.
Sexual activity was not viewed as permanently and intrinsically evil
and thus by definition an affront to God or a barrier to salvation.
At the same time, the body was not presented as the bane of
human existence—indeed, such a belief would have contradicted
Jesus' ontological nature, that is, his incarnate/bodily reality. Yet
Jesus did present a "severe" sexual ethic that broke with the social
and religious mores of his time.[47]

For instance, Jesus consistently called for a life without sex during a time when many considered fertility a blessing. Jesus went so
far as to commend the choice of some to become eunuchs. He
said, "For some are eunuchs because they were born that way;
others were made that way by men; and others have renounced
marriage because of the kingdom of heaven. The one who can
accept this should accept it" (Matt. 19:12). He also argued that
marriage was characteristic of the temporal, earthly way of life,
while celibacy was the way of eternal life: "The people of this age
marry and are given in marriage. But those who are considered
worthy of taking part in the resurrection from the dead will neither marry nor be given in marriage, and they can no longer die;
for they are like angels" (Luke 20:34).

Consistent with his counsel that, in view of the coming kingdom, fulfilling bodily needs must be secondary to spiritual readi-
ness, Jesus cautioned that it was shortsighted to worry about
"what you will eat or drink" and to "sell your possessions and give
to the poor" (Luke 12:29, 33). He especially urged his disciples
"to free themselves" of transitory, worldly ties, even "family obligations" so that they might focus on their spiritual connections and
needs (Luke 12:49-53; Mark 3:33-35).[48]

Despite the stern ascetic principles found in Jesus' teachings,
Jesus did not stigmatize the human body and sexuality. To suggest
that he condemned the body and sexuality would be just as much
of a distortion of his teachings as suggesting that he condemned
the biological family. His austere teachings, in fact, are best understood not as an absolute, provisional, or even situational ethic but
as an *urgent* ethic.[49] His ethic was defined not by a disavowal of

the sexual body; rather, it was defined by the need to free oneself from all that might hinder a person from an absolute commitment to God's approaching kingdom. Jesus was speaking to the urgency of the times. In so doing, he mandated the behavior necessary to prepare for the divine revolution that was on its way. Elaine Pagels describes the context of urgency best when she says:

> Jesus' radical message of the impending Kingdom of God left his followers no time to fulfill the ordinary obligations of everyday life. First-century Christians saw themselves partic-ipating at the birth of a revolutionary movement that they expected would culminate in the total social transformation that Jesus promised in the "age to come."[50]

Nevertheless, Jesus' teachings were vulnerable to platonized dualistic interpretation, as evidenced by the apostle Paul.

Paul was driven also by a sense of urgency to prepare for the kingdom of God. Not only because at least twenty years had passed between Paul's and Jesus' ministries during which time people had become less vigilant in regard to the kingdom, but also because of Paul's Platonist background, his sexual ethic was more extreme than that of Jesus. Paul presents marriage and sexual activity as a form of bondage. He says that both divert one's attention from what is utterly important: proclaiming the gospel and preparing for the kingdom. His most impassioned and often-quoted pleas to abstain from sexual liaisons are found in his first letter to the church at Corinth.

One of the most serious concerns facing the Corinthian church involved a prominent group of "enthusiasts" who had emerged in the community. As New Testament scholar Günther Bornkamm notes, these "spirit-filled people" believed that they had reached a perfected state of living that granted them access to the divine realm of power. Consequently, they considered themselves free not only from mortal limitations such as death but also from earthly obligations. This sense of "spiritual" freedom translated into "licentious" behavior.[51] It was to this situation that Paul was particularly speaking when he pronounced his rigid views toward sex and marriage.

The particularity of his concern notwithstanding, Paul's Corinthian ethic is representative of his overall position on sexual activity. Paul strongly advocated celibacy. Although he did not demand an abstemious lifestyle, as Elaine Pagels points out, he wished men to be, like himself, celibate (1 Cor. 7:7). For those who could not remain celibate, he advised, "it is better to marry than to burn with passion" (1 Cor. 7:9). For those who were married, Paul instructed them to fulfill their "marriage obligation," even though he recognized that such obligations could be enslaving. Thus, in spite of his directives to meet the needs of marriage, he ironically encouraged those "who have wives [to] live as if they have none" (1 Cor. 7:29). Ultimately he believed that "it was good to remain unmarried" to spare oneself the many troubles (i.e., sexual obligations and temptations) that accompany the married state (1 Cor. 7:8).[52]

Clearly, Paul had little use for sexual activity, especially outside the bounds of marriage. He made clear that unrestrained sexual activity, that is sexual pleasure, was immoral and a sin against the very body. He admonished faithful Christians to "flee from sexual immorality" while cautioning that "he who sins sexually sins against his own body" (1 Cor. 6:18).

Some Pauline interpreters have suggested that Paul's zealous disapproval of sexual activity was not an indication that he "loathed the flesh," but rather a reflection of his "urgent concern for the practical work of proclaiming the gospel" as well as a concern to prepare for the imminent kingdom.[53] While this may be the case, Paul's views toward the body and sex were certainly not positive. The body sexual had, for him, little redeeming value. Paul clearly advocated a lifestyle that was free from the distractions of the flesh. He repeatedly championed the unmarried state over the married state because he fervently believed that the unmarried person was better able to "live in a right way in undivided devotion to the Lord" (1 Cor. 7:35). Those who were married, Paul argued, were unavoidably preoccupied with "the affairs of this world" and thus were not totally devoted to God. Essentially, whether he intended it to be the case or not, Paul's unrelenting valuation of nonmarriage over marriage, celibacy over noncelibacy, devotion to God over bodily obligations, strongly implied a palpable tension, if not dualistic relationship, between the body and the soul. While he may not have "loathed the flesh," and thus may not have meant for the body and soul to be conceived as naturally incompatible forces, his sexual attitudes certainly placed them in an antagonistic relationship. That his teachings would essentially provide the foundation for sacrosanct dualistic approaches to the body and sexuality, and hence sustain a platonized tradition, was virtually inevitable.

It is interesting to note that rigid, ascetic, world-denouncing interpretations of Paul's views, such as in the *Acts of Paul and Thecla,* flourished in first- and second-century Christianity. Various Christian communities took seriously the austere values of Paul's ethic, and perhaps did follow them to their logical conclusion. They proclaimed virginity and celibacy as the *only* proper path for Christians. As a result, numerous virgin and ascetic cults emerged. Platonized Christianity, however, does not typically reflect the severe austerity of these early communities of abstinence. Rather, it mirrors Paul's more "moderated" disregard for sexual activity and thus characteristically circumscribes, but does not forbid, Christian engagement in sexual behavior. At the same time, however, platonized Christianity typically "loathes the flesh" in a way that Paul's writings invite one to do. In this regard, Orlando Patterson is perhaps correct to suggests that Paul's writings have played a pivotal role in sustaining a tradition that provides sacred covering for those who loathe black flesh.[54] Again, Paul's role in nurturing a platonized Christian tradition is not a simple matter. While Paul's sexual ethic was more disavowing of the body sexual than was perhaps warranted by Jesus' teachings, one must always bear in mind that Paul was responding to the concerns of particular congregations, like that of Corinth. Accordingly, his sexual ethic was appropriate to the issues at hand, even as it was profoundly shaped by a dualistic paradigm. Moreover, it was those who interpreted Paul's teachings who ultimately concretized a flesh-loathing, and hence platonized, Christianity.

There is no one who relied on Paul's writings more and who would also have a more significant impact on Christian theology than Augustine of Hippo.[55] In fact, Augustine "has fixed a certain reading of Paul for generations of later readers," thus allowing for his own Augustinian imprint on Christian sexual morality to be virtually unsurpassed.[56] Augustine was indeed the major conduit of platonized Christianity into the Western theological tradition.

Augustine's sexual ethic was rooted in his own struggle to control his sexual desires. Augustine believed that he was controlled by lust, especially during his adolescent years. He confessed, "Love and lust together seethed within me. In my tender youth they swept me away over the precipice of my body's appetites and plunged me in the whirlpool of sin."[57] Eventually, after suffering much internal conflict concerning his prurient life, Augustine encountered words from Paul's Epistle to the Romans, which read: "Not in revelling and drunkenness, not in lust and wantonness, not in quarrels and rivalries. Rather, arm yourselves with the Lord Jesus Christ; spend no more thought on nature and nature's appetites."[58] Heeding Paul's words, Augustine slowly changed his way of living and most significantly developed a theology based on Pauline sexual attitudes, even though Augustine may have exaggerated them.

Augustine's theology unambiguously pronounced sex as sinful. It considered sexual desire nothing less than diabolical and a reflection of humanity's fallen state. Clearly influenced by platonic dualism, Augustine argued that the body with its passions was always to be subjugated to the soul with its rationality. Sexual desire was considered a sign of the body's rebellion against the rule of reason. There was no greater proof of this than the involuntary sexual excitement of genital organs, described by Augustine as "organs of shame."[59] Augustine viewed genital organs as enemies of the mind, for these organs were servants to the worst kind of lust, sexual lust. Sexual lust, Augustine argued, ultimately leads to the suspension of reason. He put it this way:

This lust assumes power not only over the whole body, and not only from the outside, but also internally; it disturbs the whole man, when the mental emotion combines and mingles with the physical craving, resulting in a pleasure surpassing all physical delights. So intense is the pleasure that when it reaches its climax there is an almost total extinction of mental alertness; the intellectual sentries, as it were, are overwhelmed.[60]

The only way to prevent one's reason from becoming overpowered by lust was, Augustine continued, to keep one's bodily organ holy by using it only to procreate. Drawing on 1 Thessalonians 4:4–5 he said:

Now surely any friend of wisdom and holy joys who lives a married life but knows, in the words of the Apostle's warning, "how to possess his bodily instrument in holiness and honour, not in the sickness of desire, like the Gentile who have no knowledge of God"—surely such a man would prefer, if possible, to beget children without lust of this kind. For then the parts created for this task would be the servants of his mind, even in their function of procreation. . . . They would begin their activity at the bidding of the will, instead of being stirred up by the ferment of lust.[61]

Granted, Augustine's sexual ethic was only one aspect, though a pivotal one, of his theological treatise. Still, his claims about sex were instrumental in fostering platonized Christianity. To reiterate, Augustine was the key transmitter of platonized Christianity into Western theological thought. He influenced both Catholic and Protestant traditions. In so doing, he has had a significant bearing on how Paul's convictions on sex and the body have been construed, that is through a platonized dualistic framework. What, then, is platonized Christianity's sexual perspective/ethic?

Platonized Christianity advocates a dualistic sexual ethic. That is, it suggests only two ways in which to engage sexual activity, one tolerable and not inherently sinful and the other intolerable and sinful. Procreative use is tolerably good; nonprocreative use is intolerably evil. Characteristic of platonized Christianity, a third possibility is not offered. A platonized sexual ethic does not allow for sexual activity as an expression of an intimate, that is, mutually loving, relationship. For all intents and purposes, platonized Christianity severs sexual intimacy from intimate relationality. Sex is fundamentally objectified within a platonized framework. It is rendered an object of either procreation or lust, again precluding the possibility of sexual intimacy as an expression of human love (this will be addressed more fully later in this text). This rigid dualistic approach invariably gives rise to the profound denigration of the body (the vehicle of sex) and sexuality (essentially defined in terms of sexual activity) that has come to characterize a platonized Christian tradition. Accordingly, it is platonized Christianity that gives rise to Christian participation in contemptible attacks against human bodies, like those against black bodies. Not only does platonized Christianity provide a foundation for easily disregarding certain bodies, but it also allows for the demonization of those persons who have been sexualized, as will be discussed in further detail later. It is also worth noting (as will be discussed more fully later) that in the American theological scene, platonized Christianity perhaps found its most comfortable home in the evangelical Protestant tradition. This was the prominent tradition of the American South. This was the tradition that most significantly shaped the theological consciousness of those whites who were party to black lynchings. This same tradition, ironically, was also the tradition to which many early black Christians in America were converted. In this regard, platonized Christianity has had an impact on black lives not simply in the ways in which the black body has been subjugated by white culture, but also in the ways that platonized views have been integrated into the black faith tradition.

How is it, then, that "church men and church women" were able to participate without remorse or fear of betraying their Christian identity in the lynching of Richard Coleman? How was a Christian minister able to so boldly use the Bible to support his

call to lynch George White? Such Christian involvement in the
ravishing of two black bodies and many more is an almost fore-
seeable consequence of a platonized Christian tradition.

To reiterate, this is a tradition that was formed long before the
first black body was lynched. Moreover, this is a tradition that has
injured more than just black bodies. As earlier mentioned, it no
doubt contributed to early Christian persecution of the Jews and
has also contributed to Christianity's participation in the persecution of other groups such as Native Americans and women. Perhaps, the more Christianity has been used in an oppressive
manner, the easier it becomes for it to be used oppressively. Therefore, Christianity's prior tyrannical tradition of disdain for certain
human bodies may also greatly contribute to Christian participation in attacks against black bodies. Whatever the case may be, this
disturbing Christian tradition was born as central aspects of Christianity's theological core, specifically its closed monotheism and
christological paradox coalesced in a particular way with Platonic
and Stoic thought. This dubious alliance formed a dualistically
defined theo-ideological foundation, thereby allowing for a Christian tradition that demonized the body and sexuality, namely, platonized Christianity. This platonized tradition grounds itself in the
Bible, even as its approach to the Bible may be skewed by a dualistic framework. Reflective of its dualistic bias, this tradition can
easily provide sacred justification for acts such as lynching as it naturally cultivates sexualized dehumanizing demonization of certain
peoples. Indeed, as will become even clearer later, Christian support of lynching epitomizes the complex oppressing potential of a
platonized Christian tradition. So, Christian participation in vile
attacks against black people is a practical, if not inevitable, consequence of a platonized Christian tradition. This brings us, therefore, to another essential factor in Christian involvement with
depraved acts against humanity: platonized Christianity's alliance
with power. It is only as platonized Christianity becomes the religion of those with social-political power that a terrorizing Christian tradition becomes viable. The next chapter will explore
Christianity's foreboding connection to power.

2

Christianity and Power

ON DECEMBER 7, 1899, *New York World* newspaper described the
scene at Richard Coleman's lynching:

> Richard Coleman, a twenty-year-old colored boy was burned
> at the stake at *noon* today within the limits of [Maysville,
> Kentucky], in the presence of thousands of men and hun-
> dreds of women and children.
>
> Tortures almost unbelievable were inflicted upon the
> wretched negro. In all the vast crowd that witnessed the ago-
> nies of the man, not one hand was raised in humanity's
> behalf, nor a single voice heard in the interest of mercy.
> Instead, when some new torture was inflicted upon the
> shrieking, burning boy, the crowd cheered and cheered, the
> shrill voices of women and the piping tones of children
> sounding high above the roar of men.
>
> . . . The population of the whole city and country for
> miles around, *church men and church women*, professional
> and business men of eminence, people of distinguished
> ancestry, formed the mob.[1]

Richard Coleman's noontime lynching is eerily reminiscent of
another noontime murder that took place some two thousand
years earlier at the hands of another merciless crowd. The Markan
Gospel reports the events of that day:

> "What shall I do, then, with the one you call the king of the
> Jews?" Pilate asked them. "Crucify him!" they shouted.
> "Why? What crime has he committed?" asked Pilate. But

they shouted all the louder, "Crucify him!" Wanting to sat-
isfy the crowd. . . . He had Jesus flogged, and handed him
over to be crucified. (Mark 15:12-15)

Though these two events are separated by centuries, the similarities between them are striking. Both Richard Coleman's and
Jesus' reprehensible murders took place at noon. Both men were
summarily executed on a tree. Both torturous deaths were unwarranted. And both Richard Coleman's lynching and Jesus' crucifixion played to the cruel, pitiless delight of a crowd thirsty for
blood. Yet, as impressive as the similarities between the two
human atrocities are, there is an even more arresting dissimilarity.

Jesus' followers presumably were not among those voices
shouting for Jesus' crucifixion. Though witnesses to the crime, the
followers of Jesus, later to be known as Christians, essentially represented the silent victims that day as they watched the one they
believed to be the Messiah crucified before an incensed crowd.
There were Christians, however, who were definitely not so silent
on the day of Richard Coleman's lynching. They were a part of the
voices cheering on his execution. They were among the rowdy
mob of lynchers.

How is it that people whose religious identity is centrally linked
to a shameful, unmerited crucifixion could so easily roar approval
for an equally shameful and unmerited lynching? What is it that
has allowed for such a radical transformation in Christian character? How is it that Christians with a history of being persecuted
could so eagerly become persecutors? Is there something about
Christianity that presages such a disconcerting change in Christian
consciousness? Is there something about Christianity itself that
actually fosters a lynch-mob mentality?

As suggested by James Carroll's earlier observation concerning
the impact of Constantine's conversion on the church, the answers
to these questions, in large measure, trace back to 312 with events
on the Tiber River at the Milvian Bridge.[2] On the Milvian Bridge,
Emperor Constantine defeated his foe Maxentius and was able to
consolidate his power as ruler over the Roman Empire. Prior to

that crucial battle, Constantine had a remarkable vision. Constantine's earliest biographer, Eusebius, reports that Constantine provided him with the following account of that timely vision:

> about noon, when the day was already beginning to decline, he saw with his own eyes the trophy of a cross of light in the heavens, above the sun, and an inscription, CONQUER BY THIS, attached to it. At this sight he himself was struck with amazement, and his whole army also. . . .
>
> He said, moreover, that he doubted within himself what the import of this portent could be. And while he continued to ponder and reason on its meaning, night overtook him; then in his sleep the Christ of God appeared to him with the sign which he had seen in the heavens, and commanded him to make a likeness of that sign which he had seen in the heavens, and to use it as a safeguard in all engagements with his enemies.[3]

Some historians have suggested a less dramatic vision that included a "heavenly sign" but not necessarily the words "Conquer By This."[4] Whatever the precise vision, Constantine interpreted it as a signal that the Christian God would be on his side in the upcoming battle on the Milvian Bridge. He therefore ordered his troops to wear Christian symbols on their shields. Most significantly, he viewed the victory over Maxentius as a fulfillment of this vision. Consequently, Constantine became Christian—as did the Roman Empire over which he ruled.

With the conversion of Constantine, Christianity moved from being a powerless, sometimes persecuted religion, in the empire, to becoming a powerful, potentially persecuting religion. Constantine's conversion essentially created an indelible link between Christianity and power. This link has not only changed Christianity's social-political status in the Western world, but most significantly it has had a theologically transformative impact on an influential Christian tradition, namely, platonized Christianity. In this chapter I will attempt to specify the theological implications of Christianity's bond with power. The underlying assumption is that Christianity's link with power makes Christian participation in abominable acts such as lynching not only possible but theologically sustainable. Moreover, in chapter 2 I will argue that there *is* something at the theologically defining center of Christianity that makes its alliance with power especially dangerous. That something is the cross. I will point out that while the interaction between power and platonized Christianity is troubling—in that the practical distinctions demanded by a closed monotheism and christological paradox can be implemented—the interface with power and the cross, particularly in a platonized tradition, can be lethal, and has been so for black bodies. I will conclude this chapter by assessing whether or not a religion with a crucifying cross at its center is suitable for black people, and thus for me, a black female. Let us now turn to the implications of Christianity's link with power.

Closed Monotheism and Power

With Constantine's conversion, political power allied with Christian theology. As has been pointed out by other interpreters of this pivotal Christian period, Constantine's conversion signaled to Christians that their theological claims were correct: their God was the *one true* God. The truth of their God was revealed by the events surrounding the Milvian Bridge. Similar to Moses' burning-bush theophany (leading him to take on the enemies of his people) Constantine's vision of the cross empowered him to confront his political enemies. Just as God turned away the enemies of Moses and the Israelites at the Red Sea, God ostensibly defeated the enemies of Constantine at the Tiber River. The events of the Milvian Bridge seemingly vindicated Christian claims. To reiterate, for Christians the Milvian victory and Constantine's subsequent conversion were proof enough that their God—the God of Jesus—was the only true God. The Milvian events further showed Christians that their God *was* the God of Moses. Thus, Jesus was the Christ, the hoped-for Israelite Messiah. He was the "bearer of God's rule." Christians were now affirmed in their understanding of themselves as the

"True Israel."[5] In the Christian mind, the Milvian conversion event revealed that pagans and, most significantly, Jews were wrong for not affirming the ultimate truth of the Christian God. Both were in fact considered the enemies of God. In one historical moment the closed monotheism of Christianity was apparently justified. Such justification proved to be dangerous, if not deadly, for many non-Christians. Always wrong!

Constantine's conversion inaugurated a new reality for Christian life in the Roman Empire. James Carroll effectively points out that during the 125-year period following the imperial conversion, "Christians went from being 10 percent of the empire, a despised and violently persecuted minority, to being its solid majority. Christianity went from being a private, apolitical movement to being the shaper of world politics."[6] Those who were once considered the outsiders within the empire and were oftentimes viciously persecuted and killed for not renouncing their Christian beliefs were now social and political insiders, with the necessary power to persecute those whom they regarded as adversaries to themselves and their God. The once "persecuted church became the church of the powerful."[7] Fourth-century apologist St. John Chrysostom conveys this change in the church's fortunes in his perhaps exaggerated observations:

> There was a time when [the Christian church] consisted of only a few men, when it seemed to be an innovation and a novelty. There was a time when the seed of its teaching was newly planted, when there were so many wars and such great battles burst into flame from every side. But these conflicts could do nothing nor did they get the upper hand. This is all the more true now that the Church has spread over the entire world, every place, mountain, glade, and hill. It has made itself master over land and sea and every nation under the sun.[8]

Chrysostom's exuberance notwithstanding, Constantine's conversion did mark an epic change in Christian status. With this change Christians were able to act on their theological claims. They were empowered to institute the practical requirements of their closed monotheism.

Specifically, Christians had sufficient power to impress their beliefs upon others, especially since the Christian agenda corresponded to the emperor's political agenda. Religious unity was an important component of Constantine's efforts to unify his empire. For Constantine, "one empire had come to equal one religion."[9] Constantine's desire for unity translated into both a lack of tolerance for religious diversity within the empire and theological discord within Christianity. In order to achieve theological unity within Christianity, Constantine called together an ecumenical council out of which the Nicene Creed was established. As for religious unity throughout the empire, Constantine basically backtracked on what he had assented to in 313, the Edict of Milan, which affirmed religious freedom. Conversion, destruction of non-Christian property and persecution soon became the modus operandi in relation to pagans and Jews within the Constantinian empire. Christians could now impose their beliefs upon others with both religious impunity and political backing. They could demand that non-Christians assent to the Christian God—that is, convert. Most significantly, these newly empowered Christians were able to punish those who did not assent or convert. Sadly, Christians eventually began to treat non-Christians—especially Jews—in the same contemptible manner in which they had previously been treated.

Some might suggest that the early Christian persecutions of non-Christians signaled that Christians had fallen prey to what has come to be understood as a common psychological phenomenon, "identification with the oppressor." That is, once freed, the oppressed begins to take on the very characteristics of those who once oppressed them.[10] French anthropologist René Girard might even describe the persecuting behavior of the early Christians as a form of "mimetic" behavior in which Christians became so obsessed with their once rivals that they mimicked their persecuting behavior.[11] There were undoubtedly multiple contributing factors to Christian cruelty toward non-Christians. Identification with their oppressor, mimesis, and simple vindictiveness all no doubt played a role. Indeed, as suggested by these reasons for Christians becoming oppressors, it may well be a disquieting part of human nature itself that when invested with power—especially if once powerless—men and women are inclined toward abusing that power. To be sure, human history would suggest this to be the case regardless of a people's religious affiliation. Nevertheless, while there certainly may be various underlying reasons for fright-ful Christian behavior, such behavior was surely theologically moti-vated and sustained. Let us look at this more closely.

If persons actually believe, as Christians did (and perhaps many still do), that they possess the absolute/ultimate truth, then they are obligated to cling stubbornly to and fervently defend that truth. To do anything less would be to capitulate to that which they ostensibly know to be wrong and misguided. In this respect, the measure of Christians' confidence in the authenticity of their God was seen in the lengths they went to standing up for that God. So, just as early Christians felt theologically bound to stand firm in their beliefs regardless of the deadly consequences (mar-tyrdom) they no doubt thought themselves equally duty bound to oppose fervently non-Christians. What made the Christians' stance even more intractable was their view of the cosmos. For again, early mainstream Christian thought viewed the supernatural realm as a polarized reality, with the Christian God standing against and ultimately triumphing over opposing, evil forces. What God did in God's heaven, Christians presumed to do on earth—stand fast against and triumph over all enemies. Indeed, the Chris-tian earthly triumph over non-Christians was nothing less than a sign of God's ultimate triumph. In effect, Christianity's closed monotheism not only rendered Christians vulnerable to persecu-tion but also theologically predisposed them to becoming perse-cutors. This very persecuting inclination can be seen in Eusebius's passionate words concerning Constantine's rule:

> Our emperor, [Jesus'] friend, acting as interpreter to the Word of God, aims at recalling the whole human race to the knowledge of God; proclaiming clearly in the ears of all, and declaring with powerful voice the laws of truth and godliness

to all who dwell on the earth. . . . Our emperor, emulous of his Divine example, *having purged his earthly dominion from every stain of impious error,* invites each holy and pious worshipper within his imperial mansions, earnestly desiring to save with all its crew that mighty vessel of which he is the appointed pilot.[12]

At the same time that Christian monotheism invited oppressing behavior, it triggered a particularly unrelenting and vicious response toward those whom Christians considered their most dangerous, if not "intimate" rivals to the truth—the Jews.[13]

To reaffirm, Christian monotheism was completely intolerant of competing claims to truth. It was not enough, therefore, for Christians merely to proclaim the validity of their own beliefs. They had also to invalidate the beliefs of others. Essentially, they were theologically obligated to provide undisputed proof exposing the error of non-Christian ways. For the early Christians this proof translated into an imposed suffering on others. That is, Christians made to suffer those who tenaciously clung to their own god(s). Despite the fact that Christians were the cause of this suffering, they construed the suffering of non-Christians as the inevitable consequence of their giving themselves over to false gods. Christians basically interpreted the suffering of non-Christian others as God's way of dealing with God's enemies. But again, the Jews would have a special burden to bear in terms of early Christian persecution. In many respects, as suggested in the previous chapter, early Christian treatment of the Jews is the beginning of the Christian tradition of tyranny that eventually overwhelmed the black body. To be sure, many of the same dynamics were present in the Christian tradition in relationship to Jewish bodies and black bodies. For this reason, let us briefly examine Christianity's early disquieting relationship with Jewish people.

As Carroll astutely points out, the very Jewish presence challenged Christian claims to being the "new Israel." "[W]hat was to be made of—done with—the survivors of that old Israel who stubbornly refused to disappear?"[14] Furthermore, how could Christians claim that Jesus was the "fulfillment of Jewish prophecy, yet

No mention of Jewish rejection of Jesus

be repudiated by the holders of the title to that prophecy"?[15] The *True?* only seemingly practicable solution to this dilemma, in Christian eyes, was to turn Jewish prophecy against the Jews themselves. Essentially, Christians interpreted Israelite prophecy as heralding the coming of Jesus as the Davidic Messiah and proclaiming curses against those who did not regard Jesus as the Messiah. In this way, the Jews in their refusal to believe were held responsible for their beleaguered plight. Again, Christians justified their treatment of the Jews by claiming Jewish suffering as a divine act. *MUST STUDY.*

This anti-Jewish way of thinking was pervasive throughout early Christian thought. The body of writings that most expressed this thought came to be known as *Adversus Judaeos* literature. In these *Adversus Judaeos* writings, the early church fathers did indeed scrupulously turn the Hebrew prophetic tradition, the Old Testament, against the primary holders of that tradition, the Jews. As Rosemary Radford Ruether says, "anti-Judaic midrashim" on the Old Testament characterized these anti-Semitic writings.[16] Justin Martyr is an early representative of this profound anti-Semitism as he—though himself persecuted for his beliefs—justified Jewish persecution. He wrote:

> Knowing beforehand that you would be guilty of [rejecting Christ], God pronounced this curse against you through Isaias: "Woe to their soul! They have taken evil counsel against themselves saying: Let us bind the Just One, because He is distasteful to us. Therefore they shall eat the fruit of their own doing. . . . Evil shall befall him according to the work of his hands. O my people, your oppressors plunder you, and your exactors shall rule over you."[17]

Described as "the most violent and tasteless of the anti-Judaic literature of the period,"[18] St. John Chrysostom's *Eight Homilies against the Jews* turns also to the Old Testament in claiming that Jewish suffering is a divine response to their religious misdeeds. He indeed provides a long litany of Jewish sins and prophetic foretelling of punishment for those sins from the time of Moses to Constantine, as he says he will do:

I shall prove that this is true, and that God foretold everything which was going to befall the Jews. I shall do so not
only from what Isaiah said but from all things which happened to them both good and bad. . . . [19]

Eleventh-century Christian theologian Peter Abelard later captured
the long-standing contempt toward the Jews in his *Dialogue of a
Philosopher with a Jew and a Christian,* when ostensibly in support
of the Jews he observed:

To mistreat the Jews is considered [by Christians] a deed
pleasing to God. Such imprisonment as is endured by Jews
can be conceived by the Christians only as a sign of God's
utter wrath."[20]

In effect, Christianity's closed monotheism prompted a theological notion of divine *retributive suffering.* Such a notion advises
that a people's sufferings are deserved as they are just recompense
for wrongdoing. In this instance, the wrongdoing is the refusal to
adhere to the one and only true God. It was in this way that early
Christians felt justified in their actions against the Jews. Jewish suffering was considered nothing less than the inevitable and perhaps
divinely imposed consequence for rejection of the Christian God.[21]
Once again, René Girard offers insight into the psychology that
possibly prompts theological models of retributive suffering. He
argues that such a model allows persons to better accept their violent behavior toward others since they can regard it "not as something emanating from within themselves, but as a necessity
imposed from without, a divine decree whose least infraction calls
down terrible punishment."[22]

Psychological imperative notwithstanding, that Jews received
the brunt of Christian cruelty was compelled by the "logic" of certain theological claims. Specifically, as Jewish faithfulness posed a
threat to the truth of Christianity's closed monotheism the Jews'
suffering presence became an important witness to the validity of
those Christian claims. That Jews suffered reinforced the truth of
Christianity and the Christian God. Rosemary Ruether explains:

The Jew was allowed to exist, indeed commanded to exist in the Christian era, not as one with a legitimate vehicle of religion in his own right, but in the negative space of divine reprobation and as an eventual or ultimate witness to the "truth" of the Church.[23]

(As will be later argued, aspects of Jesus' existential and ontological presence challenge Christian notions of *retributive* suffering.) Both Jesus' ministry and his death on the cross in some way defy Christian instigation of or participation in the sufferings of marginalized others, especially when carried out in Jesus' name. For now, however, it is important to note the disturbing reality of a closed monotheism when it is endowed with political, social, and ecclesiastical power.

Power and a closed monotheism present a potentially deadly combination. In one sense, Christianity is not unique when it comes to monotheistic traditions. As pointed out earlier, the monotheistic nature of Judaism initially led the early Israelites to persecute non-Israelites as they considered them "foreign enemies." A review of Islamic religious history (as Islam is also a monotheistic faith) would also reveal a certain correlation between Islamic power and the persecution of non-Islamic peoples. Thus, it is perhaps the case that monotheistic traditions in general, when invested with sufficient power, are potentially oppressive. Yet in another sense, the closed nature of Christianity's monotheism makes it even more disposed toward vile disregard of others than other forms of monotheism, for example, the strict monotheism of Judaism. For again, a closed monotheism is *absolutely* and inherently intolerant of other claims to divine truth. It is concerned not simply with the loyalty of its adherents to a single God, but also with the beliefs of others. Thus, the combination of a closed monotheism and power readily suborns Christian persecution of those noncompliant with Christian claims, as was the case with the Jews. This combination would thereby initiate a theological legacy in support of the oppressive responses to non-Christians for centuries to follow. Christian responses to the treatment of American Indians as well as to the enslavement of African peoples are a part of this legacy. As Red Jacket, a nineteenth-century leader of the Iroquois, said in an 1805 oration concerning Christianity's attitude toward Native American religions, "You want to force your religion upon us. . . . You say that you are right and we are lost."[24] Chinese literary artist Frank Chin perhaps described best the persecuting tendency of Christianity's closed monotheism, when he said of Christian disrespect of Chinese religions, "I've come to believe that monotheism encourages racism whoever practices it. There is only one God and everyone else is an infidel, a pagan, or a goy."[25]

As problematic as Christianity's closed monotheism is when it comes to persons of other cultural and religious traditions, it is not the only problem for Christianity when it comes to power. There are other aspects of the Christian theological tradition that foster troubling practices when enjoined by power and thus seem to reinforce the worrisome tendencies of its closed monotheistic nature. One such aspect is the platonized approach to sexuality.

Platonized Sexuality and Power

As argued in the previous chapter, the influential Christian tradition about which we are speaking, platonized Christianity, fundamentally demonizes sexuality. Nonprocreative sexual behavior is considered reflective of un-Godly ways. At best, it signals a weakness in a person's spiritual development that proper spiritual guidance can correct, as in the case of Christians such as Augustine. At worst, nonprocreative sex is a sign of an incorrigible demonic nature, as was considered the case for pagans and Jews. In effect those judged driven by sexual desire and passion are seen as enemies of God. They are effectively demonized just as sexuality itself is demonized. Platonized views on sexuality essentially served to reify the distinctions demanded by Christianity's paradoxical christological core and monotheistic nature.

Such a disapproving approach to sexuality becomes a useful tool for a church in power. For power itself, especially inequitable power, invariably seizes human sexuality as a means of carrying out its rule. In other words, sexuality is a crucial component in the exercise of power. Michel Foucault helps us to understand why this is the case.[26]

"How is it that in a society like ours," Foucault asks, "sexuality is not simply a means of reproducing the species, the family, and the individual? Not simply a means to obtain pleasure and enjoyment?[27] Because, Foucault asserts, sexuality is integral to power. It is the axis where the human body and reproduction come together. Power can thus be exerted over a people through careful regulation of their bodies, their perceptions of their bodies, and their reproductive capacities. China

Foucault further notes the importance of sexuality to sustaining unjust power. He argues that sexuality is a mechanism by which distinctions can be made between classes and groups of people. To question or impugn the sexuality of another bolsters one's claims to superiority as it suggests another group's inferiority. Such is the case in a platonized Christian tradition. To reiterate, this tradition has argued not simply that those who are sexually driven are inferior, but that they are demonic. It is the assertion of their demonic nature that sets the stage for Christians' violent persecution of them. A platonized view of sexuality, as earlier argued, provides a "real" standard for determining precisely the enemies of God. Inasmuch as certain peoples are sexualized, they are God's enemies. Essentially, a circular logic functioned to allow Christians to discern the enemies of God. Lustful sexuality was a sign of God's enemies, at the same time that God's enemies were characterized as lustfully sexual. The fateful implication of such logic was that God's enemies needed to be acted against. It was with the acquisition of social and political power that Christians had the means to act on their platonized approach to discerning the enemies of God. Invested with social and political power, Christians were able to terrorize those whom they regarded as demonic, as supported by their perceived sexual practices.[28] Moreover, when influential Christian thinkers like Augustine irrevocably established within the dominant Christian tradition a platonized sexual ethic, the necessary theological foundation was laid for a Christian legacy

that would promote and sustain Christian participation in ravishing certain human bodies. In this instance, Foucault's observation
is sustained: sexuality and power are natural partners. Perhaps even
more to the point is the sinister potential in the partnership
between a demonized approach to sexuality and inequitable
power. For if sexuality were not regarded as a sign of depravity,
then it could not be used as a tool to denigrate and subsequently
oppress others. Nevertheless, not only does Christianity rely on
sexuality as a means of making distinctions between people, but
Christianity's involvement in the persecution of others is theologically reliant on its commitment to a platonized view of sexuality.

Christianity's platonized views toward sexuality lend themselves
to another related and equally disturbing legacy. Not only do
these views provide the foundation for Christians' direct use of
oppressive power, but they also render Christianity wholly vulnerable to being appropriated by wielders of cruel power. Platonized
Christianity effectively supplies the perfect "sacred legitimation"
for the brutal treatment of certain peoples. It provides the means
to theologically justify their demonization and concomitant dehumanization. Essentially, Christianity's platonized views on sexuality provide a sacred covering for tyranny. Christianity shelters
violent attacks against certain sexualized bodies. Correspondingly,
violent attacks against a sexualized people find their shelter in
Christianity. In so doing, Christianity all but becomes the "sacred"
cohort to dehumanizing brutality. In effect, platonized Christianity invariably becomes an element in discursive power. We will see
later how this has been the case in regard to black people. For now
it is important to recognize the potentially horrifying consequences of significant Christian claims—closed monotheism and
platonized sexuality—when they interact with power. These claims,
when emboldened by social and political power, encourage the
merciless treatment of powerless peoples.

As potentially dangerous and destructive as Christianity's closed
monotheism and platonized sexuality are when empowered, there
is another more central element of Christianity that can become
even more lethal when invested with power, and that is the crucifying cross.

The Cross and Power

When Christianity acquired social and political authority, something even more unsettling occurred. What is now Christianity's chief symbol, the cross, became a sign, even a weapon, of power. What originally pointed to the crucified history of Christians came to mark the crucifying force of Christianity. The historical victims of the cross became terrorizers in the name of the cross. The cross became a shield for Christian imperialism. It was a critical symbol in the theological justification for hostile aggression against non-Christian peoples. Christians used the reality of Jesus' death on the cross as an impetus and an excuse to persecute others. Constantine's conversion is again implicated in this alarming turn of events.

James Carroll astutely notes that with Constantine's conversion the cross became more prominent within the "Christian imagination."[29] Carroll argues that while the apostle Paul certainly established the cross and crucifixion as essential to Christian salvation, the cross was not the sole salvific marker. The waters of baptism were also an important sign of Christians dying with Christ and thus being saved by his death. In this respect, Carroll says that "water not wood" had a "hold on the Christian imagination." This was borne out by the fact that the cross was not initially a pervasive Christian symbol. In early Christianity, palm branches, doves, monograms of Jesus, and the Greek word for fish (ichthys) were more popular symbols than was the cross.[30] After the conversion of Constantine, however, the place of the cross seemingly changed. The cross became not only central in the Christian imagination but also more determinative of Christian salvation and most vital in establishing Christian dominion within the empire.

As mentioned earlier, when Constantine came to power he was intent on creating political and religious unity within his empire. This desire prompted him to call together the first ecumenical council of bishops. This council eventually produced the Nicene Creed. Within this creed not only was the integrity of the incarnation protected, but the role of the cross/crucifixion to Christian salvation was firmly and irrevocably established. The creed clearly states:

We believe in one God, Father, Ruler of all, Maker of heaven and earth. . . . And in one Lord Jesus Christ . . . who for us human beings and for our salvation came down from heaven and was incarnate from the Holy Spirit and Mary the Virgin and became human; and was crucified for us under Pontius Pilate, and suffered.[31]

It is important to note that this confession moves directly from the incarnation to the crucifixion. In keeping with a platonized Christian tradition that renounces the earthly/bodily realm (as this tradition presupposes the body as evil), the central focus of the creed is not the life and ministry of Jesus (the implications of which will be discussed later in the book), but the fact of Jesus' crucifixion.[32] The creed implies that God became incarnate, that is, embodied in order to be crucified.[33] As noted by Carroll, the significance of the crucifixion is perhaps further evidenced by the fact that the only historical detail mentioned in the creed refers to the crucifixion. Specifically, the creed remarks that Jesus was "crucified under Pontius Pilate."[34]

Essentially, the Nicene confession suggests that what matters most in Christianity's inaugural history, and concomitantly for Christian salvation, is not how Jesus may have lived but the fact that he was crucified. If it had not been the case beforehand, then certainly after the Nicene Creed the crucifixion—hence the cross—was firmly established as decisive to Christian salvation. To be sure, historically Jesus' death on the cross has been the center of attention in dominant Western theological doctrines of atonement.[35] Not only did the cross take on more salvific meaning after Constantine's conversion, but it also more significantly shaped the Christian relationship with non-Christians—above all with the Jews.[36]

Once more, the cross was a major symbol in Constantine's conversionary vision—so much so that Constantine ordered his troops to wear the symbol not only into the battle at Milvian Bridge but also into subsequent battles.[37] Basically, through Constantine, the cross of Christian salvation came together with the sword of Christian imperialism. The historical consequences of this were quite deadly, again, especially for the Jews.

Reinterpreting, if not misinterpreting, the historical circumstances surrounding Jesus' crucifixion, prominent early Christian
thinkers began to place Jesus' death in the hands of the Jews as a
people. The tendency to do this was already well established
within the New Testament gospel tradition. In varying degrees,
responding to particular crises in their own communities while
also trying to minimize conflict with contemporary Roman
authorities, each of the four gospellers exaggerated and oversim-
plified the Jewish role in Jesus' crucifixion. They presented
Pilate—who in actual fact was a very tyrannical, powerful leader—
as a reluctant participant, almost a victim, of Jewish mania to bring
Jesus to death. Thus, the early church fathers virtually took up
where the gospellers left off. Specifically, the *Adversus Judaeos*
writings pointedly blamed the Jews for the crucifixion of Jesus. No
one did this more decisively than John of Chrysostom. He said:

> You did slay Christ, you did lift violent hands against the
> Master, you did spill his precious blood. This is why you have
> no chance for atonement, excuse or defense. . . . Your mad
> rage against Christ, the Anointed One, left no way for any-
> one to surpass your sin. This is why the penalty you now pay
> is greater than that paid by your fathers.[38]

Unsurprisingly, these writings were not innocuous. This anti-Jewish literature sustained, if not instigated, social, political, and ecclesiastical attacks against Jews. Again, with imperial power on their
side, Christians were able to act on the anti-Jewish rhetoric of the
Adversus Judaeos literature. Christians were empowered to make
the Jews pay for their alleged crime against Jesus. As Rosemary
Ruether explains,

> All of this might have remained theoretical, however, if
> Christianity and Judaism had both remained minority reli-
> gions in a pagan . . . state. . . . In the fourth century, how-
> ever, Christianity became the religion of the Greco-Roman
> Empire. What had previously been theology and biblical
> hermeneutics now was to become law and social policy.[39]

What we find is that after Constantine's conversion the cross partnered with power in a most insidious fashion. When conjoined with power, the once redemptive cross of suffering became a "retributive" cross of tyranny. What once signified salvation now signaled terror for those designated as the enemies of Christ— pagans, but especially Jews. While it may be argued that the use of the cross to terrorize is a perversion of its true meaning (this argument will be explored further in chapter 3) it is important to recognize how the cross itself renders Christianity highly susceptible to being used as an instrument of murderous tyranny.

Whether understood historically or theologically, the cross is unquestionably the site of a violent execution with a sacrificial undercurrent. It is the sacrificial undertone of the cross that portends problems for Christianity when Christianity is aligned with power. René Girard's anthropological insight into the meaning of sacrifice helps us to understand the sacrificial character of the cross and thus why the cross and power make for a dangerous combination.

According to Girard, sacrifice is the end result of a subtle process defined by "mimetic desire." Girard contends that human beings naturally desire what their neighbor, known as the mimetic rival, has. There comes a point, however, when that desire is frustrated. One is blocked from attaining the desirable object of one's rival. Such frustration, which Girard terms "scandal," leads to mimetic rivalry and eventually to violence. In order to stem the tide of violence "those involved in this tangle of rivalry turn their frustrated desire against a [single] victim, someone who is blamed, who is identified as an offender causing scandal."[40] This innocent victim is then violently sacrificed to "quell the violence" and to curb the rivalrous frenzy of a community. Thus, the sacrificed victim is at once portrayed as the source of violence (hence he must die) and the source of peace (because he died). It is in this way that sacrifice has both a practical and mythological quality.

Practically speaking, the sacrifice prevents the eruption of interminable community conflicts. It is necessary to resolve these conflicts; otherwise the community lapses into crippling and violent chaos. The sacrifice of an innocent victim is the resolving mechanism, as it prevents the sacrificing community from turning against itself. The sacrifice "restores tranquility and strengthens social ties."[41] Girard explains that through making a sacrifice, "society is seeking to deflect upon a relatively indifferent victim, 'a sacrificeable' victim, the violence that would otherwise be vented on its own members, the people it most desires to protect."[42]

Every sacrifice, according to Girard, also has a mythological quality in that the sacrifice acquires religious meaning. The mythology surrounding a sacrifice suggests that the sacrifice itself satisfies a supernatural/divine reality. In many instances Girard suggests the sacrificial victim, who was initially demonized for causing the communal chaos, is later deified for restoring peace as a result of being sacrificed. If the sacrificial victim is not mythologically deified, then in the very least the mythology makes clear that a particular deity demanded the sacrifice.[43] In this regard, sacrifice becomes "an act of mediation between a sacrificer and a 'deity.'"[44] In effect, a certain mythology emerges around the sacrifice that religiously legitimates it. Mythology thus serves to shelter the community from its own violence. As mentioned earlier, religious mythology allows persons to better accept their violent behavior toward others since they can regard it "not as something emanating from within themselves, but as a necessity imposed from without."[45]

Whether or not one agrees with the details of Girard's theory of sacrifice in terms of its origin in mimetic desire, his theory does help clarify the sacrificial quality of Jesus' death on the cross, both historically and mythologically. Girard in fact refers to Jesus' crucifixion as an exemplar of sacrifice. He offers an interpretation of the events surrounding the crucifixion that suggests that Jesus' death quelled the rage and violence of a hostile crowd. Whatever frustrations they may have had with the political and religious leadership of their day, they vented them onto Jesus, an innocent victim. In this regard, Jesus became the "sacrificial victim" that allowed for a certain peace and cohesiveness to return to the first-century Roman world of which he was a part. Thus, Girard argues, the crucifixion of Jesus served a practical purpose—as is characteristic of communal sacrifices. Yet Girard also carefully points out that Jesus' deification emerged not from the crucifying crowd but from a minority group who split off from the crowd and thereby attested to Jesus' resurrection. In this regard, Girard argues that the crucifixion of Jesus is different from other models of sacrifice. In fact, he says the resurrection of Jesus actually exposes the false nature of sacrificial mythology, if not the injustice of sacrifice (about which more will be said later). For now it is important to note that while the recognition of Jesus as divine may have involved a different process from most sacrificial deifications/ mythologies, a mythology of sacrifice did emerge around Jesus' crucifixion.

Classic Western atonement theories developed a sacrificial mythology of Jesus' crucifixion as they have argued that Jesus was crucified for the sake of human salvation. For instance, in keeping with the belief that there was a cosmic battle between God and other evil forces, second- and third-century theologians like Origen developed the theory that Jesus' death was a divine trick employed to pay a "ransom" to Satan in an effort to regain authority over sinful humanity.[46] Disputing the notion that God would ever be unjust to the point of resorting to tricks, let alone that anything was owed to Satan, twelfth-century theologian Anselm of Canterbury argued that Jesus, the incarnate one, was sacrificed in order to repay a debt incurred as a result of human sin, owed not to Satan but to God. Yet the debt, while owed by humans, was far too great for humans to pay. It was so great, in fact, that only God could repay it. It was for this reason, then, that God became incarnate, that is, the God/Man. Why the God/ Man, Anselm asked? In order, Anselm answered, to expedite the repayment of the human debt to God. This repayment is sealed with the death of Jesus.[47]

St. Thomas Aquinas built on Anselm's approach in his theory of "satisfaction." St. Thomas argued that the death of Jesus was sufficient satisfaction for the sin of humanity. As such, the love displayed by Jesus' suffering far outweighed the sin of those who crucified him. [48]

A younger contemporary of Anselm, the aforementioned Abelard, also stressed the love of God as the principal factor in

Jesus' death. He specifically put forth a theory of "moral influence," which suggested that, as a result of Jesus' death, human beings would be so moved by God's love for them (a love that sacrificed God's Son) that they would in turn open their hearts to God.[49] The sixteenth-century reformers continued these theories of sacrificial atonement. John Calvin stressed that it was "no ordinary example of incomparable love" that Jesus "cast away all care of himself that he might provide for us." Calvin argued that because of Jesus' obedient act of "substitution" on the cross, the source of human salvation is found in "the death of Christ." [50]

Essentially, what we find in Christianity's classical atonement tradition is that Jesus' crucifixion has come to be understood as some form of divine mediation, that is, a sacrifice made to or required by God as compensation for human sin. In this respect, Christianity—not unlike other ancient religions—has at its center human sacrifice, replete with sacrificial mythology. It is this sacrificial center and accompanying mythology that make it most susceptible to becoming a religion that perpetuates brutal human terror. Let's look more closely at how this is the case.

To reiterate a point made earlier, Christians (that is, the followers of Jesus) ostensibly were not a part of the crowd that demanded Jesus' sacrifice, even though they acquiesced to it by their silence. Nevertheless, as even Girard aptly points out, the followers of Jesus were initially, for all intents and purposes, victims of the crucifying event. Ironically, however, it was their status as victims that presumably set the stage for them later to become crucifiers. Christians would eventually take on the voice of the crucifying mob. It is, according to Girard, almost unavoidable. Girard goes on to say, "The more one is crucified, the more one burns to participate in the crucifixion of someone more crucified than oneself."[51] So much is this the case that Girard notes that even Jesus recognized that his followers would one day join his persecutors, as he quotes Jesus as saying to his followers, "You will all be scandalized because of me."[52]

Again, whether or not one agrees with Girard's explanation, the fact remains that Christian history reveals "a tendency of Christians themselves . . . to lose themselves and merge into the mob of persecutors," if not themselves become persecutors.[53] This is clearly evident in early Christian treatment of the Jews.

However one might explain it, it seems that having a human sacrifice at the center of Christianity further allows Christians to participate in the sacrifice of others. To be sure, given Christianity's crucifying center, human sacrifice is not an inherently abhorrent concept to Christians. As seen in traditional theories of atonement, Western Christianity has theologically embraced the possibility of there being "ultimate" (as in divine) value in the sacrifice of a human being. As harsh as it may sound, Christianity's classical atonement tradition makes Christians at least open to the notion that humans can serve as "sacrificial mediators" between God and humanity—either as a way of exorcising evil from a particular community or as a way of pleasing God. While the Constantinian empire may have put an end to crucifixions, such a ban did not halt Christian participation in human sacrifice. We will indeed see this harsh reality played out in relationship to black human beings.

Notwithstanding the fact that the Christian God may have very well decried sacrifice (as we will attempt to argue in chapter 3), Jesus' crucifixion ostensibly does provide a model of human sacrifice. In effect, Jesus' death on the cross, coupled with the theology surrounding that death, set into motion a potential pattern of divinely accepted, even required, sacrifice. The only thing needed to make this pattern real was the same thing needed to carry out the sacrifice of Jesus, namely, social-political and ecclesiastical power.[54] Recognition of the need for power to carry out a sacrifice also makes something else perfectly clear—the victim of sacrifice must be socially, politically, and possibly ecclesiastically powerless.

Girard convincingly argues that the sacrificial victim *must* be powerless. If the sacrifice is to effectively stop the violence of a community, the victim must be one who is marginalized and powerless within the community so that there is no danger of violent reprisals. Girard also notes that this marginalized victim is typically "demonized" to further support the rightness of the sacrifice. The implication of having a powerless, demonized victim is again that

→ yes. true of lynchers.

those who perform the sacrifice are powerful and moreover consider themselves to be acting in God's stead. The sacrificing community is thus typically endowed with a certain social and political,
if not religious, authority. It at least holds power over the community of the one to be sacrificed. Hence, whatever it is that causes
"sacrificial desire," in order for that desire to be successfully acted
on one needs power. Once endowed with power, therefore, Christianity's potential to become a terrorizing religion of sacrifice was
unleashed. In other words, empowered Christians possessed not
only the theology to legitimize sacrifice but also the power to commit a sacrifice. Again, it is important to remember that the cross is
pivotal in Christianity's participation in the terror of sacrifice.

With particular respect to the Jews, Christians justified their
treatment of others as a divine recompense for their participation
in Jesus' crucifixion. Given the theology that developed surrounding Jesus' death, it would seem that the Jews would have
been celebrated—not castigated—for their alleged role in assuring
human salvation. But such was not the case. Christians were able
to blame the Jews for Jesus' crucifixion, while at the same time
theologically rejoicing in his death. It is in the "rejoicing" over
Jesus' death that the theological support for human sacrifice is
found. For again, the classical atonement tradition provides a theological paradigm for accepting human sacrifice as a means for salvation. In short, Jesus' crucifixion with its surrounding atonement
"mythology" creates the possibility for Christians to persecute,
indeed sacrifice, designated "others" with religious impunity. The
recognition of this leads us to the horror of lynching.

The Cross and Lynching

The relation between Jesus' crucifixion and black lynching has
long been acknowledged. Various black literary artists have provided some of the most chilling insights as they have portrayed
black lynching in the shadow of Jesus' cross. There is perhaps no
poet who has written more about the parallels between black
lynching and Christ's crucifixion than Countee Cullen. In 1922
he wrote "Christ Recrucified":

The South is crucifying Christ again . . .

> Christ's awful wrong is that he's dark of hue
> The sin for which no blamelessness atones;
> But lest the sameness of the cross should tire,
> They kill him now with famished tongues of fire,
> And while he burns, good men, and women too,
> Shout, battling for his black and brittle bones.[55]

There is perhaps no poem that does more to relate the pathos of black lynching and to highlight theologically the connections between black lynching and the cross than Cullen's epic poem, *The Black Christ*. In this 1929 narrative poem Cullen painstakingly tells the story of the Black Christ through the life of a young black man, Jim. Jim is lynched and crucified as a result of his love for a white girl and his subsequent killing of a white man who discovered him and the white girl together. As Cullen tells Jim's story, he reveals the agony and trials of faith that Jim's surviving brother and mother, "Job's dark sister," endure in relation to Jim's life and fate, just as he has told of Jim's own struggle with a God who would stand by while black people are summarily lynched. Throughout the poem one is struck by how Cullen retells Jesus' crucifixion story (and even resurrection, since in the end Jim is resurrected) through the black experience while also commenting on atonement explanations. The poem's opening lines immediately relate Jesus' crucifixion to black lynching. Cullen writes:

God's glory and my country's shame . . .

> How Calvary in Palestine,
> Extending down to me and mine,
> Was but the first leaf in a line
> Of trees on which a Man should swing
> World without end, in suffering
> For all men's healing, let me sing.[56]

The closing lines of Cullen's poem affirm the connection between the cross upon which Jesus was crucified and the trees upon which black people are lynched:

Somewhere the Southland rears a tree,
(And many others there may be
Like unto it, that are unknown,
Whereon as costly fruit has grown).
It stands before a hut of wood
In which the Christ Himself once stood—
And those who pass it by may see
Nought growing there except a tree,
But there are two to testify
Who hung on it . . . we saw Him die.
Its roots were fed with priceless blood.
It is the Cross; it is the Rood.[57]

Similarly, Claude McKay, in his poem "The Lynching," describes black lynching as a sacrifice made at the behest of God. In this poem the reader is left to ponder God's role in black lynching just as one contemplates God's role in Jesus' crucifixion. McKay writes:

His Spirit in smoke ascended to high heaven.
His father, by the cruelest way of pain,
Had bidden him to his bosom once again;
The awful sin remained still unforgiven.
All night a bright and solitary star.
(Perchance the one that ever guided him,
Yet gave him up at last to Fate's wild whim)
Hung pitifully o'er the swinging char.
Day dawned, and soon the mixed crowds came to
    view
The ghastly body swaying in the sun
The women thronged to look, but never a one
Showed sorrow in her eyes of steely blue.

And little lads, lynchers that were to be,
Danced round the dreadful thing in fiendish glee.[58]

In "Christ in Alabama," Langston Hughes takes this connection between black lynching and the crucifixion one step further

and places the incarnation, that is, Christ, in the period of the
lynching white South. As he does so, he closes the distance
between Christ's crucifixion and a black man's lynching. Hughes's
poem makes clear that they are one and the same, even as he too
seemingly indicts a God who would demand such a human sacrifice. Such a God for him could only be white. Hughes writes:

Christ is a nigger,
Beaten and black:
Oh, bare your back!

Mary is His mother:
Mammy of the South,
Silence your mouth.

God is His father:
White Master above
Grant Him your love.

Most holy bastard
Of the bleeding mouth,
    Nigger Christ
    On the cross
    Of the South.[59]

Even before Cullen's, McKay's, and Hughes's poetic theological reflections on lynching, W. E. B. Du Bois also wondered what
kind of God could tolerate, let alone demand, such a high price of
human life to be paid. In 1906, after witnessing a race riot in
Atlanta where white mobs viciously killed and assaulted several
black people, Du Bois wrestled with God in "A Litany at Atlanta."
He wrote:

Bewildered we are and passion-tossed, mad with the mad-
ness of a mobbed and mocked and murdered people; strain-
ing at the armposts of Thy throne, we raise our shackled
hands and charge Thee, God, by the bones of our stolen
fathers, by the tears of our dead mothers, by the very blood

of Thy crucified Christ: What meaneth this? Tell us the plan;
give us the sign!
Keep not Thou silent, O God![60]

In a later writing Du Bois queried the motivation of people who
would lynch. In *The Prayers of God,* he wrote:

For this, too, once, and in Thy Name,
I lynched a Nigger—

A few lines later, Du Bois makes clear that to "lynch a Nigger" is
to in effect lynch Jesus:

Thou?
Thee?
I lynched thee?[61]

Early black artists and thinkers on lynching capture the diffi-
culty of affirming a religion or a God that would in any way support lynching. That Christianity and its God in fact do this is made
clear to these black writers by the very fact of Jesus' crucifixion—
to them nothing less than a first-century lynching. Moreover, also
not lost to these writers is the fact that lynching is so often carried
out in a part of the country known for its Christian religiosity and
by those who themselves profess to be "good" Christians.

Orlando Patterson provides an in-depth analysis of the fundamentalist religion of the South that he says supported, if not
fueled, the lynching mentality. He argues that just as Christ's crucifixion was considered redemptive for humanity, black lynching
was seen as redemptive for the post–Civil War South after its
humiliating defeat in the war. He suggests that it is telling that the
Southern defeat of Reconstruction was referred to as "Redemption" and that the leaders of that defeat were called "Redeem-
ers."[62] He goes on to draw a parallel between the notion of Satan
in fundamentalist Christianity and the demonization of black people. He specifically argues that by characterizing black people as
subhuman beasts and by equating blackness with a sinful, satanic

nature, the lynching of black people became for white southerners equivalent to casting out Satan from their midst. Patterson explains: "Afro-Americans became to the body politic what Satan was to the individual and collective soul of the South. For both the same metaphor of a 'black' malignancy to be excised was employed."[63] Patterson ends his discussion by noting the centrality of the cross as a symbol of white supremacy in general. He says: "Here there is no room for doubt. The cross—Christianity's central symbol of Christ's sacrificial death—became identified with the crucifixion of the Negro, the dominant symbol of the Southern Euro-American supremacist's civil religion."[64]

The link between the cross and black lynching that Patterson and various black literary artists realize points to the insidious relationship between human oppression, especially black oppression, and Christian theology. Essentially, black lynching epitomizes the potential horrors that a platonized Christian tradition can uphold. Two things are worth noting in this regard. First, platonized Christianity in fact found its most comfortable home on the American scene in evangelical Protestantism. This is the form of Christianity that is most prevalent in the South, and thus is reflected in the hymns sung and sermons heard by everyday Christians. Patterson is therefore correct in highlighting the relation between white Southern religiosity and black oppression. This shall be more thoroughly discussed in part 2 of this book.

Second, that lynching exemplifies the brutal potential of a platonized tradition is illustrated through the matter of sexuality. The means by which white society confirmed its belief in black people's inferior and satanic nature was by characterizing black men and women as overly sexual beings. The black male was considered a rapacious brute and the black female a seductive Jezebel. As discussed earlier, to sexualize a people is an effective mechanism for maintaining control and power over that people. Such was the case in terms of white social control of black people.[65] In fact, historically marginalized and oppressed people in general have borne the burden of being a sexualized people. We see this in the case of the Jews. Christians at one time supported their persecution of the Jews by accusing them of all manner of behavior, such as pornog-

Qnon nows!

raphy and conducting "perverse" rituals with the blood of Christian boys whom they had murdered.[66] Historiographers John D'Emilio and Estelle Freedman have also noted that by the seventeenth century, sexuality had become a "powerful means" by which white Americans subjugated various nonwhite peoples.[67] As for black people, consonant with their sexualized depiction, sexual crimes became a common pretext for their lynching. Given this link between sexuality and black lynching and violent attacks against other sexualized bodies, Girard's observations concerning the relationship between sacrificial violence and sexuality become germane, especially as they help to further enunciate the implicit danger of platonized Christianity.[68]

Girard compellingly argues that human sexuality often incites a violent response. He shows this in terms of marriage and community relationships. He specifically points out that sexual breaches often lead to the most violent reactions. He says, "Sexuality leads to quarrels, jealous rages, mortal combats. It is a permanent source of disorder even within the most harmonious of communities."[69]

Given the tendency of sexuality itself to inflame violent responses, a platonized Christian tradition again becomes particularly vulnerable to encouraging and perpetuating sacrificial violence. For again, platonized Christianity characteristically sexualizes Christian outsiders and enemies. As suggested by Girard's analysis, to sexualize a people is not only to demonize them but also to make them susceptible to violent attack. Similar to sacrifice itself, the sexualization of a people has both a mythic and a practical quality. Mythologically people are demonized; practically they are killed. Generally speaking then, the sexualization of a people serves a dual purpose in a platonized Christian tradition. It allows for the religious legitimation of their vile treatment at the same time that it compels violence against them. A sexualized people is thus virtually fodder for violent sacrifice. The twofold repercussion of sexualization is seen in black lynching. That a dominant Christian theological tradition, that is, platonized Chrstianity, supported black people's sexualization and demonization (a subject to be taken up in the discussion of religious racism later in the book) no doubt further guaranteed black people's violent demise, even as Christianity's platonized tradition served to legitimate such a demise. It bears repeating that sexual misconduct was often given as an excuse for the lynching of black men.[70]

In general, platonized Christianity is implicated in the oppression of certain peoples. Because this tradition sexualizes those it demonizes, it leaves those who have been sexually demonized susceptible to being sacrificed even as it leaves its adherents vulnerable to becoming the sacrificers. It is in this way that the cross in a platonized tradition becomes even more troublesome. It provides a theological anchor for sacrifice as it in fact symbolizes the sacredness of sacrifice, especially for the sexualized terror fostered by a platonized Christian tradition. Once again, the suitability for black people of a religion with a crucifying cross at its center must be questioned.

In James Weldon Johnson's novel *The Autobiography of an Ex-Coloured Man,* the main protagonist, a mulatto whose light-skinned complexion allows him to pass for white, witnesses a lynching. He provides this poignant description of his reaction to white human beings transformed into "savage beasts" as they bring a black man to a torturous death:

> It was over before I realized that time had elapsed. Before I could make myself believe that what I saw was really happening, I was looking at a scorched post, a smouldering fire, blackened bones, charred fragments sifting down through coils of chain; and the smell of burnt flesh—human flesh— was in my nostrils.
>
> I walked a short distance away and sat down in order to clear my dazed mind. A great wave of humiliation and shame swept over me. Shame that I belonged to a race that could be so dealt with.[71]

Later in his reflection on the lynching, the protagonist further wonders how such savage "beating and murder of scores of innocent people" could take place "in the streets of a civilized and *Christian* city."[72]

This scene in Johnson's novel clarifies the question that this book seeks to answer. Just as Johnson's protagonist wondered how it was possible for him to belong to a race that could summarily be lynched, black people must question how it is possible to belong to a religion that easily provides a theological cover for lynchers. Moreover, how can a lynched people belong to a religion with a sacred lynching at its center?

Even if there are certain factors inherent in Christianity, and even particular to Christianity's crucifying center, that mitigate Christian participation in acts such as lynching, these factors clearly do not preclude such participation. It is for this reason that we must at least recognize the cross as an extremely troublesome, if not irredeemable aspect of Christianity. While the cross in and of itself may not precipitate deadly terror, the cross invested with power does. If nothing else, the cross, when empowered, makes it almost theologically irresistible for people not simply to inflict unwarranted suffering on others but also to sacrifice their very lives. The cross can easily spell the sacrifice of innocent, powerless people. The Christian cross and power thereby represent a deadly union. And so it is an almost predictable fate for Christians to be amongst the rowdy mob cheering for the noontime lynching of Richard Coleman. The noontime lynching that took place some two thousand years earlier makes such Christian involvement virtually a fait accompli given Christianity's relationship to power.

In 1887 British historian Lord Acton, in denying that any one class of people was more "unfit" than another to govern, said, "Power tends to corrupt and absolute power corrupts absolutely." Acton argued that power was the most serious threat to liberty. In this regard, he clearly surmised that a tendency to abuse power was inherent in human nature. Perhaps Lord Acton's observations were correct. History certainly reveals that power can make tyrants of people. If this is indeed the case, then a religion endowed with social and political power almost inevitably presents a dangerous imperialistic threat. What we have certainly found in relation to Christianity is that power is a theologically distorting, if not corrupting, influence. For all intents and purposes, Christianity and power should not mix, regardless of what may or may not be the natural inclinations of human beings. Christianity and power do not make for a desirable partnership. Given Christianity's theological core—that is, closed monotheism, christological paradox, and crucifying cross—it is a partnership that needs to be avoided. To reiterate, power allows Christians to act on the distinctions demanded by Christianity's monotheistic and paradoxical nature as well as to act on the deadly ramifications of the cross. For Christianity to align with power is thus for Christianity to invite trouble and perhaps invariably become an oppressing force. In effect, then, it is power as it interacts with the core theological elements of Christianity that allows Christians, with a history of being persecuted, to become ruthless persecutors so easily. Power, in many respects, becomes the triggering agent in Christianity's unsettling history. More specifically, Christianity—particularly a platonized Christian tradition—is unquestionably deadly for black people when it is allied with social and political power. Therefore, in assessing the viability of Christianity for black people, another question must be addressed: Is there anything about Christianity itself that could resist and even prevent this alliance with power, thereby opening the possibility for Christianity to be not simply suitable but perhaps intended for those who are powerless, such as black people. This question will be addressed in chapter 3, as this chapter will try to assess the integrity of Christianity's theological core with particular respect to power.

3

A Heretical Tradition

ON APRIL 28, 1899, the *Kissimee Valley Gazette* described Sam Hose at the time of his Sunday afternoon lynching:

> Holt [sic] went to the stake with as much courage as any one could possibly have possessed on such an occasion, and the only murmur that issued from his lips was when angry knives plunged into his flesh and his life's blood sizzled in the fire before his eyes.
> Then he cried, *"Oh, my God! Oh, Jesus."*[1]

On June 24, 1921, the *Baltimore Afro-American* described the events at John Henry Williams's Saturday night lynching:

> Flames flared up and found their way to Williams' body. Now and again he cried aloud and his body went though horrible contortions. For a time the winds carried the flames and smoke directly in his face so that he could not speak. Later the winds shifted and members of the mob, unaffected, recognized the hymn he sang as, "Nearer My God to Thee."[2]

There is perhaps no greater tragic irony than the scene that was surely played out at numerous black lynchings when both the lynchers and the lynched ostensibly cried out to the same God, the God of Jesus Christ. Just as those doing the lynching no doubt believed that God was on their side in their act of human sacrifice, so too did the ones being lynched believe that God was with them as they were being "sacrificed." At the same time that a Sam Hose

71

or a John Henry Williams was crying out to God, there were no doubt voices coming from the mob of lynchers also calling out to God. Indeed, one witness to Sam Hose's lynching reports "an old white-haired man screaming 'God bless every man that had a hand in this and thank God for vengeance.'"[3] This leads to the question, Whose voices were most representative of the God of Jesus Christ? Is this God most reflected in the pleas of the powerless victim or in the shouts of the powerful lynchers? For whom is Christianity most suited?

If one follows the theological logic of Christianity's classical atonement tradition, then the Christian God is one who in some way accepts human sacrifice.[4] A crowd that lynches, therefore, would not immediately repulse such a God. A God that sanctions a human sacrifice as brutal as crucifixion can serve as a divine ally for those who make such a sacrifice—even a sacrifice as horrific as lynching.

But what then about those who are sacrificed? How does the Christian God respond to their pleas? Does this God have any sympathy for the lynched? Is the God of Jesus Christ really, as the classical atonement tradition implies, a God that could in some way accept an act of human sacrifice? Or does the atonement tradition actually distort God's role in the crucifixion and hence God's tolerance for sacrifice? At stake is whose witness at the lynching tree is most revealing of the Christian God and hence of Christianity: that of the lynchers or that of the lynched? The answer to this question is perhaps found at the scene of sacrifice that took place some two thousand years before the scenes of black lynching: Jesus' crucifixion.

Whether or not they had them in mind at the time of their own executions, both Sam Hose's and John Henry Williams's final few words from the trees upon which they were lynched are a haunting echo of Jesus' last words from the cross upon which he was crucified. As if prefiguring the report of Sam Hose's plaintive words, the Gospel of Matthew reports that Jesus cried out, "My God, my God, why hast thou forsaken me?" (Matt. 27:46). And just as John Henry Williams seemed assured of God's care for him even unto death, Jesus was assured of the same as he reportedly said right before his death, "Father into thy hands I commit my spirit" (Luke 23:46). Is the similarity in the words of sacrificial victims centuries apart reflective of more than just two victims' familiarity with Jesus? Are Sam Hose's and John Henry Williams's pleas simply prayerful attempts to imitate Jesus, or do their pleas imply a more profound connection between themselves and the one crucified two thousand years earlier? Are the words of Hose and Williams divinely revelatory as the words of Jesus were perhaps similarly revelatory? Do these words cried out from a tree as well as from a cross provide us with any insight into the meaning of the Christian God concerning this God's relationship to the vulgar mistreatment of human bodies, especially black bodies? This chapter will argue that they do. The prevailing assumption of chapter 3 is that there is more than a coincidental familiarity between black lynch victims and Jesus. There is in fact a theological bond between the two.

Chapter 3 argues that it is with the crucified and the lynched that God identifies, not in a way to abide their torturous sacrifice but in a way to decry it. This chapter maintains that the crucifixion decidedly reveals the Christian God as one who sides with victims of unscrupulous power. Likewise, the cross distinctly indicates that Christianity is a religion most suited for those who are socially, politically, and even ecclesiastically dispossessed, if not demonized. This chapter thus contends that Christianity's alliance with power is anti-Christ. This will be shown by exposing the heretical nature of platonized Christianity, for inasmuch as platonized Christianity denounces the body, it betrays Christianity's incarnational identity. Such a betrayal allows for and, in fact, makes probable Christianity's collusion with unjust forms of power. Corresponding to this argument, chapter 3 will also reveal the heretical nature of atonement theories that suggests divine forbearance for any form of human sacrifice. Such theories reflect the kind of theological distortion acceptable within platonized traditions. In the end, this chapter maintains that Christianity's alliance with dominating power is antithetical to the Christian religion itself. Such an alliance essentially violates the christological integrity of Christianity's theological core. It is in this way that chapter 3 will

bring us closer to appreciating the soundness of the black faith tradition, and how it is that I, a black woman, am Christian. Let us
begin this chapter by examining the heretical nature of a platonized Christian tradition.

The Heretical Nature
of Platonized Christianity

The belief in Jesus as Christ/Messiah is the unique claim of the
Christian faith tradition. This belief is predicated on the theological presupposition that Jesus is the incarnate One, that is, that God
became flesh in him. This incarnational claim represents the chris-
tological/ontological paradox of Christianity's theological core.
This paradox is carefully explicated in the classical christological
tradition. As discussed in chapter 1, this tradition affirms that in
Jesus two different natures came together, the divine and the
human. The Chalcedonian confession specifically clarifies that
ontologically Jesus is both "*fully* God and *fully* human." This confession remains faithful to New Testament testimony concerning
Jesus. For instance, in the Second Letter to the Corinthians Paul
confirms Jesus' divinity as he states, "God was reconciling the
world to himself in Christ" (2 Cor. 5:19). According to gospel
accounts, Jesus' divine nature is made explicit from his very birth,
as it is said that he was conceived not by man, but by the Holy
Spirit.[5] Furthermore, while the New Testament tradition does not
provide a complete biographical account of Jesus' life, his full
humanity is definitely attested to. For instance, the intensity of
human emotion and bodily need that the gospels report Jesus
experiencing profoundly reveals his humanity. The Gospels
describe his pain and grief (Luke 19:41; John 11:33-36), his
weariness (John 4:6), his hunger (Mark 11:12) and his thirst (John
19:28). What is witnessed to in the New Testament accounts and
subsequently affirmed by the christological tradition is that Jesus
embodies an ontological paradox; he is at once human and divine.
Hence, he is God incarnate.

Just as the fact of the ontological paradox is affirmed as significant to Christian faith, so too is the relational character of that paradox. In this regard, the christological tradition again remains true to New Testament witness concerning Jesus. The Chalcedonian confession expressly states that neither Jesus' divine nor his human nature is confused or changed by the other. The *integrity* of each nature is maintained in who Jesus is as Christ. Again, such a creedal claim is consistent with the New Testament gospels as they report both signals of Jesus' full divinity—for example, the dove descending from heaven at the time of his baptism (Mark 1:9-11), his authority to forgive sins (Mark 2:1-12), his transfiguration (Mark 9:2-8)—and also signs of his full humanity (his hunger, thirst, grief). The point is that Christian faith relies on both the recognition of Jesus as the incarnate One and the affirmation that his divine and human natures authentically and mutually coexist within him. Thus, the christological tradition makes clear that even while Jesus harbors an ontological paradox, he is not at odds with himself. Simply put, for him to be both divine and human—that is, God incarnate—does not mean that he possesses "two warring natures," but rather that he possesses two complementary natures. In recognizing this christological actuality, the heretical quality of a platonized Christian tradition becomes evident.

Most fundamentally, the incarnation itself, that which was expressly affirmed at the Nicene council, absolutely defies any theological notions of there being an innate antagonism between divinity and humanity. The incarnation signals that the body/flesh is not an imposition to that which is divine. As I have argued in other places, that God became embodied in Jesus attests that the body can provide—and in the case of Jesus did provide—a perfect vehicle for divine presence.[6] Christianity's unique and central affirmation that God became incarnate thereby serves to deny the validity of theological claims that construe the body as an inexorable source of evil. In this respect, the incarnation unquestionably disputes a platonized Christian tradition since this tradition characteristically demonizes the body and the flesh.

To review, platonized Christianity considers the body a vessel of human sin—and the putative worst sin of all, sexual lust. In the platonized tradition the body is regarded as that which separates human beings from God. It is seen as a mortal trap for the divine soul, something the soul must somehow overcome. In effect, the body is deemed an albatross to all that is holy. Platonized Christianity, therefore, fosters a sacrosanct denigration of the flesh. Given platonized reasoning, it is no wonder that platonized Christianity is so often implicated in violent attacks against certain human beings (more to be said about this later). For again, this tradition does not hold the body in high esteem. The body is seen as a hindrance to God. And so it follows that those persons who are summarily essentialized according to their bodies are likewise considered God's enemies. For again, as platonized Christianity constructs sacrosanct antagonistic relationality between the body and the soul it correspondingly projects hostile relationality between certain groups of people—that is, between those people considered governed by their soul and those considered controlled by their body. It must be remembered that as it does this it unequivocally betrays the incarnational distinctiveness of Christianity's theological core.

Once more, that God became embodied signals that the body is not a reality that needs to be overcome. It is not the nemesis of the soul nor is it the vessel of all that is evil. Rather, it is a receptacle for divine witness; it is an instrument for divine revelation. The incarnation thereby makes clear that the body, far from being intrinsically evil, is what potentially participates in making the ways of God known in human history. In other words, the mark of one's humanity (i.e., body), is not offensive to God, but is taken on by God so that the fullness of God may be revealed. At the very least, the essential incarnational character of Christianity manifestly rejects representations of the body/flesh opposed to the soul/divine. Correspondingly, the very fact of the divine incarnation insinuates a sacred respect for *all* human bodies in that *any* human body potentially serves as a vessel for divine revelation. That God became flesh in Jesus should thereby preclude Christianity's theological demonization of the body and hence explicit and implicit Christian involvement in the violent disregard for certain human bodies. To appreciate the significance of the incarnation does not mean an undue worship of the body, but it does mean recognition of the body's utter sacred value and, hence, the sacred value of all human life.

Not only does Christianity's incarnational identity oppose theological notions of the intrinsically "evil body," but it also contests dualistic conceptualizations of difference. As mentioned above, the Chalcedonian confession insist that the two different natures of Christ are not in any way dualistically related to each other. Each nature—humanity and divinity—maintains its own integrity. Neither one overpowers, dominates, or extinguishes the other. At the same time that the Nicene/Chalcedonian tradition clarifies the reality of Jesus' ontological paradox, it also suggests that it is as the two natures exist in concert with one another that Jesus is a perfect revelation of God, that is, Christ. Fittingly then, during the debates that led to the Chalcedonian confession, those views that were construed as diminishing the fullness of either nature were proclaimed to be heretical. For instance, early on the road to a christological settlement, Docetism was rejected because it was seen as devaluing Jesus' humanity, while Arianism was rejected for devaluing the divinity of Jesus.[7] Both views threatened the integrity of the incarnation itself. The classical christological tradition thus affirms that it is only as divinity and humanity *fully* and mutually exist in relationship that God is "perfectly" revealed in human history through Jesus.

In a sense, not only are the christological settlements logically and naturally related to the later trinitarian resolutions about the Godhead, but they prefigure those resolutions. During the trinitarian discussions, the Greek concept of *perichoresis* became important. Introduced into the debate by the Cappadocian Fathers, it allowed for the unique identity of each person within the Godhead—that is, the Father, Son, and Holy Spirit—to be preserved while it also maintained that each person shared in the work of the others. *Perichoresis* basically suggested an eternal relationship of mutuality and reciprocity within the Godhead itself. That is, while each person had its own function, those functions were respected by the other persons, even as the respective functions could not be fully carried out independent of the other persons. The Nicene/

Chalcedonian christological tradition suggests a similar *incarnational perichoresis*. While each of Jesus' two natures maintains its own identity and each manifests itself in Jesus in a particular way, each nature is dependent on the other if Jesus is to be Christ. Just as the trinitarian *perichoresis* suggests a perfect dance of mutuality and reciprocity within the godhead, the same is suggested in regard to Christ—a perfect dance of mutuality and reciprocity vital to the incarnation itself.[8] Moreover, just as the trinitarian reality by definition defies dualisms (by virtue of the fact that a dualism implies two things in relation and a trinity by definition means three things in relation), so too does the incarnational reality. For again, the fact of the incarnation means that that which is of God/divine is not dualistically opposed to what is human/flesh.

Thus, once more it becomes clear that a platonized Christian tradition substantially betrays the integrity of Christianity's christological/incarnational paradox. As platonized Christianity pits the body against the soul, divinity against humanity, it is at odds with the incarnation. It belies a Christ who is at once fully divine and fully human. Inasmuch as the body is considered a natural antagonist to that which is divine, platonized theological constructions do not allow for the two different natures of Christ to coexist respectfully and mutually. Given this, platonized Christianity must be considered just as heretical as the positions banned during the Nicene/Chalcedonian debates since, like them, it does not allow for Jesus to be a fully *embodied* revelation of God. Platonized Christianity essentially denies the body's indispensable positive value to the incarnation.

Ironically, however, to say, as platonized Christianity does, that the body must in some way be denied or kept in check so that divinity can be effectively manifest is actually to concede the powerful nature of the body. For it is to suggest that if the body is given space to exist naturally, it would in due time obfuscate the witness of the divine. The implication is that "humanity" is ultimately more powerful than "divinity," and thus the mark of one's "humanity"—the body—must be severely constrained in order for "divinity" to be made fully known. This of course is not the intended message of platonized Christianity, but it is perhaps a

logical extension of this tradition. Why else would so much theological imagination be spent denouncing and trying to curb the
demands of the body if the power of the body itself was not
feared? In fact, it is often the case that the thing that one attempts
to suppress the most is the very thing that one also most fears.
Given this understanding, it appears that it is not the "weaknesses"
of the flesh that platonized Christianity attempts to circumvent,
but rather the very strength of it.

In sum, platonized Christianity does not construct a theological paradigm in which the body and soul can equally coexist. Even
as platonized Christianity purports to protect the integrity of the
soul, by vanquishing the body, it actually undermines divinity's
very sacred authority. It concedes that the body overwhelms the
soul; hence, divinity is enfeebled by humanity. That platonized
Christianity ultimately distorts the character of divine nature is
consistent with its dualistic approach. Dualistic approaches by definition distort the integrity of at least one, if not both, compo-
nents of a relationship involving difference. To reiterate, dualistic
paradigms do not permit a complementary difference to exist
between two things. The Chalcedonian confession, and hence the
christological tradition, challenges such platonized notions as it
resists a dualistic conception of the incarnation, that is, the ontological paradox. This brings us back to the conceptualization of
difference.

The practical implication of the christological tradition rejecting a dualistic conceptualization of the incarnation is that it
advances a nondualisitic model for the negotiation of relationships
of difference. The classic christological tradition does not, in and
of itself, project "wrong relationality." Rather, it puts forward a
theological/christological model that demands mutuality of relationship and thus a respect for difference—perhaps even human
difference. With this said, that it does so *is* absolutely remarkable.

Men with ecclesiastical and political power took part in the
christological councils. Bishops were the only ones permitted to
participate in the ecumenical gatherings. In fact, one of the main
instigators of the Nicene debates, Arius, was not allowed to argue
his theological position before the Nicene council because he

lacked sufficient ecclesial-political clout—he was not a bishop. Bishop Eusebius of Nicomedia had to speak for him. Again, the men at the ecumenical councils were men of power with at least three objectives: consolidating their authority, protecting the authority of the emperor, and preserving Christian unity at a time when Christians were just beginning to enjoy a peaceful existence within the empire. The point being made is that theological difference was not to be acknowledged let alone respected.

In effect, Emperor Constantine's motivation for calling the first ecumenical council set the tone for this and subsequent christological councils: unity was to be achieved at all costs and thus difference was not to be tolerated. This tone was evident in how theological dissenters were treated. For instance, those bishops who refused to sign the creed agreed upon at Nicaea were summarily deposed, declared heretical, and later banished from their cities by Constantine. Much disquieting intrigue continued on the road to Chalcedon, but in the end, even as it came after his death, Emperor Constantine's agenda for the empire was realized. Ecclesiastical and political power coalesced to achieve uniformity of theological and political conviction throughout the Roman Empire. And so, given the social and political climate that inspired the ecumenical councils, it is most astonishing that these councils could possibly produce—even unwittingly—christological understandings that preserve the nondualistic impulse of the incarnation, ideas that appreciate difference. Yet they did. In recognizing the ontological paradox as essential to the incarnation, the Chalcedonian confession affirms a relationship of mutuality and respect as characteristic of that paradox. It essentially emphasizes a paradoxical relationship—that is, it delineates difference—yet it does not construe that difference in a dualistic manner.

What we find, then, is that the difference at the heart of Christianity's theological core, a difference that is fundamental to the faith tradition itself, can be conceived in a manner that does not prescribe "dualistic epistemology" or "dualistic relationality." Recalling a point made earlier, a paradox does not automatically signify a dualism. Thus it seems that even with a christological approach that starts from above—one that begins with the fact of

God descending to earth to become incarnate in Jesus—a nondualistic Christology can be affirmed. In other words, a high Christology, one that stresses the ontological nature of Christ, can in fact produce a nondualistic model of relationality.

Perhaps I am pushing this interpretation of the Nicene/Chalcedonian christological tradition too far. For regardless of what may be the nondualistic tendency of the ontological paradox as affirmed in this tradition, this tradition has readily given way to dualistic interpretations. This tradition has, in effect, become platonized. It must be kept in mind that the Nicene/Chalcedonian tradition is the very tradition of Augustine, the theologian considered most responsible for the infusion of a platonized viewpoint into Western Christianity. Even if one were to accept that the Nicene/Chalcedonian tradition itself does not specifically convey dualistic ways of thinking and acting, one must acknowledge that this tradition has quite easily given way to, if not suborned, both dualistic epistemology and relationality, as has been well argued by various scholars such as Carter Heyward.[10] Moreover, the Nicene/Chalcedonian tradition has allowed for, and even sustained, a collective theological consciousness defined by dualistic relationality and subsequently one that easily colludes with inequitable power. One must thus ask, how is this the case? How is it that this classical christological tradition, one that ostensibly espouses nondualistic constructions of difference, has so easily surrendered to platonized theological frameworks and hence become aligned with unjust power?

As noted in chapter 1, that Christianity's very theological core begs for delineation of difference certainly makes Christianity vulnerable to dualistic perspectives. Yet vulnerability is not compliance. That is, to be vulnerable to particular perspectives does not mean that those perspectives must be inexorably adopted, especially if there are mitigating factors, as in the case of Christianity. Specifically, as just shown, the incarnation itself contests dualistic constructions. And so, how is it that, irrespective of Christianity's prevailing nondualistic center, a dominant Christian tradition governed by a "dualistic epistemology" was able to emerge? At stake is not simply that a dualistic framework defines a predominant strand of Christianity (platonized Christianity) but that this dualistic framework is characterized by unjust relationality. The essential question, therefore, is: How does a religion that theologically upholds a relationship of mutuality and respect at its very core become so theologically corrupt that it supports disreputable dehumanizing relationships that culminate in the defilement of human bodies? The answer to this question is perhaps found in what the Nicene/Chalcedonian tradition fails to do.

For all of its merits, the Nicene/Chalcedonian tradition overlooks the historical reality of the incarnation. It recognizes only one essential christological paradox while ignoring the other. It does not acknowledge the aforementioned *existential* paradox also at the heart of Christianity's incarnational reality. In other words, it fails to appreciate Jesus' earthly ministry. According to the classical christological tradition (again commonly recited in churches in the form of the Nicene Creed), it was enough that God became incarnate in Jesus. This divine act was sufficient proof of Jesus being Christ. Jesus' ministry as the "bearer of God's rule" is virtually dismissed in the Nicene Creed and thereby rendered inconsequential to his messiahship. To repeat a point made in the previous chapter, this creed moves directly from Jesus' birth to his crucifixion and resurrection. Missing from the creed is any reference to Jesus' ministry. It is in this way that the classical christological tradition actually betrays the New Testament gospels' portrayal of Jesus. (This failure to take Jesus' ministry seriously will become significant to platonized Christianity's impact on black life, via evangelical Protestantism. For ironically, while evangelical Protestantism emphasizes the literal significance of the Bible, it— true to a platonized hermeneutic—devalues the ministry of Jesus. (More will be said about this later.)

While the four gospels certainly provide distinctive interpretations of Jesus, they do show a remarkable similiarity. The gospels, even in their differences, all focus on Jesus' ministry. They actually pay little attention to the fact of his birth and rarely speak of his ontological reality apart from his earthly ministry. The earliest canonical gospel, Mark, does not even include a birth narrative. It is only John, the latest of the four gospels, that opens by highlighting Jesus' preexistent reality.[11] In effect, the gospels' portrayals of Jesus as Christ resist high christological interpretations of Jesus' significance. They challenge any understanding of Jesus as the incarnate One that principally concentrates on his ontological reality (the fact of the divine/human encounter) thereby devaluing his existential reality and his ministry. In short, the gospels make clear that the meaning of Jesus as God incarnate is found not only in that he was a fully embodied divine/human reality but also that he *acted* in human history.

If we are to be theologically instructed by the emphasis of the gospels, then the fact that Jesus acted in human history was just as important to his being Christ as his ontological reality. Thus, to construct a Christology that makes Jesus' ministry virtually inconsequential is to fail to appreciate the meaning of the incarnation itself. So ironically, even as the Nicene/Chalcedonian tradition serves to affirm the fact of Jesus as the incarnate One, it does not apprehend Jesus' full significance as God incarnate. But most significantly, because this tradition basically discounts what Jesus *did* through his body (and accordingly for the bodies of others) it tacitly provides theological license for the development of a Christian tradition that disregards the sanctity of various human bodies, such as the black body.

In general, to ignore Jesus' ministry—namely, his existential paradox—is to dispense with the defining factor in determining Christianity's appropriate relationship to social/political power, and hence Christians' proper relationship to peoples oppressed and marginalized by such power. For Jesus' very ministry challenges any Christian collusion with disreputable power. Consequently, a Christian tradition grounded in christological interpretations that substantially ignore the ministry of Jesus sets itself up for suspect involvement with dehumanizing power since such a tradition has basically abandoned anything that might check these involvements. At the same time, a tradition that ignores the ministry of Jesus lends itself to a platonized approach as the devaluation of the body in this approach compels a similar disregard of Jesus' ministry. Finally, such a tradition is apt to interpret the crucifixion in such a way that supports and possibly suborns the violent derision

of certain human bodies. For as we will soon see, it is only in recognizing and realizing the meaning of Jesus' existential paradox
that the theological import of his crucifixion can be properly
appreciated and accordingly that the sacredness of human bodies
becomes clear. In short, to ignore the existential paradox of the
incarnation is to set Christianity on a course that opposes its
unique christological identity—the incarnation itself, Jesus Christ.
Let us now look more precisely to see how this is the case.

Power as Anti-Christ

Jesus' existential paradox is just as important to his being Christ as
is his ontological paradox. Indeed, it can be argued that his existential reality is more crucial, given that it is not largely a matter
of theological speculation, as his ontological reality is. As already
stated, all four canonical gospels emphasize Jesus' public ministry.
In so doing, they make clear that this ministry was first and foremost preoccupied with the imminent coming of God's kingdom.
The gospels report that through his preaching, teaching, and
interactions with all manner of people, Jesus clarified the character of God's kingdom at the same time that he summoned people
to prepare for its arrival. In this way, who he was as an existential
paradox becomes evident. His human existence is altogether consumed with divine matters. His earthly ministry is thoroughly
focused on the heavenly realm. To recognize Jesus as an existential paradox is to realize that through him God's ultimate dominion over the earth is disclosed. Hence, Jesus' ministry is the
christological key for determining the meaning of God in and for
human history. It is also crucial to discerning the theological significance of the crucifixion. Let us thus examine this ministry
more closely.

According to the New Testament gospels, Jesus' ministry was
disruptive of the social-political status quo. It was so in at least two
noteworthy ways: First, by associating with those who were
socially marginalized and demonized such as Samaritan women,

tax collectors, and lepers (John 4:1-42; Luke 7:36-49; Luke 19:1-10; Mark 1:40-45), Jesus disregarded cultural and religious relational boundaries. Second, by asserting the authority of God over earthly authorities, Jesus challenged the very rule of power itself (Matt. 7:24-28; Mark 12:12-17; Luke 20:45-47). Essentially, the gospels' overall portrayal of Jesus' ministry—even allowing for each gospel's nuanced interpretation—is one in which Jesus boldly and passionately rejected the conventions and supremacy of prevailing social, political, and religious power.

Not surprisingly, then, Jesus' ministry created much enmity between himself and the ruling forces of his day. His noncooperation with accepted mores and customs along with his insolence in respect to earthly authority was unacceptable to the governing leaders. Jesus' presence was perceived as a threat to their rule and accordingly to social stability. Thus, in the end, the political and religious authorities of the first-century Roman world cooperated with one another to rid themselves of Jesus' menacing presence.

While the precise offense triggering Jesus' arrest and eventual crucifixion may always remain unclear, his consistent challenge to prevailing power unquestionably sealed his fate. In fact, Jesus' final arrival into Jerusalem at the time of Passover ensured that this challenge would reach a climax. For at as important a time in Jewish religious life as the Passover, when many Jews would be making the pilgrimage to Jerusalem, both Pontius Pilate (the Roman governor) and Caiaphas (the Jewish high priest) were sure to be there. Hence Jesus' presence served as a direct affront to each of them even as it allowed them to join together in solving the Jesus' problem. And so it was, according to the gospel accounts, that the political and religious leadership of the day collaborated—perhaps incited by the crowd gathered in Jerusalem—to crucify Jesus. That Jesus was crucified makes even clearer the nature of his ministry.

In the first-century Roman world, crucifixion was arguably the most brutal form of punishment available. Political, not religious, authorities most often employed it. Moreover, crucifixion was characteristically reserved for slaves and captured enemy soldiers, though others that the state held in particular contempt might also be crucified. Crucifixion—whatever the particular justification for its use in individual cases—generally indicated the class and social status of the crucified ones. Those crucified were considered outcasts or a threat to social stability. In this regard, the extreme nature of crucifixion can be taken as a sign of how worthless and troublesome to established order the victims were perceived to be. Given this understanding of crucifixion, it was a fitting fate for Jesus. For again, in the name of promoting the kingdom of God, Jesus associated with social outsiders and challenged the very rule of power. In short, Jesus was crucified because he identified with the "crucified" class of people and because he jeopardized social and political stability. The crucifixion of Jesus thereby reaffirms both whom Jesus was for and what Jesus was against. He was for those rendered of no value by dominant power and he was against such power. Essentially, that Jesus was crucified underscored his solidarity with those broken and exploited (if not also demonized) by power and his opposition to subjugating, dehumanizing power.

It is in appreciating these general grounds for Jesus' crucifixion, even if we are unable to know the specific reasons for it, that the revelatory significance of his ministry and the theological import of the crucifixion itself are found.

Inasmuch as Jesus was God incarnate, Jesus' ministry reveals a decidedly *partial, active* God. This is not a God who is passive or impartial to the complex inhumane realities associated with inequitable power. The God incarnate in Jesus is One unequivocally identified with those exploited by power and One unambiguously against abusive power. More particularly, through his ministry Jesus reveals God's absolute denunciation of two types of relationships necessary to keep unjust power in place: the *dualistic relationality* inequitable power constructs between certain groups of people and the *congenial relationality* inequitable power seeks with sacred authority.

Divine opposition to dualistic relationality is disclosed in Jesus' refusal to set himself over and against those whom political and religious rule considered the unacceptable "others." As earlier noted, Jesus reached out to a Samaritan woman, lepers, tax collectors, and the like. In so doing, Jesus not only showed solidarity with those cast out by power but most significantly defied the over-and-against dualistic relationality constructed by power. Essentially, he refused to treat as "others" those marginalized and demonized by the rules and customs of political and religious authority. Jesus' ministry thereby invalidates any Christian appropriation of dualistic relationality. In this regard, the existential paradox of Christianity's christological core makes explicit the nondualistic impulse of its ontological paradox. Put plainly, the incarnation unquestionably denounces the practice of dualistic relationality. Therefore, Christian support of any form of dualistic relationship, which by definition create hostile, even deadly, interactions between groups of people, becomes theologically indefensible—especially if one gives serious consideration to the ministry of Jesus.

Not only does Jesus' ministry deny sacred status to dualistic relationality, but it also reveals profound divine opposition to the congenial relationality that oppressive power seeks with sacred authority. This is most clearly demonstrated in one of Jesus' last acts before his arrest—the running of the money changers out of the temple (Mark 11:15-18). His attack on the symbiotic relationship between political and religious authority bespeaks God's predisposition toward Pilate/Caiaphas–like alliances. In short, it condemns such an alliance. In so doing, Jesus' act signifies that sacred legitimation is not to be given to corrupt, exploitative power. This implies at least two things regarding Christianity's connection to power—one practical, the other more theoretical. First, practically speaking, Christian leaders are not to provide for or join in the ways of abusive social/political leadership. There should not, in effect, be a congenial relationship between the two.

Second, and perhaps most fundamentally, Christianity is not to provide a theological shelter for the contrivances of power. Recalling Foucault's analysis of power mentioned in chapter 1, Jesus' act in the temple impugns Christianity's participation in discursive power. Simply put, just as the temple was not to provide a safe harbor for money changers, Christianity is not to provide a theological canopy for the productions of unjust power. Once more the implication for platonized Christianity is strong. For inasmuch as the platonized tradition has provided for both *implicit* and *explicit* Christian involvement in human oppression, it contradicts God's revelatory partiality, that is, God's unequivocal opposition to unfair power as revealed in Jesus.

Before leaving this scene of Jesus in the temple, it is perhaps also worth noting what Jesus interrupted from being sold in the temple, that is, innocent animals for sacrifice (doves, oxen, and sheep). If these items of sale are of any particular importance to the gospel report, perhaps Jesus' protest portends God's disposition toward "sacrificial acts"; that is, it implies what the crucifixion event makes clear—God is against the sacrifice of the innocent. Not to make too much of this scene theologically, let us focus on what it does clearly indicate—divine opposition to the congenial relationality often enjoyed by inequitable power and sacred authority.

In effect, then, who Jesus is as an existential paradox reveals a God whose presence in human history opposes the complexities of unmerited power, be it the particular dualistic or congenial relationality necessary for such power to prevail. Interestingly, while Jesus, through both his ontological and existential realities definitely opposed relationships that promoted unjust and hostile opposition between people, he projects a sacrosanct oppositional relationship—that is, the relationship between God and oppressive power. This brings us to the theological significance of the crucifixion.

Inasmuch as Jesus was "the bearer of God's rule" he was a perfect embodiment of what God was for. Jesus perfectly revealed God's presence in history as well as the nature of God's ultimate dominion over history. Therefore, for God to have in any way participated in or condoned Jesus' crucifixion would place God on the side of those who contested Jesus and his ministry and therefore against God's very self. Essentially, for God to approve, accept, or tolerate in any way Jesus' crucifixion suggests an inexplicable act of divine self-opposition.

Furthermore, any divine warrant for the crucifixion also belies the incarnation itself as it defies that which the incarnation demonstratively affirms: the sacred value of the human body. To reiterate, crucifixion by all accounts was one of the cruelest acts that could have been perpetrated against human beings. The bodies of the crucified ones were considered of no account and thus viciously and purposely defiled. Yet the incarnation suggests that all human bodies are to be respected as potential vessels for divine revelation. The incarnation basically repudiates any form of demonizing disrespect of the body/flesh. Jesus' actual ministry in fact demonstrated sacred regard for the body/flesh.

The gospels report that Jesus' ministry routinely involved the healing of certain bodies. Accordingly, they never report that Jesus defiled the bodies of others. As if to emphasize the divine regard for the human body, Luke portrays Jesus as restoring the ear of one of those who was sent to arrest him after one of his disciples cut it off (Luke 22:50-51). The overriding point is that who Jesus was as the incarnate One, both ontologically and existentially, reveals a sacred regard for the flesh. In this respect, any divine sanction of the crucifixion would contravene this central aspect of the incarnation. And so what we find is that the reality of the incarnation suggests not divine warrant but divine opposition to Jesus' crucifixion. To repeat, for God to affirm in any way the crucifixion of Jesus would set God against God's very self both in terms of God's incarnate presence in human history and God's ultimate reign over human history. Atonement theories that suggest that God in some way enjoined the crucifixion of Jesus for salvific purposes are therefore at best christologically misguided, and at worst christological heresies.

Atonement Tradition Revisited

There is no doubt that Jesus' crucifixion is a central part of the Christian story. There is also no doubt that Christianity's emphasis on the crucified Jesus has perpetuated human suffering both physically and otherwise (more will be said about this in relationship to the black body later). In many respects, Jesus' crucifixion has become a "stumbling block" throughout Christian history as it is often implicated in Christianity's troubling legacy. In fact, to have a violent unjust execution at the center of the Christian story has been difficult to account for theologically, especially for those people whose bodies are often violently and unjustly harmed.

Various theologians have given voice to the problem of the crucifixion for a suffering, historically demonized people. Most notable among them are womanist theologians. They have variously attempted to articulate a life-sustaining and empowering theology for black women whose bodies have especially been abused by the perverse complexities of white patriarchal rule. Delores Williams is arguably the earliest and most consistent womanist voice to call for a "re-imagining" of the Christian story for black women. She has been unrelenting in her critical reassessment of the crucifixion's meaning for Christian faith in general and black women's faith in particular.

During the 1993 Re-Imagining Conference, Williams stirred up much theological controversy when she asserted, during a question-and-answer session, "I don't think we need a theory of Atonement at all. . . . I don't think we need folks hanging on crosses and blood dripping and weird stuff."[12] While this has perhaps been the most often quoted portion of Williams's response, and certainly the part that ignited the most debate, often left out when recounting this response is her critique of the "classical" atonement tradition. Williams explained in her answer, "I think Jesus came for life and to show us something about life and living together and what life was all about. Atonement has to do with death."[13] For Williams, theories of atonement are by definition attempts to provide divine legitimation for the death of Jesus. What Williams's response at the Re-Imagining Conference summarily captures is her fuller valuation of the crucifixion and its significance for black women.

Williams's assessment of the crucifixion and its accompanying atonement tradition begins with an appreciation for black women's oppression, which, she says, is characterized by "surrogacy." Though Williams makes a distinction between the "coerced" surrogacy experienced by black women during slavery and the "voluntary" surrogacy they have experienced postslavery, both forms of surrogacy bespeak an imposition of white patriarchal systems and structures of oppression—what she refers to as the "demonarchy" that encumbers black lives.[14] So for instance, Williams points out that during slavery black women's bodies were used as "surrogates" for white women's bodies not only in terms of "suckling white babies," but also in terms of satiating the rapacious sexual desires of white men. During the postbellum period Williams explains that significant numbers of black women have continued to serve as surrogates for white women given the jobs most available to them, that is, nannies and domestic workers. Williams argues, however, "God did not intend the surrogacy roles [black women] have been forced to perform."[15] It is for this reason that Williams maintains that the meaning of Jesus' crucifixion within the Christian tradition must be rethought.

Williams rightly points out that an undue emphasis has been placed on Jesus' crucifixion as a means of atoning for human sin. She specifically argues that atonement frameworks for understanding the crucifixion characteristically cast Jesus in a surrogacy role. That is, through his death Jesus serves as a surrogate for humanity, thus making up for human sin and securing human salvation. It is in this way that Jesus' suffering and death on the cross are understood as sacrificially redemptive. Williams asserts, however, that atonement theories of the crucifixion are not only a misreading of the Jesus story, but most importantly they are detrimental to black women. She convincingly argues that these theories allow for, if not compel, black women to interpret their own oppressive surrogacy as redemptive. Williams therefore challenges womanist theologians "to respond meaningfully to black women's historic experience of surrogacy oppression, [by showing] that redemption of humans can have nothing to do with any kind of surrogate or substitute role Jesus was reputed to have played in a bloody act that supposedly gained victory over sin and/or evil."[16] In so doing, the meaning of the cross in black faith as well as in the Christian story must be construed in such a way that redemption is found—as God intended it to be—in a life of peaceful, productive, and "abundant relationality," not through a life of exploitative surrogacy (i.e., sacrificial suffering). Williams puts it plainly:

Humankind is, then, redeemed through Jesus' *ministerial vision* of life and not through his death. There is nothing divine in the blood of the cross. God does not intend black women's surrogacy experience. Neither can Christian faith affirm such an idea. Jesus did not come to be a surrogate. Jesus came for life, to show humans a perfect vision of ministerial relation that humans had very little knowledge of. As Christians, black women cannot forget the cross, but neither can they glorify it. To do so is to glorify suffering and to render their exploitation sacred. To do so is to glorify the sin of defilement.[17]

In perhaps the most extensive study of the cross in the African American experience from a womanist perspective, JoAnne Marie Terrell takes issue with Williams's disregard for atonement theological constructions and hence for what she perceives as Williams's underestimation of the cross's significance in black lives. While she agrees with Williams that the notion of God requiring the death of Jesus needs to be revisited, Terrell believes that Williams does not fully appreciate the importance of "traditional notions of Atonement" for black church people and correspondingly does not appreciate the meaning of the atonement in the gospels.[18] Drawing on the gospel tradition, Terrell specifically argues that while God does not "sanction" the violence of the cross, God did indeed send Jesus into the world for "honorable" purposes, even though the world received Jesus badly. With this in mind, she argues that while the cross is certainly a reflection of the "egregious nature of every historical crime against humanity and the Divinity," it is more significantly "about God's love for humankind in a profound sense." She explains that the cross "testifies to the exceedingly great lengths to which God goes to advise the extent of human estrangement (from God and one another)." It is for this reason, Terrell offers, that the cross has special meaning for black women. She maintains that the crucifixion is a reminder of "God's decision to be *at-one*" with black women in their suffering, even as the "empty cross [the resurrection] is a symbol of God's continuous empowerment."[19] Thus in direct response to what she calls the "rhetorical impetus" of Williams's critique[20] Terrell states:

> It is no slight on the intelligence of black women when they confess [faith in the crucified Christ]; rather, it reflects on what they say they need and what they say Christ's real presence, mediated through the gospel, provides—redemption and release from the self-alienation and social alienation they experience in their workaday lives.[21]

Drawing on her own life experience, Terrell concludes by providing a "sacramental" understanding of sacrifice. In this regard, Jesus' suffering and death on the cross serve to empower those who suffer to live their lives not according to the violent ways of their oppressors or as victims, but rather in identification with the profound love of God. She states,

> This is what I think it means to witness *sacramentally* to the character of God: loving ones' own, *not* loving others uncritically and, most important, *not* being defined by one's victimization but by one's commitments [even if that means suffering and death].[22]

Clearly, I agree with Williams and Terrell that the classical atonement tradition has misconstrued the theological and perhaps even historical meaning of the crucifixion. This tradition has without a doubt contributed to a Christian theological consciousness that has granted sacred meaning to suffering and sacrifice, thereby providing a sacred covering for Christian participation in and acceptance of the sacrifice of certain human bodies. Even though the particular theories of "ransom," "satisfaction," and "moral influence" have long ago lost their "normative" status in Western theological thought, they set in motion the prevailing theological hermeneutic for interpreting the crucifixion. Sacrificial and/or redemptive suffering motifs characterize this hermeneutic. We will see later in this book the particular ill effects that this sacrificial/redemptive hermeneutic has had on the black body, not simply in terms of the way the black body has been reviled by others, but also in the way it has been regarded by black people as well as the way in which black people have regarded other human bodies. And so, without question a re-evaluation of the cross's theological significance is needed.

An important aspect of such a reevaluation, however, must be an understanding of how an atonement tradition that allows for the defilement of certain bodies could have possibly emerged and become so influential within a religion that at its very core maintains the sacredness of all human bodies. It is only in understanding this that the theological significance of the crucifixion will become even clearer and most important that we can begin to appreciate the special meaning the cross has for a suffering people, especially black people. Let us first, then, attempt to discern what it is that helped to form the troubling atonement tradition.

Questions of what to do with a Messiah that was executed and a God that presumably failed and in large part compelled the atonement tradition. Indeed, these very questions helped to shape the way the gospelling communities told the story of Jesus' crucifixion. Essentially, the classical Western atonement tradition, carrying forth from the gospels themselves, was and perhaps continues to be an attempt to make sense out of a crucified Messiah. This very concern suggests an underlying problematic: a narrow assumption about the meaning of divine power.

Given the fact that Jesus, the One who was claimed as Messiah, suffered a humiliating fate, an atonement tradition emerged to try to provide theological justification for it. In so doing, this tradition attempted to interpret the crucifixion in a manner consistent with a "powerful" God. Essentially, early Christian thinkers were unable to reconcile notions of the "one true powerful Christian God" with the utter powerlessness associated with being crucified. The problem within this early influential atonement tradition is the implicit, yet fundamental, concept of power. Within this tradition power is apparently conceived in relation to finite, mundane realities. Missing is a realization that the essence of God's infinite power might be very different from that of finite human power. Thus, seemingly shaped by the sociopolitical models of power in their own time, "classical" atonement theories suggest a dominating, authoritative perception of power. In this respect, the classical atonement tradition reflects the imperialistic reality of the Constantinian and post-Constantinian Christian church. Power is understood as that which triumphs over and defeats its enemy. It is associated with those who are socially, politically, or religiously dominant. With such a presumptive notion of power, it was inconceivable that the One "True" Christian God as perfectly revealed in Jesus could meet the crucified fate of society's most powerless. Hence, classical atonement theories emerged that attempted to explain the crucifixion of Jesus by assigning authoritative redemptive power to suffering, that is, suggesting that the crucifixion was a reflection of God's controlling command so as to offset any notion that it was a sign of God's weakness. However, in assigning the crucifixion to God, such theories violated the integrity of the incarnation both ontologically and existentially as earlier explained.

The question thus remains, How are we to understand the significance of the crucifixion? Can it be understood in such a way that does not imply the sanctity of sacrificial suffering and death, yet preserves the authority of God and at the same time appreciates the special importance it might have for suffering people, particularly black people? As this question implies, I agree with Terrell that given the oppressive reality of black life, the crucifixion has a special significance for black people that must always be appreciated. Black women and men relate intimately to and rely on the cross as they navigate the harsh realities of black living in America. Black theologians such as James Cone and before him Howard Thurman have provided the most compelling and comprehensive analysis of the existential importance of the cross for black faith.[23] The cross's significance is indeed witnessed to by Sam Hose and John Henry Williams at the time of their lynchings (about which more will be said later). Yet I also agree with Williams in her assessment that redemptive perceptions of the cross (which as we will later see characterize black faith) have been detrimental to the overall well-being of black life. And so again, we are compelled to ask if the crucifixion can be understood in a way that maintains the integrity of the incarnation and hence does not sanction certain

sacrificial human suffering. Or is the cross an unmitigated draw-
back when it comes to Christianity being a religion suitable for a
powerless people? Is there any positive, empowering value for a
suffering people to be found in a religion with an unjust execution
at its center? I contend that there is.

It cannot be stressed enough that any proper understanding of
Jesus' crucifixion must be first grounded in an appreciation of his
ministry. Such an appreciation makes unambiguously clear that
Jesus categorically identified with those who suffered at the hands
of dominating power and accordingly opposed those who wielded
such power. To repeat a point made earlier, that Jesus was crucified in effect concretized whom Jesus was for and what he was
against. As such, the crucifixion of Jesus the incarnate One trans-
forms conceptions of power when it comes to God.

The crucifixion reveals at least two interrelated Christian theological fundamentals: the *revelatory privilege* of the "least
regarded" and the defining integrity of divine power. Recognition
of the revelatory privilege associated with the "least regarded"
provides telling insight into divine power.

That Jesus was crucified not only reaffirms God's partiality for
the oppressed; it also reifies that this partiality is much more than
an impassive identification with those least regarded in society.
The crucifixion unquestionably reveals a *compassionate solidarity*
with them. Jesus is *with* the powerless in their very dehumanizing
condition, even to the point of crucifixion. It is in this way that we
can speak of the *kenosis* of Jesus.

Central to the affirmation that God became incarnate in Jesus
is the notion of *kenosis*. Deriving from the Pauline christological
testimony found in Philippians 2:5-11 that Jesus emptied himself
of his divinity even to the point of his death on the cross, *kenosis*
has come to signify Jesus' sacrificial obedience to God. However,
when understood in the context of Jesus' full ministry as it led to
his crucifixion, *kenosis* signifies not Jesus emptying himself as if to
be sacrificially obedient to God, but rather his divestment of anything that would obstruct his absolute compassionate solidarity
with the most oppressed. Such an act of compassionate solidarity
gives sacred meaning to the lives of those least regarded.

By taking on their dishonored life condition, God, through Jesus, exalts them as an indispensable, vital witnesses to God's self-disclosure. In this regard, God's partiality for the powerless is not simply a signal of God's opposition to dehumanizing power, but also an emphatic statement concerning the fundamental nature of divine revelation. Divine revelation comes through those who are rendered powerless. The powerless have "revelatory privilege" in that it is through them that God chooses to make God's self known. This concept of revelatory privilege is of course similar to what other theologians have variously described and which I have affirmed in other places, as God's "preferential option for the poor."[24] What is being emphasized here in this particular denotation "revelatory privilege," is that the very condition of the powerless tells us something about not only God's presence and movement in history but also God's very self. In this particular regard, it tells us something about the intrinsic quality of God's power. For made clear through Jesus is that the power of the incarnate God is best reflected in the condition of those rendered powerless. It is reflected through the crucified class of people. This of course raises the question, What kind of power is it that is crucified on the cross? In order to answer this question one must view the crucifixion in conjunction with the resurrection. The theological meaning of the crucifixion depends, in other words, on its inextricable relation to both Jesus' ministry (as explained above) *and* Jesus' resurrection. When understood in conjunction with the resurrection the character of God's power as well as God's affirmation of the powerless becomes clear.

Through the resurrection of Jesus, God repudiates dominating, inequitable power. This type of power invariably denigrates human bodies even to the point of death. Moreover, the resurrection confirms what the classical atonement tradition seems to overlook—that God's power is expressed altogether differently than human power. The essential quality of God's power is indeed evident in Jesus' own responses to his crucifixion. For instance, Jesus does not enjoin the oppressive tactics of his accusers. As seen in the gospel reports, he refuses to respond to the charges against him, thus not giving any credence to the authority of his executors or to the way in which they exercise that authority (see Mark 15:1-5). Furthermore, he does not respond in kind to the violent, life-destroying acts of prevailing authorities. Instead, Jesus responds to his crucifixion in an irenic, yet unassailable fashion. Most strikingly, he does not call for retribution on the crowd that called for his crucifixion. It is not that he acquiesces to his suffering; it is rather that he projects a different model of power—the divine power that comes through the powerless. God's power, unlike human power, is not characterized by force or might. It is not a presumptuous, triumphal, forceful kind of power. It does not claim authority by ruthlessly imposing itself on human bodies. Rather, it seeks to preserve the sacred integrity of the human body and hence the sanctity of human life. In general, this is not a power that acts in a way to humiliate, denigrate, or defile the bodies of others. It is perhaps for this reason that according to the gospels' report Jesus pronounced forgiveness from the cross as opposed to vengeful retribution for those who crucified him. Even from the cross Jesus portrays a divine power that refuses to respond to body-destroying acts in kind.

What Jesus points to in his responses to his crucifixion, the resurrection makes clear. The resurrection is God's definitive response to the crucifixion itself. It clarifies the essential character of God's power—it is power that values human life. Thus, God's power never functions in a way that profanes the bodies of people. Accordingly, the resurrection of the crucified one establishes that God does not in any way sanction the suffering and profane treatment of those rendered powerless in society, that is, the "crucified" class of people. Their lives are not to be used as sacrificial vehicles for any reason. The resurrection in effect asserts the "wrongness" of the crucifixion. In so doing, it disavows any notion that the sacrifice of the human body is expressive of divine power. What the resurrection *does* avow is one of the central tenets of the incarnation itself: the sacredness of the human body and concomitantly the sanctity of human life. It cannot be said enough: the resurrection asserts God's power as a body-affirming force. Hence, the theological meaning of the crucifixion is not found in the cross alone, that is, through the death of Jesus.

Rather the meaning of the crucifixion is found in conjunction with the resurrection—thus it is found in Jesus' very life. The resurrection in effect points us back to Jesus' life, that is, his ministry.

It is also important to recognize that this emphasis on the resurrection, and hence on the life/ministry of Jesus repudiates the religiocultural bias and oppressive practices historically associated with Christianity's closed monotheism. For what is established in Jesus' life is a way of living that affirms the sacred value of all human life, respects all human bodies, and thus renounces any behavior that demeans the life and bodies of others. In this regard, any salvific significance in following Jesus is found not in the efficacy of his death for all who would proclaim him as Christ, but in abiding by the life that he led, that is, by adhering to his ministry. Again, to do so would virtually alleviate the oppressing potential of Christianity's closed monotheistic core. But once more it bears repeating that platonized Christianity does not do this, for it tends to ignore the centrality of Jesus' ministry for Christian living.

So clearly this rendering of the crucifixion-resurrection event has strong implications for the Christian theological and historical tradition. Most notably, to understand Jesus' crucifixion in relation to both his ministry and resurrection allows the positive value of the cross for a suffering people to become clear. Specifically, though an unjust crucifixion is central to the Christian story, it does not set Christianity on an inexorable course of tyranny against those who are most powerless in society. Neither does it suggest that the powerless must accept the exploitation of their bodies as a form of redemptive sacrifice. When understood fully, the cross points to God's special regard for the powerless as well as God's absolute denunciation of crucifying power. The crucifixion/resurrection makes plain that a concern for the powerless is central to the Christian story and thus a concern requisite for any theology that identifies itself as Christian. Furthermore, the crucifixion/resurrection event unmistakably invalidates theological notions that suggest that God wants, requires, or approves of the sacrifice of human bodies. As earlier stated, models of sacrificial/redemptive suffering are rendered heretical as they betray the message of the incarnation. To repeat, the incarnation attests to

the sacredness of the human body. It is thus the act of the resurrection—not the crucifixion—that best affirms the revelatory significance of the incarnate God.

This particular interpretation of the crucifixion's meaning for
the Christian story accords with Delores Williams's conclusions,
for she also draws attention to the centrality of the resurrection.
Uniquely emphasized in my understanding, however, is the importance of the powerless as vessels for God's revelation concerning
the value of human life and concomitantly the character of God's
power. In contrast to JoAnne Terrell, my understanding of the
crucifixion does not project any divine meaning onto human sacrifice. I affirm as historical fact that those who opposed Jesus were
the ones who crucified him. They alone were responsible for his
death. I also affirm that the crucifixion was a fait accompli of his
ministry, though this is perhaps a debatable point. Therefore, I
strongly contest any notion that God was party to or sanctioned
in any way Jesus' crucifixion. Simply put, people who wielded
inequitable power—not God—crucified Jesus. Any divine meaning to be found in the act of crucifixion itself relates to God's *compassionate solidarity* with the powerless, not to God's acceptance
of their crucifixion. This again is made clear by the fact that God
responded to the crucifixion not with approval of this evil attack
on a human body, but with the resurrection, a body-affirming act.
If there is redemptive meaning to be found in the crucifixion/res-
urrection event, therefore, it is to be found not through the sacrifice of the human body, but through the reclamation of it.

This theological rendering of the crucifixion also accords with
René Girard's anthropological analysis of sacrifice. Girard concludes that Jesus' crucifixion demonstrates the Christian God's
repudiation of human sacrifice. He expressly argues that the full
divinity of Jesus is revealed through Jesus' becoming the "victim"
of "sacrificial violence." As victim, Jesus discloses God's utter
alliance with those who suffer at the hands of unscrupulous power
as well as God's triumph over crucifying power. Girard poignantly
states that the resurrection is a "spectacular sign of the entrance
into a world of power superior to [the crucifying power demonstrated by earthly power]."[25] Essentially, Girard argues that the

crucifixion establishes Christianity as a religion that should have at its very center a concern to protect the "value" of society's innocent victims, that is, those persons most susceptible to sacrifice.[26]

Ironically, even in their questioning of God's role in lynching, black literary artists have also essentially attested to Jesus' status as victim and thus his special affinity with black people. This can be seen in Langston Hughes's aforementioned poem, "Christ in Alabama," where Hughes speaks of the "Nigger Christ."[27] There is perhaps no writer, however, who more passionately portrays this ironic connection that Jesus has to black people than W. E. B. Du Bois. In his short stories, "The Son of God" and "The Gospel According to Mary Brown," Du Bois presents Jesus as a black man who offends white power and is subsequently crucified.[28] In the latter, Du Bois writes of the sentiments leading to his Jesus character's, Joshua's, crucifixion: "Bitter, ever more bitter, grew the White Folk at his silent protest—his humble submission to wrong. They seized him and questioned him." The story continues with the mob yelling, "Kill the nigger." With that, Joshua is crucified. Du Bois's depiction of the crucifixion scene enunciates the sense of Jesus' victim status and thus his *compassionate solidarity* with black victims:

And so swiftly he was sentenced for treason and inciting murder and insurrection; quickly they hurried him to the jail-yard, where they stripped him and spit upon him, and smote him on the head, and mocked, and lynched him. And sitting down, they watched him die.[29]

Essentially, in appreciating Jesus' profound tie with victims of crucifying power, it can be soundly concluded that inequitable forms of power are intrinsically anti-Christ. They have been shown to be so in several significant ways. First, it was inequitable power that attempted to push Jesus—"the bearer of God's rule"—out of the world. The prevailing power of the first-century Roman world was in actual fact against Christ, as the crucifixion clearly attests. Second, the conceptual influence of inequitable power greatly contributes to troubling, if not heretical, interpretations of the

crucifixion event. Third, inequitable power almost invariably projects dualistic relationality between groups of people, degrades the
bodies of those people it has "othered," and thereby opposes the
incarnational reality of Christ. In the end, to take seriously both
the ontological (i.e., his divine/human nature) and the existential
(his ministry) paradoxical realties of Jesus as the incarnate one is
to conclude that inequitable power is anti-Christ, which means it
is adversative to Christianity itself.

What then can be said concerning the contrasting "Christian"
witness that undoubtedly took place at the many lynching trees
where black people met a cruel death? The lynching scenes such as
those of Sam Hose and John Henry Williams graphically drama-
tize the conflict between two different views of Christianity. One
view is that of the powerless, who, as mentioned above, have a special connection to Jesus, as they both find themselves victims of
inequitable power. It is from this victimized, powerless vantage
point that the meaning of the incarnation is best revealed. The
other view is that of the oppressing powerful, a perspective that
has been established as being inherently anti-Christ. Moreover, it
is from the vantage point of the powerful that Christianity most
easily becomes platonized. As argued in the previous chapter, with
its disregard for the body and devaluation of sexuality, platonized
Christianity attracts and is attracted to power, especially inequitable power. And most critical, platonized Christianity almost
invariably invites the violent sacrifice of certain people as it provides sacred legitimation for their sexualized demonization. Essentially then, the Christian drama played out at the lynching tree is
a haunting display of the vile pursuits that can find shelter in a platonized Christian tradition—especially when that tradition is
invested with power. It would thus seem that the most lethal of
alliances is that between power and platonized Christianity. In this
regard, lynching becomes an example of the evil height that such
an alliance can reach.

Whose witness then—that of Sam Hose and John Henry
Williams or that of their lynchers—is most reflective of the God of
Jesus Christ? Inasmuch as the incarnate Jesus defines Christianity's
theological core, and inasmuch as the crucifixion of Jesus is cen-

tral to the Christian story, then it is the witness of Hose and Williams that is most revealing of the God of Jesus Christ. Hose and Williams *do* share a special theological bond with Jesus. Just as Jesus is a perfect revelation of the Christian God, so too are Hose and Williams. They, along with other victims of cruel power, have revelatory privilege when it comes to the very God of Jesus Christ. It is in this way that Christianity is a religion best suited for the victimized powerless and not the victimizing powerful. For again, it is the powerless who best bear witness to the meaning of the incarnate God in human history. Thus we must reassert that "power" is of the anti-Christ and platonized Christianity is heretical. The two together, power and platonized Christianity, are nothing less than blasphemous when it comes to the God incarnate in Jesus. Left now to revisit is the prevailing question for part 1 of this book: What is it about Christianity? This question will be answered in our summary review of the theo-ideological foundation of a terrorizing Christian tradition.

Excursus

WHAT IS IT ABOUT CHRISTIANITY? Is there something about Christianity itself that suggests a disreputable, dehumanizing legacy? Christianity is a closed monotheistic religion. It is defined by a christological paradox. And Christianity is a religion with a violent crucifixion at its very center. Each of these theological characteristics has greatly contributed to Christianity's implicit and explicit participation in acts of human terror. Part 1 of this book has shown us that Christianity's theological core has made it vulnerable to becoming platonized and makes it—especially when platonized—exceedingly dangerous when empowered. It is in fact this empowered, influential, platonized Christian tradition that is regularly implicated in Christianity's disreputable legacy, particularly when it comes to the black body. So the answer to the question, "What is it about Christianity that allows for its involvement in the defilement of the black body?" while not simple, is clear: it is Christianity's very theological core. This core, inasmuch as it highlights "difference" and features a "sacrifice," makes Christianity susceptible to a platonized theo-ideological distortion that coheres well with inequitable dehumanizing power.

Yet, even as this core makes Christianity susceptible to corruption, the very incarnational character of this core sets the parameters for how difference should be construed and for how the crucifixion should be regarded. Thus, the defining incarnational character of Christianity's theological core actually contests the very corrupting influence of platonized thought and unjust power. Specifically, Jesus the incarnate One not simply protests the advent of a terrorizing Christian tradition but absolutely repudiates it. Jesus as Christ, both ontologically and existentially, opposes Christianity's adoption of a platonized hermeneutic, connection of this to power, and the oppressive body-devaluing tradition that ushers forth from the mutual impact of both. It is Jesus Christ, then, who renders a platonized tradition and all that issues forth from it antithetical to the "truth" of Christianity. In effect, Jesus Christ makes clear the blasphemous nature of a Christian tradition that cultivates or sustains shameful treatment of any human body. The underlying assumption in coming to this conclusion is that to recognize the incarnate Jesus as what makes Christianity unique is also to affirm Jesus' normative status in regard to Christianity. Thus, while Christianity's very theological core makes it vulnerable to becoming a religion that terrorizes, the incarnational character of that core renders terrorizing forms of Christianity absolutely illegitimate. With this in mind we can now directly revisit the question: What is it about Christianity that makes it acceptable to black faith? The answer is clear: Jesus Christ. It is Jesus as the incarnate One that invalidates oppressive forms of Christianity and thus allows for black women and men to affirm a Christian identity at the same time that their bodies are ravished in the name of Christianity.

The paradox of affirming the very religion that others use to justify their shameful treatment of you is poignantly dramatized in scenes of black lynching. It is also this paradox that makes the answer to what it is about Christianity when it comes to black people a complicated issue. The point of the matter is that regardless of what may be its heretical nature, the platonized version of Christianity is a very influential one. Platonized Christianity has indeed found its most comfortable home in evangelical Protestantism. It is in this way that it has not only aligned with "whiteness" in such a way as to humiliate and destroy the black body, but it has also significantly shaped black faith subsequently affecting black people's regard for their own black bodies and the bodies of others. At the same time, it has been this platonized faith that black people have relied on to sustain and empower them in their struggles against whiteness. So even though platonized Christianity may be seen as heretical and easily dismissed on a theo-ideological level, it cannot be so easily dismissed on a theo-practical level. Again, it represents a prevalent form of Christianity and has thereby greatly influenced black lives. Part 2 of this book will thus examine more directly what has been generally asserted at this point: platonized Christianity's complicity in black oppression. Part 2 will substantiate how it is that a platonized tradition has provided for Christianity's implicit and explicit involvement in ravishing the black body.

Part II
What Is It about Black Faith?

4

Christian Theology and White Ideology

No two persons better understood the complex interactive social-cultural and political nuances of the white attack on the black body than Ida B. Wells and W. E. B. Du Bois. Not only was Wells a pioneering leader protesting lynching, but she also daringly refuted the myth that it was black male desire for white women that precipitated these hideous crimes. She strongly insinuated that it was actually the reverse. In an 1892 editorial for her paper, *Free Speech*, she wrote: "Nobody . . . believes the old thread-bare lie that Negro men assault white women. If Southern white men are not careful they will over-reach themselves and a conclusion will be reached which will be very damaging to the moral reputation of their women."[1] Further exposing the hypocrisy of lynching, Wells brazenly noted:

> I found that in order to justify these horrible atrocities to the world, the Negro was being branded as a race of rapists, who were especially mad after white women. I found that white men who had created a race of mulattoes by raping and consorting with Negro women were still doing so wherever they could, these same white men lynched, burned, and tortured Negro men for doing the same thing with white women; even when white women were willing victims.[2]

Du Bois too understood the "white" lie behind lynching. Affirming the findings of the Southern Commission on the Study of Lynching (1933) that black male rape of white women was only a subterfuge for the violent rampages against black men, Du Bois wrote, "white men have disguised themselves to impersonate Negroes and fasten crime upon them."[3] As astute as Wells and Du Bois were about the duplicity involved in white violence against black bodies, they were equally perceptive concerning the relationship between Christianity and such violence. During her 1849 antilynching crusade in Bristol, London, Ida B. Wells was asked about the role of American churches in the fight against lynching. She responded, "American Christians are too busy saving the souls of white Christians from burning in hell-fire to save the lives of black ones from present burning in fires kindled by white Christians."[4] Some seventy years later, W. E. B. Du Bois also expressed dismay concerning the white Christian response to white racist tyranny. Du Bois wrote, "We have curled our lips in something like contempt as we have witnessed glib apology and weary explanation. Nothing of the sort deceived us. A nation's religion is its life, and as such white Christianity is a miserable failure."[5]

In their decries concerning the Christian response to black oppression, both Wells and Du Bois insightfully recognized the peculiar alliance between whiteness and Christianity. Their remarks point to the seemingly easy relationship between white culture and the Christian tradition. Du Bois aptly identified this alliance as "white Christianity." What they both were in fact witnessing was the natural coherence between a platonized Christian tradition and white culture. It is this correspondence between platonized Christianity and white culture that has proven particularly devastating for the black body. Chapter 4 will thus explore the comfortable yet disturbing connection between platonized Christianity and white culture. In this chapter, white culture is understood as that culture—with its language, values, beliefs, and artifacts—that serves to secure white supremacy. It is a culture built on a specious belief in white people's superiority and the inferiority of those who are not white. In this respect, it is the lifeblood of white racist thought and practice.[6] This chapter will examine the link between white culture and platonized Christianity. An underlying assumption of this chapter is that eighteenth-century Enlightenment discourse provided the essential metanarrative that stimulated white culture and platonized Christianity's bond with each other.

The chapter will proceed by initially focusing on the emergence of "religious racism" in the eighteenth and nineteenth centuries as a Christian response to the Enlightenment challenge. It will specifically be argued that the compatibility with the theology of platonized Christianity, the Enlightenment narrative, and the ideological underpinnings of white culture made the advent of religious racism almost certain. This chapter will continue by looking at the role of platonized Christianity in shaping the collective theological consciousness of "everyday" white Christians. The section develops, as has been previously noted, that platonized Christianity found its most comfortable American home in the very influential evangelical Protestant tradition. The Great Awakenings will provide the prism through which evangelical Protestant theology will be examined. Again, the Enlightenment metanarrative will serve as the backdrop for understanding the development of this theology in relation to white culture. While this chapter by no means argues that evangelical Protestantism exclusively suborns white tyranny against black bodies, or that it necessarily leads to racist practices (for indeed many white evangelical Protestants have been in the forefront of racial and social activism), this chapter does recognize two important things. First, there are aspects of evangelical protestant thought, as it is platonized, that make it susceptible to collusion with white racism. Second, the vibrancy of this evangelical manifestation of platonized Christianity has uniquely impacted black lives.[7] In the end, chapter 4 maintains that whiteness and platonized Christianity create an unholy alliance, even as whiteness and Christianity are incompatible, thus making clearer the dangers of platonized religious traditions for marginalized people in general and black people in particular. We will also by chapter's end move even closer to determining the allure of Christianity for black people as well as for me. Before proceeding, however, it is necessary to note what will not be discussed in this chapter—namely, the role of Christianity in legitimating slavery.

The use of Christianity by the white slaveholding class to support the slavocracy is perhaps the most blatant example of Christianity's collusion with white culture. To be sure, the use of Christianity to support slavery exposes the dangers inherent in the classical christological tradition as this tradition ignores the ministry of Jesus.[8] Moreover, the various theological arguments used to justify the enslavement of African peoples (for instance, that enslavement was necessary to introduce the African "heathens" to the one true God of Jesus Christ) reveal the potential problems inherent in a closed monotheistic religion like Christianity as earlier suggested. Reinforcing this point, historian Forrest G. Wood astutely observed that Christianity's support of slavery was inevitable, given the implications of its monotheistic core. Woods says, "It is inherent in every monotheistic faith that there are only truth and error, good and evil. . . . Since the dark-skinned heathen obviously did not belong on the side of truth and good, the Christian assigned him . . . to error and evil."[9] Given Christianity's profound involvement in justifying slavery, Du Bois was right in his assessment that "American Christianity was the bulwark of American slavery."[10] Indeed, Christianity's role in maintaining slavery has long since been established and thus does not need to be reiterated in this book.[11] Furthermore, as devastating for the black body as Christianity's sanction of slavery was, Christianity made an even more insidious bond with white culture. Platonized Christianity's concurrence with white supremacist ideology fostered a religious racism that continues to influence black lives when it comes to the black body, the bodies of others, and black faith. Let us thus continue chapter 4 by examining the problem of "religious racism."

Platonized Christianity and Religious Racism

White Cultural Ideology and Enlightenment Discourse

In order to fully comprehend how platonized Christianity gave way to religious racism, one must first have a basic appreciation of two things: the ideology of white culture and the prevailing narrative of the eighteenth-century Enlightenment. Thomas Jefferson helps us to understand both. Historian Winthrop Jordan insightfully comments, "Thomas Jefferson was not a typical nor an ordinary man, but his enormous breadth of interest and his lack of originality make him an effective sounding board for his culture."[12] It is in this regard that Jefferson's remarks on black people are most instructive.

Because he believed that the enslavement of human beings violated the natural rights granted to them by their Creator, Jefferson was ambivalent, if not guilt-ridden, about his own personal involvement in the slave system. Though he "trembled" about how God looked upon a nation of slaveholders, he was not fearful enough to free his slaves.[13] Moreover, his disdain for slavery did not ameliorate his attitude toward black people. Jefferson steadfastly maintained that black people were irrevocably inferior to whites in all aspects, "body and mind." He made his position clear in his "Notes on the State of Virginia." In this 1781 essay, written in reply to inquiries made to him by the secretary of the French Legation in Philadelphia, Jefferson seems to take special care to comment on the intellectual and sexual capacity of black women and men. He says, for instance, that the appearance and passionate nature of the black female makes her so highly sexual that male apes prefer her to female apes. He declares, "as uniformly as is the preference of the Oran-utan for the black woman over those of his own species." Jefferson goes on to ascribe to the black male lascivious ways similar to those he attributed to the black female: "They are more ardent after their female," he says, "but love seems with them to be more an eager desire than a tender delicate mixture of sentiment and sensation."[14] Jefferson continues by making clear that not only are black people driven by sexual passion but they also have no capacity for reason. He says:

Comparing them by their faculties of memory, reason, and imagination, it appears to me that in memory they are equal to the whites; in reason much inferior. . . . They astonish you with strokes of the most sublime oratory; such as prove their reason and sentiment strong, their imagination glowing and elevated. But never yet could I find that a black had uttered a thought above the level of plain narration . . . Their love is ardent, but it kindles the senses only, not the imagination. Religion, indeed, has produced a Phyllis Whately [*sic*] but it could not produce a poet.[15]

Influenced by the Enlightenment demands for scientific proof (to which we will return later), Jefferson offers that any conclusions concerning black people's inferiority "in the faculties of reason and imagination, must be hazarded with great diffidence." Nevertheless, he continues, "I advance it, therefore, as a suspicion only, that blacks, whether originally a distinct race, or made distinct by time and circumstances, are inferior to the whites in the endowments of body and mind." Jefferson essentially summarizes his assessment of black people when he says, "In general, their existence appears to participate more of *sensation* than *reflection*."[16]

Even though Jefferson's views toward black people would come under attack from various quarters, Jordan notes, "Until well into the nineteenth century Jefferson's judgment on that matter, with all of its confused tentativeness, stood as the strongest suggestion of [black] inferiority expressed by any native American."[17] Thus, Jefferson's comments also reflect several factors that figure in platonized Christianity's complicity in the emergence of religious racism. Let us now look to see how this is the case.

Jefferson's comments reflect the fundamental ideology of white culture. This is an ideology formulated to maintain the notion of white supremacy. To review what was earlier noted, the defining principle of this white supremacist ideology is the hyper/bestial sexuality of black women and men. They are considered, as Jefferson advises, an "ardent people." White culture, in fact, depicts black men as rapacious predators—"mandingo bucks," and black women as promiscuous seductresses, "Jezebels." This oversexed caricature of black people has allowed for the black body to be controlled and exploited in ways that have benefited white racist society. For instance, it permitted white slaveholders to rape black women with impunity, thereby increasing the slaveholder's capital. Philosopher Naomi Zack explains:

black female slaves became objects of sexual desire to white slave owners because money could be made if they bred them, and more could be made if they themselves bred them. For a white slave owner to breed his black female slaves himself, he would have to have sex with them—ergo, the black female slaves were sexualized because they were literal objects of sexual desire, albeit primarily for monetary reasons.[18]

Essentially, white cultural hyper/bestial sexualization of black men and women allowed for white society to both control and profit from the black body, even if that meant rape, castration, and lynching. The hyper/bestial sexualization of black people and the reasons for it have been well documented so time will not be spent reiterating it here.[19] What will be examined, however, particularly in our effort to better understand the interplay between platonized Christianity and white cultural ideology, is another aspect of Jefferson's comments. For not only did he suggest that black people were overly sexual—that is, "ardent"—but he also stressed that they lacked reason. His emphasis on their lack of reason was telling of the Enlightenment world of which Jefferson was a part. The Enlightenment "spirit" in fact provided the metanarrative that propelled platonized Christianity's collusion with white culture in the development of religious racism, and so let us briefly examine it.

The eighteenth-century Enlightenment period, which began in Europe and spread to the American colonies, signaled a new age in the quest for truth and knowledge: the Age of Reason. This was an age where "reason" reigned. In 1784 Immanuel Kant pronounced the motto for the Enlightenment as, "*Sapere aude!* [Dare to know] Have courage to use your own reason!"[20] Unfettered reason was considered the key to human progress. One needed only to "Dare to know." The only limitation on reason, and hence on human progress, was thought to be self-imposed. A truly enlightened person was one who freed him- or herself from the fetters of beliefs or systems of beliefs that were not themselves reasonable. It was in this way that religion came under attack, as we will see later. Important to understand for now is that reason was the standard of authority. As John Locke said, "*Reason* must be our last Judge and Guide in every Thing."[21] Reason *was* the adjudicating principle in determining the merit of an argument, the validity of an area of study (e.g., psychology or religion), and the worth of an individual. If an argument was not "rational," it was discounted as advancing any knowledge. If a field of study put forth claims that were not compatible with those reached by reason alone, then it too was discredited for being "unreasonable." And if human beings were shown lacking in reason, and indeed incapable of growing in reason, then they were at best regarded as inferior beings, perhaps right above the beast, and at worst regarded as subhuman, in fact beast.[22]

For Jefferson, black people's lack of rational "capacity" did not impeach their humanity, but it did strongly attest to their irretrievable inferiority. To reiterate, Jefferson cautioned that blacks were capable of "sensation" but not "reflection." This distinction no doubt reflects John Locke's influence on Jefferson's thought. It is said, in fact, that Jefferson "worshiped" the thought of the Enlightenment thinker Locke.[23]

Locke argued against the notion of "innate ideas." He maintained that all knowledge starts in experience. Experience, he said, produces knowledge by way of two "fountains"—sensation and reflection. Without oversimplifying the complexity of Locke's analysis concerning knowledge and ideas, it is safe to say that according to his analysis, sensation represents a lower level of knowledge acquisition than does reflection. Sensation is knowledge derived strictly from senses. It is knowledge gained directly from "External, Material things." Sensations have to do with the sensible world and how "particular sensible Objects, do *convey into the Mind*."[24] Reflection represents a higher order of knowing. Reflection is knowledge acquired as a result of "inward operations," of the mind, as Locke put it, "Operations of our own Minds within." Children, Locke said, are not capable of reflection. He said that reflection does not come "till [persons] come to be of riper Years; and some scarce ever at all."[25]

For Jefferson, the ability for reflection never comes to black people. He said that they are incapable of such "inward"/rational operations of the mind. Again, this rational incapacity did not, for Jefferson, render black men and women inhuman, but it did render them inferior beings, particularly in relation to white people. The underlying assumption is that white people are the quintessence of rationality. In accordance with white culture, whiteness is essentially synonymous with rationality, while blackness is synonymous with irrationality and hyper/bestial sexuality. It was largely on these grounds that Jefferson confidently proclaimed that blacks, even with a change in circumstance, would never be equal to whites.

Without a doubt, Jefferson's arguments concerning black intellectual inferiority are convoluted, in that they sometimes seem to contradict his own views concerning the equality of all human beings in creation. Furthermore, Jefferson's views were widely criticized by opponents of slavery who believed that any sign of black intellectual inferiority was due to the condition of slavery, not to any innate lack. Needless to say, Jefferson's thoughts concerning black people along with the debate these thoughts incited require their own careful study beyond the scope of this book.[26] That notwithstanding, his comments about black people remain important to this study because they indicate the Enlightenment "standard" by which black people were judged, and the very avenue by which platonized Christianity found common cause with white culture.

To reiterate, Jefferson's pronouncement concerning black people's lack of rational ability reflected a chief assumption of white culture: whether for innate or environmental reasons, black people were a people governed not by reason but by emotion or passion (in the words of Jefferson, "sensation"). Black people were thus designated a people controlled by their bodies, not by their minds. In an Enlightenment and post-Enlightenment world, such a designation supported black people's continued dominated state. If, as John Locke said, "it is the *Understanding* that sets Man above the rest of sensible Beings, and gives him all the Advantage and Dominion which he has over them," then white people, "rational beings," must have dominion over black people, "sensible beings."[27] Such a view is also consistent with the Platonic idea that certainly informed the Enlightenment spirit concerning the supremacy of reason. For Platonic thought, especially as expressed in Plato's *Republic*, requires that in an orderly society "body" people must be ruled by "mind' people. Thus, in Plato's republic, the philosopher, the embodiment of one governed by reason, was to be the king, the ruling force in society. In a world where white people are considered the paragons of reason and black people the models of passion, according to the Enlightenment spirit it follows that white people should rule over black people—mind over body/reason over passion.

What we find, then, as exemplified by Jefferson's comments, is how the ideology of white culture coalesces with Enlightenment thought in such a way as to guarantee white control and even exploitation of the black body. For while the Enlightenment obsession with reason led to recognition of the "unreasonableness" of religion (to be explored later), it did not lead to a similar recognition regarding the "unreasonableness" of white culture. Indeed, inasmuch as white cultural assumptions concerning black people could be supported by science, they passed the test of the Age of Reason. It was thus this interface between white cultural assumptions and Enlightenment principles that gave rise to scientific racism. In fact, Jefferson's caution in "hazarding" black inferiority presages scientific racism in that it begs for scientific investigation into the matter.

During the Enlightenment, science was king. It was the field of study above all others because it was thought to embody reason. For any claim to be taken seriously it had to be legitimated by science. Frederick Douglass astutely described this period as "an age of science." He went on to say, "[Science] must explore and analyze, until all doubt is set at rest."[28] Thus, the claims of white culture regarding black inferiority "willed" scientific validation. In this regard, the "Foucauldian" analysis of power is apt. It is important at this point to recall this analysis. Michel Foucault argues that power "wills" its own knowledge to sustain itself. Inequitable power produces certain forms of knowledge to validate the various inequities and structures of domination intrinsic to it. Accordingly, inequitable white power rooted in notions of black inferiority necessitated scientific legitimation, thus the advent of scientific racism. Subsequently, various specious forms of science emerged that ostensibly "proved" black people's inferiority.[29] In many respects, owing to the spirit of the Enlightenment, science fueled and kept alive the vital ideology necessary for white exploitative abuse of the black body. The vitality of white culture is, thus, in many respects a legacy of the Enlightenment as the Enlightenment secreted the scientific racism that provided a "rational" canopy for white supremacist practices.

The Production of Religious Racism

The Enlightenment would spawn another protector of white maltreatment of the black body. For, not only would white cultural ideology and the Enlightenment philosophy come together to generate scientific racism, but all three would intersect with Christianity to produce religious racism. Again, Jefferson's comments help us to understand how this occurred.

In order to support his claim that black people were incapable of reason/reflection, Jefferson attacked the intellect of various prominent black people. It is in this attack that the Enlightenment challenge to Christianity becomes clear, and it is also this attack that augurs platonized Christianity's role in the production of religious racism.

As Jordan aptly points out, for many—particularly those involved in the antislavery movement—Phyllis Wheatley provided proof of "the Negro's mental equality."[30] She thus became the perfect target for Jefferson in making the case for black people's mental inequality. In his attempt to diminish her intelligence, Jefferson alleged that she was a product of religion, not reason; thus, she was not to be considered a poet.[31] He went on to say that Ignatius Sancho, a slave whose *Letters, with Memoirs of His Life* was published in 1782, "has approached nearer to merit in composition; yet his letters do more honor to the heart than the head . . . and show . . . strong religious zeal."[32] In these assaults on black intelligence, Jefferson clearly criticizes religion. He implies that religion is antithetical to reason. Religion appeals to the heart (that is, sensations); hence it is suited for black people, a people defined by sensation. Many people may have thought that this was the reason why significant numbers of black people were converted to Christianity, as we will see later in the book. For now it is important to note that the characterization of religion as appealing to the senses as opposed to the mind made it acceptable for black people to display talents that resulted from "religious zeal." Jefferson's estimation of religion is again representative of the Enlightenment spirit.

If science was the hero of the Enlightenment, then "religion was the principal villain."[33] If religion was once considered the supreme arbiter of truth, with the advent of the Enlightenment, science was. Religion was deemed one of the chains around reason that needed to be broken. One of the guiding principles of the Enlightenment was that "man is an adult, dependent upon himself."[34] Religion—in particular, Christianity—made "man" too beholden to God. In addition, religion—especially Christianity— was hampered by nonrational claims. With its emphasis on revelation, its belief in miracles, its story about creation, and its discussions of the supernatural, religion seemed often to defy common sense just as it went beyond what could be proven. Kant perhaps captured the Enlightenment attitude toward religion best when he wrote that there is much about religion that "prevents men from being, or easily becoming, capable of correctly using their own reason."[35] Central to the Enlightenment agenda, therefore, was an assault on religion.[36] In view of that assault, the Enlightenment presented a special challenge to Christianity.

Christianity was put on the defensive. It had to prove itself "reasonable." It had to show that its essential character was compatible with reason and thus could stand up to rational critique. One of the Christian responses to the Enlightenment attack was the appearance of essays that attempted to demonstrate that Christianity was in fact an "enlightened" religion. For instance, on the European scene John Locke published "The Reasonableness of Christianity." In this essay he suggested that the Bible witnessed to a faith that did not contradict reason but rather established a rational moral religion. For Locke, the fact that God existed was a conclusion that could indeed be reached by reason. In his "Essay Concerning Human Understanding," he had already stated that God's existence was "equal to mathematical Certainty." He went to say, "it is plain to me, we have more certain Knowledge of the Existence of GOD, than of any thing our Senses have not immediately discovered to us. . . . I mean there is such a Knowledge within our reach, which we cannot miss, if we will but apply our Minds to that."[37] As for Jesus, Locke asserted in "The Reasonableness of Christianity" that Jesus showed those who believed in him a way to a better, moral life. With respect to various Christian doctrines such as the Trinity, Locke found that they could not be supported by reason, just as he found no support for them in the Bible. Locke essentially epitomized the "rational" Christianity that emerged during the Enlightenment, not only in Europe but also in America. This was a Christianity that had to survive the scrutiny of reason. This was thus a Christianity that emphasized an impersonal God and morality. As religious historian Martin Marty noted, "in order for Christianity to survive in an Age of Reason it had to adopt a "new vocabulary" where "the mind mattered more than the heart, reason more than revelation, morals more than miracles, public virtue more than private salvation."[38]

Benjamin Franklin as well as Thomas Jefferson reflected the "enlightened" approach to Christianity that emerged in America. They both advanced a kind of "public religion" that emphasized a "common morality."[39] In a letter in 1790 to Ezra Stiles, then president of Yale, Franklin provided what he called the "fundamental principles of all sound religion." He expressed them as follows: there was a God who "ought to be worshipped," "that the most acceptable service we render to [God] is doing good," and that the "soul of Man is immortal" to be treated justly in the next life in respect to conduct in this life. As for Jesus and Christianity, Franklin offered, "I think the system of morals and his religion, as he left them to us, the best the world ever saw or is likely to see."[40]

Jefferson's view of religion and Christianity was very similar to Franklin's. In accordance with Enlightenment demands, Jefferson stressed that the truth of religion would emerge after the scrutiny of "reason and free inquiry." Presumably after subjecting Chris-

tianity to such a test, he concluded that Christian doctrines such
as the Trinity were incomprehensible, in fact, "gibberish."[41] But,
like Franklin, Jefferson suggested that the truth of Christianity was
found in Jesus and the simple life and morals that he put forth.[42]

In general, the Enlightenment explosion of reason no doubt
overwhelmed Christian thinkers. Somehow they had to find a way
for Christianity at least to survive the onslaught of critique, if not
regain a measure of authority. What Franklin's and Jefferson's
Enlightenment versions of Christianity indicate was that Christianity did indeed secure an authoritative space for itself during the
Enlightenment. It did this by deemphasizing those aspects of the
religion that pushed the envelope of reason while emphasizing the
religion's moral precepts. Various interpreters of the Enlightenment have suggested that during an Age of Reason Christianity
was able to find common cause with "disciples" of reason (i.e.,
philosophers) on the grounds of "morality."[43] While this interpretation may in fact accurately reflect significant Christian responses
to the Enlightenment, it certainly does not tell the whole story.
The Enlightenment had a more insidious impact on Christianity.
Indeed, the Enlightenment's obsession with reason coincided
with an influential strand of Christianity in a way that allowed for
the explosion of religious racism. Specifically, the platonized
Christian tradition's exaltation of reason and detestation of the
body permitted Christianity to claim authoritative space during an
age absorbed with reason in another way, on the "backs of black
people." Let us look to see how this was the case.

As we have seen, the Enlightenment's valorization of reason
imposed itself on Christianity in such a way as to force it to show
its worth. Platonized Christianity was theologically well suited to
this challenge. First of all, it shared in the Enlightenment's regard
for reason. Within a platonized tradition, reason accords with the
soul. It is the avenue by which one can become closer to God.
Thus, within platonized Christianity, as previously argued, the
mind is virtually divinized. Clearly, then, a fundamental theological
assumption of platonized Christianity was commensurate with the
defining principle of the Enlightenment. But this intrinsic compatibility did not necessarily manifest itself by way of theological

apologia sanctioning the Enlightenment elevation of reason. It most notably manifested itself in a more deleterious manner. For perhaps more significantly, platonized Christianity was not only able to find common cause with the Enlightenment in a mutual embrace of reason, but it was also able to team up with science. If the Enlightenment fomented an antagonistic relationship between science and Christianity, then the platonized Christian tradition amended that relationship. It was able to do this because it corresponded to something that the Enlightenment did not readily challenge and that science, the champion of the Enlightenment, legitimated: white cultural ideology as it pertained to black people. Hence, we see the confluence of white cultural ideology, Enlightenment thinking, and scientific racism spawning religious racism.

To reiterate, white culture asserts that blackness is virtually synonymous with hyper/bestial sexuality and thus correspondingly adversative to reason. Platonized Christianity asserts that sexuality is a cauldron of evil and opposes the human connection to God. As such, platonized Christianity maintains that sexuality encumbers reason, as the body/flesh encumbers the mind/soul. By maintaining the evilness of sexuality, platonized Christianity potentially provides a theological cover for any claims that people governed by sexual desires at the expense of reason are innately evil and need to be controlled. Platonized Christianity essentially suggests—commensurate with the Enlightenment spirit—that reason must be freed from the imposition of sexuality. The practical consequences of this thinking are deadly for a sexualized people, in this instance, black people. For platonized Christianity, at least implicitly, supports white cultural debasement of black men and women as well as white domination over them. But it cannot be stressed enough that perhaps most alarming of all is that, taken to its logical extreme, platonized Christianity suborns white attacks against the black body even though they may be fatal. For again, platonized Christianity demonizes the body and sexuality, thereby implying the demonization of sexualized people. Inasmuch as sexuality is considered evil, so too are oversexual black people. Therefore, if black people are evil by nature, then to eliminate them from society—as in to execute/lynch them—is a way of exorcising evil from a particular community. In the language of the Enlightenment, it is a way of freeing reason, that is, whiteness, from one of the obstacles that prevent it from flourishing, that is, blackness. Once again it becomes clear that platonized Christianity's theology of sexuality not only sanctions black people's dehumanization but also suggests their violent demise.

Unfortunately, platonized Christianity's support of white cultural ideology did not remain implicit. Perhaps driven by the aforementioned challenge of the Enlightenment to religion in general, and science's challenge to Christianity in particular, various Christian thinkers found it necessary that Christianity find common ground with science. Platonized Christianity provided an effective way for this to happen. The unquestionable common ground was race. Subsequently, though science consistently denounced various Christian fundamentals, such as the "monogenesis" of all human beings, Christianity supported science in its conclusions concerning blackness, even as that support might involve rethinking black people's place in the order of creation. It was in this way that religious racism was born. Before looking more closely at religious racism, it is important to note a certain irony concerning its development.

The authoritative space that Enlightenment philosophy theoretically granted to Christianity was moral space. Prominent Christian thinkers gladly accepted that space. And so it is ironic that what Enlightenment scholars theoretically advanced as Christianity's secure (hence reasonable) foundation—the moral ethic of Jesus—was in reality not the space that Christianity occupied. In actuality, Christianity did not stand on moral ground. It cannot be forgotten that even as Christian apologists, such as Jefferson, proclaimed the incontestable moral core of Christianity, they also supported slavery. Just as much an indictment of Christianity's moral authority, and more enduring in terms of its rhetoric, was the emergence of "religious racism." Owing to a prevailing platonized Christian tradition, Christianity was able to make an immoral alliance with scientific racism in support of white cultural ideology and practices. Thus, while prominent statesmen like Benjamin Franklin and Thomas Jefferson were putting forth a "public religion" that could comfortably exist in an enlightened world, there was a subaltern level of Christian discourse being maintained that perhaps had more of an influence on the "everyday" white Christian. This was the discourse of religious racism. This discourse, similar to Jefferson's notion of Christianity, conformed to the Enlightenment demands of science while also unabashedly supporting the conventions of white culture. Let us now look at "religious racism" more closely.

Science, in its attempts to show the reasonableness of white cultural assertions concerning black people's inferiority and the resultant dehumanizing treatment of them, proceeded to provide proof that black people were in fact of a different origin than white people. In doing this, science forthrightly challenged Christian claims concerning the single origins of all humankind. Various scientists argued that in the short span of time that the human species supposedly existed, it was virtually impossible for such a wide variety of human beings to have developed. Motivated by their desire to give proof of black people's intrinsic inferiority, if not inhumanity, prominent nineteenth-century scholars such as Josiah Nott and Louis Agassiz stridently argued—to the "surprise and dismay" of some—that there were an "*indefinite* number of original and distinctly created races of men.*"*[44] Such an assertion ostensibly provided a sound foundation for the enslavement and overall brutal treatment of black women and men. According to the logic of these "polygenesis" theories, such treatment was fitting for a people whose place in the human family was tenuous at best. Obviously the "science" of polygenesis accorded well with white cultural ideology. But it was not attractive to Christian apologists for black inferiority owing to one serious flaw: it contradicted biblical testimony concerning the origins of the human race.

As earlier mentioned, one of the ironies of platonized Christianity is its approach to the Bible. The platonized tradition is most typically manifested in fundamentalist versions of Christianity that maintain a "literal" approach to the biblical witness. Every word of the Bible is taken to be true because it is believed to have come directly from God. The irony is that this literal approach often does not translate into an appreciation of Jesus' ministry. If the words and deeds of Jesus' ministry were indeed taken literally, then platonized Christianity would be more apt to condemn—not sanction—oppressive ideologies. With this said, the platonized approach to the scripture is perhaps best understood as a "selective" literalism. It takes literally those aspects of the Bible that conform to and at least do not contradict a platonized hermeneutic, that is, a hermeneutic that reveres the soul and diminishes the flesh. Such an approach to the Bible was certainly operative for the outspoken Christian apologists of white cultural thought and practices. This meant that while platonized Christian thinking naturally cohered with white culture and, thus, found common cause with scientific racism in its legitimation of this culture, it parted company with science concerning the matter of human origins. On this matter, the truth of science and biblical truth were at odds. For a platonized Christian tradition, biblical truth was the only truth that mattered. And biblical truth said that all human beings shared common origins. Yet, platonized Christianity did not exist in a social, cultural, or historical vacuum. It was a part of an "enlightened" world. Therefore, in order for it to maintain any measure of authority and vibrancy it had to find some common ground with science, even on this matter of black origins. It cannot be stressed enough that the common ground was black inferiority. On this point, both scientists and Christians could agree. The task for platonized Christianity was to support this white cultural presupposition without contesting the "truth" of the biblical witness. The challenge was thus set for religious racism. Once again we turn to Thomas Jefferson to discern how the challenge was met.

It cannot be pointed out enough that Jefferson epitomized the duplicitous reality of Christianity as it found its way in a world defined both by the ideology of the Enlightenment and by white culture. Essentially, Christianity attempted to maintain its authority in relation to both. As pointed out above, it was a platonized Christian tradition that was best able to do this if it could overcome its disagreement with science about human beginnings. Jefferson showed how this was possible. At the same time that he touted Christianity's moral authority, he also affirmed white cultural ideology, thereby responding to science's attack on single human origins. As a way of settling the conflict with science, Jefferson offered that each "race" of animal was created not in completed form but with a divinely prescribed range within which it could develop. He explained it this way:

> Every race of animals seems to have received from their Maker certain laws of extension at the time of their formation. . . . Below these limits they cannot fall, nor rise above them. What intermediate station they shall take may depend on soil, on climate, on food, on a careful choice of breeders. But all the manna of heaven would never raise the mouse to the bulk of the mammoth.[45]

If we are to draw from his comments concerning animals in general to people in particular, then the implication is that black people were created with a range of capability beneath that of whites. To be sure, in his observations about animal formation Jefferson indicates the approach of religious racism: it is one that affirms that God relegated blacks to an inferior status without affirming multiple human origins. Religious racism achieved this by advancing one of two basic theses: that God cursed black people or that they were a part of the created order of beasts, not humans.)

The idea of a divine curse was based on the Genesis story of Noah and his sons. In this story, Noah—after recovering from a drunken stupor—is told that his youngest son, Ham, the father of Canaan, gazed upon him while he was naked. For this offense Noah pronounced a curse upon Ham and his descendants, "Cursed be Canaan, the lowest of slaves will he be to his brothers" (Gen. 9:25). The transfer of the Hamitic curse to black people was primarily grounded in an erroneous notion that the name Ham signified "blackness." This very notion that Ham was black, however, presented problems in relation to the text itself. (Left unexplained was how Ham could be black, but his parents and his brothers were not.) If it was argued that God made Ham black as the curse was pronounced, then it also had to be concluded that Noah anticipated the divine curse of blackness and named his

youngest son accordingly. Not only did both of these understandings go beyond the story as presented in the Bible, but they also
defied biological laws of science. Notwithstanding the seemingly
insurmountable problems, the belief in the curse of Ham was pervasive and persistent. That this belief was so widespread points to
the function it served. First and foremost, it suggested that black
enslavement was divinely ordered. Consequently, that blacks were
enslaved was the "fault" of God, not white people. But perhaps
most significantly over time, the Hamitic curse provided theological justification for white cultural ideology. This curse affirmed
that black people were an inferior people because they were a
divinely cursed people. Moreover, the reason for the curse further
supported the notion that blacks were innately a people moved by
"passion," not reason. For surely it was not lost on the believers in
the curse that Ham succumbed to a base instinct by looking at his
father, while the other brothers seemingly responded in a more
rational manner by preventing themselves from looking at the
naked father. Finally, the Hamitic curse, though challenged by science, still permitted Christianity to join with science in affirming
black inferiority. Besides, the problems that science had with the
particularities of the Hamitic theory were no more insurmountable than the problems Christianity had with theories of polygenesis. Obviously, more important than the particular problems that
Christianity and science had with each other was their agreement
that black inferiority was an unalterable given. As one black pro-
tester against religious racism observed, "white theologians were
'wholly absorbed in cutting and trimming theological garments to
suit their various patrons,' patrons who were most often invested
in upholding the tenets of white supremacy."[46] Frederick Douglass also noted the lengths to which science or other fields of
study would go in order to support notions of black inferiority. He
said, "It is the province of prejudice to blind; and scientific writers, not less than others, write to please, as well as to instruct, and
even unconsciously to themselves, (sometimes) sacrifice what is
true to what is popular."[47] Significantly, then, despite the vigorous
critique that science and Christianity mounted against each other
concerning the origins of humanity, both fields' tenacious com-

mitment to white cultural ideology made partners of those who might otherwise have remained enemies.

Another major way in which Christianity sanctioned notions of black inferiority was by suggesting that black people were not human but were in fact beasts. In 1867 Buckner Payne (who wrote under the pseudonym Ariel) released a pamphlet entitled, *The Negro: What Is His Ethnological Status?* In this essay, Payne refutes the curse of Ham by first simply stating, "That the negro is a descendent of Ham, the youngest son of Noah. This is false and untrue."[48] After describing the "prominent characteristics and differences" between white and black people, he then takes great pains to show that black people could not have been the progeny of Noah.[49] He finally concludes that though the Negro was on the ark with Noah, he "entered the ark as a beast," and therefore concludes that black people are not human but "the noblests of the beast creation." In calling black people "the noblests" of beast, Payne makes two things abundantly clear. First, their nobility is based on the fact that they have language, and therefore they are actually only "slightly" higher than baboons and monkeys. Second, and most importantly, that black people are beasts means that they have "no soul to be saved."[50] Ironically, Payne's thesis received the most criticism from other Christian thinkers who were just as committed as he to the idea of black inferiority. The central problem they had with Payne's argument, however, was that it rendered black people "soulless," thereby eliminating the possibility of conversion. It must be remembered that one of the mainstays of a platonized tradition is the ability to save wayward souls through conversion to another way of living. More particularly, one of the justifications of slavery hinged on "christianizing" the once "heathen" African. Payne, however, was not the only one to put forth such a thesis. Perhaps the most notorious of religious racists was Charles Carroll. At the turn of the century he produced two books, *The Negro a Beast* (1901) and *The Tempter of Eve* (1902), which basically affirmed—perhaps with greater detail and attention to scripture—Payne's argument.

In *The Negro a Beast*, Carroll takes special care to affirm the truth of "the Scriptural School of Divine Creation" and to denounce "the Atheistic School of Natural Development." In this discussion he directly confronts the claims of science that heaven and earth are "the result of natural causes working without design to accomplish their formation."[51] Leaving no doubt about his contempt for the Enlightenment's regard for reason, he says that reason actually gives no answer to the matter of creation. It is revelation, he argues, that provides the answer to the when and why of creation. Yet, while dismissing the authority of reason, Carroll consistently clarifies Christianity's compatibility with science. For instance, he says that the knowledge gleaned from revelation conforms to science. He puts it this way:

> Reason gives no answer. . . . Reason is powerless to guide us, and it would seem that any further advance that we may attempt must be merely speculative; Revelation generously comes to our assistance with that sublime assurance that, "In the beginning God created the heaven and the earth."
>
> Thus Revelation, in harmony with Science, and with Reason, emphatically confirms the teachings of each, that there is a God . . . a Creator . . . there was a definite plan of creation; a creation successive—extending through "six days."[52]

After establishing the divine creation, Carroll goes on to specify the "Negro's" place in it. He specifically argues that through Adam and Eve white people are connected to God in a way that black people are not. He reinforces this point with an illustration entitled, "The Morning of Creation." This illustration shows a decidedly white Adam and Eve in the Garden with a ray from "Heaven" connecting to them. In the ray are inscribed the words, "Direct Line of Kinship with God." Beneath the picture is the question, "Where does the line of kinship between God and Adam and Eve connect with the Negro?"[53] Combining the testimony of scripture with the findings of scientific racism, Carroll gives an unmistakable answer to his question; black people are among the lower order of animals. He says, "Let us bear in mind that the Negro, the lower apes and the quadrupeds, all belong to 'one kind of flesh,' the 'flesh of the beast.'"[54] Carroll ends his book with a resounding affirmation of Payne's position that the Negro is a soulless beast in his chapter entitled, "The Bible and Divine Revelation, as well as Reason, All Teach That the Negro Is Not Human."[55]

Carroll goes even further in his next book, *The Tempter of Eve*. In this book he establishes not only black people's nonhumanity but also their intrinsic lascivious nature. He does this by identifying the tempter in the Garden as black. Different from others who had made similar arguments, Carroll argued that the tempter was "a negress, who served Eve in the capacity of maid servant."[56] Through cunning, the "negress" tempter got Eve to distrust and disobey God, thereby causing both her and Adam to eat of the forbidden fruit. The penalty that follows Eve's, and subsequently Adam's, succumbing to temptation serves to strengthen the notion that black women are oversexed seductive temptresses; thus, dealings with them are characterized by "matters of the flesh." In the end, Adam and Eve recognize that which they were innocent of before, their nudity, and women are relegated to painful childbirth. Typical of Carroll, he supports his interpretation of the temptation with a graphic, racially charged illustration.

Carroll certainly was not the first, nor was he the last, Christian apologist for black inferiority to place black people in the Garden of Eden in the form of the serpent.[57] However, given the voluminous quality of his books, the numerous supporting illustrations, and the care by which he attempted to show that "scriptures were in absolute harmony with sciences at every point," Carroll's books were undoubtedly the most comprehensive to be written on the subject. They certainly received significant responses from both the religious and scientific communities. For instance, Reverend W. S. Armistead wrote an equally voluminous tome, also replete with illustrations, refuting Carroll's claim that the "Negro was a beast." Interestingly, however, even though Armistead painstakingly showed how Carroll's books corrupted the truth of both the Bible and science in declaring the Negro a beast, he made clear in his declaration that the "Negro was human" did not mean he considered Negroes equal to whites.[58] Nevertheless, what we find, regardless of the merits of Carroll's arguments, is that his books epitomize the way in which a platonized Christian tradition is able to sustain and generate dehumanizing portrayals of black women and men.

The emergence of religious racism bears witness to the troubling predisposition of platonized Christianity: the tendency to align with inequitable dominating power. As pointed out in the previous chapter, given the platonized tradition's theology of the sexual body, it is inclined toward a coalition with oppressive power. In this respect, platonized Christianity's vilification of sexuality coincides with the manner in which unjust power dehumanizes those it subjugates, that is, by sexualizing them. Essentially, platonized Christianity emboldens oppressive power in its sexualized denigration of certain human bodies. It should also be noted that platonized Christianity's approach to the Bible makes its alliance with unscrupulous power even more possible. For again, this is an approach that virtually ignores Jesus' ministry of compassionate solidarity with the oppressed. In this respect, platonized Christianity eschews the moral foundation on which many based Christianity's authority in an age marked by reason. Most significantly, however, religious racism was virtually inevitable, given platonized Christianity's compatibility with two dominant cultural narratives: the Enlightenment narrative on reason and the white cultural narrative on black people. Moreover, with its production of religious racism, platonized Christianity was able to provide a sacred canopy for both white cultural ideology and scientific racism. Oddly enough, while religion was struggling to find its way in eighteenth- and nineteenth-century America, platonized Christianity effectively came into its own. It colluded with the discourse of both the Enlightenment and white culture to form an impressive configuration of "discursive power." Essentially, the interplay between Enlightenment philosophy, white cultural ideology, and platonized Christianity ensured the continued violence against the black body.

Religious racism is one of the explicit ways in which platonized Christianity supported white tyranny against black men and women. Important to ask, however, is what kind of impact the discourse of religious racism had on "everyday" white Christians. Was religious racism simply a "scholarly" movement, or did it reach down into the pews, thus helping to shape the prevailing theological consciousness?

The extent to which the publications of religious racism

reached "everyday" people is uncertain. Mason Stokes notes, "anecdotal accounts suggest that *The Negro a Beast* was widely circulated, particularly in the South." In further support of its influence on everyday white Christians, he cites a door-to-door subscription campaign to distribute the book as well as resolutions passed by various white church bodies decrying its popularity.[59] If we draw from Frederick Douglass's remarks about the popularity of scientific racism, then we might also assume the same popularity for works of religious racism.[60] Whatever the actual popularity of writings like Carroll's may have been, what we know for sure is that there were numerous preachers who generally agreed with the various arguments that characterized religious racism, especially the Hamitic curse. Thus, it can be reasonably conjectured that whether or not they read the actual literature, numerous white Christians were exposed to the arguments of religious racism. Moreover, given their already platonized theological consciousness along with their white racist ideology, they were certainly prepared to accept such arguments. For the expression of Christianity in eighteenth- and nineteenth-century America, especially in the South, was evangelical Protestantism. As mentioned earlier, it was through evangelical Protestantism that platonized Christianity found its most comfortable home in America. Thus, shaped by an evangelical Protestant theology, white Christians were primed to accept not only the discourse of religious racism but also vicious attacks against the black people. Let us now look more closely at evangelical Protestantism as an expression of platonized Christianity, particularly as it regards the black body.

Platonized Christianity and Evangelical Protestantism

The Great Awakenings

By all accounts evangelical Protestantism erupted in America with the emergence of the eighteenth- and early-nineteenth-century Great Awakenings. These Awakenings have defined the essential theological foundation for evangelical Protestantism. In so doing, these Awakenings represent the beginning of platonized Christianity's prevailing influence on the American theological consciousness. As been noted by many scholars of evangelical thought, not only did evangelical Protestantism emerge as a "quintessentially American faith," but it continues to be the most significant theological influence on American life and culture.[61] It is for this reason that we will examine the Great Awakenings in terms of the theology they advanced. For in doing so we see even more clearly platonized Christianity's fatal flaws when it comes to the black body, even as we come to appreciate the collective theological consciousness that has perhaps allowed for Christian participation in acts as vile as lynching. Before examining this theology, however, we must first acknowledge some important caveats concerning this discussion of the Great Awakenings and the evangelical tradition to which they gave birth.

The Great Awakenings were a complex and rich phenomenon in American life and culture. While the First and Second Great Awakenings bore similarities to each other, they also were quite different. They were, for instance, both characterized by emotional gatherings fueled by spirited preaching. But, while mass meetings and large gatherings were typical of the First Great Awakening, smaller camp meetings typified the second. In addition, the First Great Awakening, which erupted around the 1730s, was centered in the New England colonies. The Second Great Awakening, often referred to as the "Great Revival," emerged in the early 1800s. Its primary focus was the southern and western regions of the country. Some have gone so far as to suggest that it was the Second Great Awakening that "turned the American South into perhaps the most distinctively and self-consciously religious region in Christendom."[62] It should also be noted that at the same time that revivals were flourishing in the South and West, a "new phase of the Great Revival" emerged in the North. This northern movement characteristically launched a series of social reforms based on central evangelical principles, to be examined shortly. The point is that the Great Awakenings "took many shapes, forms, expressions and colors."[63] In this regard so too does the evangelical Protestant tradition that it spawned.

It cannot be stressed enough that while the evangelical Protestant tradition advanced the Great Awakenings' platonized theology, a theology that has fostered collusion with white racism, various aspects of this platonized evangelical tradition also prompted vigorous protests against black oppression. There in fact was no stronger voice of protest against slavery than the one considered the "father of modern evangelicalism," Charles G. Finney.[64] The evangelical Protestant tradition is a complex tradition, theologically and otherwise. Its complexity is seen in that it maintains platonized notions that support black people's oppression even as it puts forward theological principles that prompt it to contest that same oppression. It is no doubt because of the complexity of this tradition that black men and women have been attracted to it at the same time that they have been harmed by it.

This particular discussion of evangelical Protestantism does not pretend to capture the intricate depth of evangelical Protestant thought. What it does do is highlight that which lends itself to the support of black tyranny while acknowledging that the "racist" strands of evangelical Protestantism do not represent the whole of the tradition.   true

Most particularly, what this discussion does advance is that even in its diversity there was a common theology that characterized the Great Awakenings and accordingly continues to influence evangelical Protestant thought significantly. Moreover, this is a theology that lends itself to promoting attacks on certain human bodies, in this instance the black body. This discussion further recognizes the theology of these early revivals as that which has especially characterized Southern religion and is pervasive within the black faith tradition. As William Martin states in his study of the religious right in America, "It is difficult to overstate the impact of the Great Revival on the development of Southern Culture."[65] Again, given the profound influence of revival theology on the collective theological consciousness of white Christians in the South (the home of slavery and lynching), along with its influence on the black Christian tradition (to be examined later), an examination of it is significant for this study. Once more, this Great Awakening theology reflects the advent of an influential platonized Christian tradition in America. Hence, by examining the theology of the Great Awakenings, even with broad strokes, we are better able to appreciate the practical impact of a platonized Christian tradition on the white consciousness and the black body. Let us now explore platonized Christianity as it emerged in the Great Awakenings.

What has come to be known as the First and Second Great Awakenings was indeed a series of revivals. The purpose of these revivals was to convert people to a "Christian" way of living. Preachers such as Englishman George Whitefield and American Jonathan Edwards led the revivals. Both of these men exemplified characteristic aspects of this revival movement. George Whitefield represented the "itinerant" aspect of the movement. He was an Anglican priest who came to the American colonies to raise money for an orphanage that he started in Georgia. As a leader of the First Great Awakening, he traveled through the colonies with his message for wayward people to convert to a holy, Christian life. Whitefield was considered by many to be one of the greatest preachers of his time. His style was reportedly very spirited and played to the emotions of his audience. One of Whitefield's contemporaries said that his voice and preaching style were such that he "could melt an audience merely by `pronouncing 'Mesopotamia.'"[66] Needless to say, Whitefield's mesmerizing style accorded well with the intent of the revivals, which again was to convert.

If Whitefield was the "itinerant" Great Awakening evangelist, Jonathan Edwards was the "stay-at-home" one. He was considered a "religious thinker and evangelical preacher who towered above all the others."[67] Edwards not only attempted to convert people from his New England pulpit but also provided scholarly reflections on the rationale and value of the revival movement.

Whether or not great numbers of people were actually converted to Christianity during this period of revivals is a matter of dispute. However, one population of people that is known to have been converted in significant numbers is blacks. Though we will return to this in the next chapter, it is always important to bear in mind that black Christianity even in its diversity "is largely a product of Awakening style or revivalistic religion."[68] For now, however, let us focus on the theological content of this movement. For again, it was through these Great Awakenings that platonized Christianity would come to significantly shape the theological consciousness of white and black Christians.

Perhaps the best way to understand the theology of this "revivalistic religion" is to recognize what its promoters claimed to be fighting against. On the one hand, their emotive style of preaching and the revival mode of taking the message directly to the people bespoke their belief that colonial churches had become too formal and learned. On the other hand, the message that they preached suggested what they believed to be the state of the times. According to many of the revivalist preachers, America was in the midst of "evil times." Tellingly for them, it was not primarily, if at all, slavery and other societal forms of white cultural oppression that made these times evil. Rather it was the "individual" spiritual decay of the populace, white and black. This spiritual decay was ostensibly characterized, in the words of Edwards, by "youth . . . addicted to night walking . . . frequent[ing] the tavern and engag[ing] in unspecified lewd practices."[69] The spiritual decay that this evangelist claimed to define prerevival America was marked by a "worldly" lifestyle where people indulged in bodily pleasures. The preachers of the Great Awakenings responded to these times of "spiritual decadence" by naming such behavior evil and against God, calling for people to repent and thereby lead a more abstemious lifestyle. Such a lifestyle was considered more befitting a Godly people. The more prurient life was considered a sign of Satan's influence.

Jonathan Edwards expresses this theology in a 1741 sermon entitled, "The Distinguishing Marks of a Work of the Spirit of God." Edwards says that when the spirit of God is at work, "[it] operates against the interests of Satan's kingdom, which lies in encouraging and establishing sin, and cherishing men's worldly lusts."[70] Edwards clarifies his point by drawing upon the First Epistle of John (2:15-16):

"Love not the world, neither the things that are in the world: If any man love the world, the love of the Father is not in him: for all that is in the world, the lust of the flesh, and the lust of the eyes, and the pride of life, is not of the Father, but of the world." So that by the world the apostle evidently means everything that appertains to the interest of sin, and comprehends all the corruptions of lusts of men, and all those acts and objects by which they are gratified.[71]

George Whitefield made a similar point in a sermon entitled, "Marks of a True Conversion," when he simply said, "if we are really converted, we shall be loose from the world."[72] Essentially, within this Great Awakening theology that came to shape evangelical Protestantism in America, the measure of one's salvation was marked by one's ability to be converted from the world. True piety was characterized by "self-denial" and resistance to bodily temptations, not the least of which was sexual pleasure. Jonathan Edwards, in fact, considered male genitalia, "a constant reminder of the 'peculiar need' of bridling and restraint."[73] Another preacher of evangelical theology whose ministry actually predates the actual Great Awakenings, Cotton Mather, prayed that God would not hold against his children the act he participated in to conceive them.[74]

There are at least two main interrelated emphases of Great Awakening theology: conversion and "holy" living. The latter, of course, is a sign of the former. Both of these principles are upheld by what was believed to be the ultimate authority, the Bible. With these two emphases the platonized nature of this evangelical theology is clear.

Platonized theology tends to exploit the closed monotheistic core of Christianity by making very clear distinctions between those who are of God and those who are not. Those who are of God are Christians and accordingly lead a Christian, that is, pure, lifestyle. Platonized Christianity makes sacrosanct divisions of the world and its people. Commensurate with this platonized tendency, the preachers of the Great Awakening tried to arouse people to convert to a Christian life by admonishing them to remain virtuous in their living. Anything less than virtuous living was considered a betrayal of their Christian/Godly identity. Most importantly, unholy living would jeopardize their very salvation. Thus, characteristic of a platonized Christian tradition(the Great Awakening advanced a theology that was primarily concerned with freeing the souls of people from the evil doings of their bodies.) On the whole, the theological content of the Great Awakenings was a platonized theology. Matters of body—that is, wanton and lustful behavior—were considered evil and an affront to God. People were therefore called to convert from their sinful/worldly ways to a more spiritual, hence sober, way of living.

As we will see, such platonized thinking had definite implications for the way black people were treated, especially as this thinking corresponded to white cultural ideology and its attendant practices. Thus, what we will find when examining platonized Christianity as it manifested itself in the Great Awakenings is jarringly similar to the way it was manifested in religious racism. In short, the proponents of the Great Awakening had much in common with the advocates of religious racism when it came to the matter of race, no doubt owing to the fact that the same theology informed them both. This similarity begins with how they both generally responded to the Enlightenment's challenge and subsequent implications for response for black people.

Great Awakening Theology and the Enlightenment

The revivals exploded onto the American scene almost simultaneously with the advent of the Age of Reason. It would at first glance seem that these two movements would be diametrically opposed to one another, given the Enlightenment disposition toward religion. Yet they were not. For while the revivals appealed to the hearts and emotions of people in order to effect conversion, reason was elevated as a marker of a converted life. Conversion meant nothing less than turning away from the "excesses" of the body, that is, lewd behavior, toward the virtues of the mind, that is, reason. Whitefield makes this clear in a sermon about the sin of drunkenness: "What renders drunkenness more inexcusable, is, that it robs a man of his reason. Reason is the glory of a man; the

chief thing whereby God made us to differ from the brute creation."[75]

Edwards went even further in trying to show the "reasonableness" of evangelical theology as he diligently attempted to show
that reason and revelation actually cohered because they were
both gifts from God. He preached, "GOD is the Author of all
Knowledge and Understanding whatsoever."[76] Moreover, in
addressing the emotional nature of the revivals, Edwards cautioned that the good convert would never "[lose] their rationality
to enthusiasm."[77] What we see in the early evangelical manifestation of platonized Christianity is similar to what we saw in religious racism—a strong concern to show the compatibility
between Christianity and reason. The credibility of the early evangelical movement in an "enlightened nation" rested not simply on
the authority of the Bible but also on its ability to show itself "reasonable." It was able to do this because it fundamentally embraced
a theology that for all intents and purposes sanctified reason.

It is interesting to note another aspect of the Great Awakening
theology that was perhaps incidentally compatible with the
Enlightenment spirit but certainly telling of a platonized Christian
tradition. The Great Awakenings focused on the individual. The
message itself was aimed directly at the individual without the
mediation of church structures or clergy. Moreover, the message
was not chiefly one of social transformation but one of individual
salvation. In addition, even though the revivals would attempt to
incite conversion "emotionally," conversion was to essentially
result from the individual's free choice, even if this was a circum-
scribed choice. For as noted by Martin Marty, the choice meant
"you must choose Jesus Christ, must decide to let the Spirit of
God work in your heart and—note well!—you may and must
choose *this* version of Christianity against *that* version."[78] The version to be chosen, of course, was a platonized version.

This emphasis on the individual and freedom was compatible
with, if not reflective of, the Enlightenment's emphasis on the
same. There was without question a "profoundly radical individualism at the heart of the Enlightenment."[79] The individual was the
center of truth and knowing as reflected in Descartes' credo, "I
think therefore I am." The rights of the individual to "life, liberty,

and the pursuit of happiness," were to be protected. But most significantly, the individual was to be the arbiter of his or her own
existence. This meant, for instance, that religion was not to be
imposed on an individual by any civil or religious authority. Locke
made the point in his *Letters Concerning Toleration* when he
argued that the "care of the souls" is not to be the responsibility
of any "civil magistrate . . . because no man can so far abandon the
care of his own salvation as blindly to leave to the choice of any
other. . . . All the life and power of true religion consist in the
inward and full persuasion of the mind; and faith is not faith without believing."[80] In America, this individualism of the Enlightenment translated into "religious disestablishment," whereby
churches were expected to support themselves without governmental assistance. This philosophy of "religious disestablishment"
accorded well with the attitude of revivalist preachers. They
believed that individuals, not clergy or institutions, should be
responsible for their own spiritual lives.[81] Admittedly, the Enlightenment's acceptance of the individual's right to seek happiness
and pleasure unquestionably conflicted with the evangelical
emphasis on self-denial. Yet the shared focus on the individual certainly provided another significant point of contact between the
spirit of the Enlightenment and the theology of the Great Awakenings. But more to the point of this discussion, the Great Awakenings' emphasis on the individual further indicated the
platonized nature of this movement.

With its unique emphasis on saving the souls of individuals,
Jesus' ministry to the oppressed and socially marginalized was
clearly a subsidiary concern for the Great Awakening. To be sure,
Jesus' ministry was not regarded as a primary exemplar of a Christian life. Instead, the emphasis of Great Awakening theology is
more reflective of the Pauline tradition. One will recall from previous discussions that this tradition stresses the significance of
leading a chaste life. Furthermore, as also mentioned earlier, the
Pauline tradition provides one of the earliest examples of platonized Christianity. In general, a platonized approach to the
Bible, drawing on Pauline texts, encourages a concern for the care
of human souls but not necessarily for the sanctity of human bodies. The practical result of this selective platonized approach to the

Bible was that it enabled the revivalists, with relative impunity, to focus their attention on individual salvation while virtually ignoring the inhuman social conditions to which black people were subjected. It did not, in other words, readily lend itself to an advocacy for the sanctity of black bodies. This leads us to perhaps the most disturbing similarity between the revivalistic theology and religious racism.

If religious racism explicitly affirmed white cultural notions of black inferiority, then the theology of the Great Awakening did so implicitly, particularly as it did not refute them. As has been well documented, evangelical preachers in the main did not protest slavery (except of course in the North where a slave economy was not central). Indeed, more often than not they affirmed the positive good of slavery by asserting that it provided for the evangelizing of Africans. Moreover, in order to gain access to the enslaved population, they also suggested to slaveholders that conversion to Christianity would not make the slaves eager for freedom, but quite the contrary, it would make them better slaves. Whitefield wrote, for instance, "I believe masters and mistresses will shortly see that Christianity will not make their negroes worse slaves."[82] The wider point, however, is that the theology of the Great Awakening did not compel a denunciation of white cultural thought and its accompanying practices. In many respects, the nature of the movement itself undoubtedly served to reinforce for some the notion that blacks were driven by "passion." For again, the emotive revival style appealed to the hearts of people not necessarily to their heads. That blacks would be attracted to this revivalistic movement, therefore, was probably no surprise to the many whites who believed them controlled by passion (we will explore later the various reasons why this movement was actually attractive to black people). "Religious zeal" as Jefferson had remarked, was certainly befitting black women and men. The Great Awakenings' emotional appeal, especially as it attracted black people, coincided with white cultural ideology. (The implication, in the illogic of white racist ideology, was that the whites attracted to the movement were attracted for reasons other than the emotional style of it.) There were also other practical implications for black people.

First, the belief that it was a pure soul that marked a Christian life and hence effected salvation no doubt served to exonerate many white Christians from any "spiritual" anxiety they may have had concerning their treatment of black people. They could, for instance, own slaves with assurance of their salvation as long as they believed in Jesus and led "chaste" lives. There were, of course, those who were at least troubled by the contradiction of being Christian and owning slaves. George Whitefield, himself a slave owner, did argue that inasmuch as slaves were spiritually equal to whites, they should not be treated cruelly. With that said, however, he also asserted that cruel treatment of the slaves could "have the positive effect of heightening their sense of their natural misery," thus prompting their conversion.[83] Characteristically, then, a change in a white person's soul did not augur a change in their attitudes toward black bodies. The Great Awakening theology that shaped their Christian consciousness certainly did not require such an attitudinal change. In this sense it makes it most remarkable that there were those evangelicals who did indeed advocate against slavery.

Second, even as this theology did suggest a certain spiritual equality, in that all souls were the same before God, it was not forgotten—even by some of the preachers of this theology—that black bodies signaled inferiority. As Winthrop Jordan says, "the men who insisted upon this equality were always compelled either to disregard or to belittle the fact that however much the Negro's soul might resemble the white man's, his skin did not."[84] Noting how these revivalist preachers never lost sight of the bodies of blacks, Jordan quotes one of the preachers as commenting, "while many of their sable faces were bedewed with tears, their withered hands of faith were stretched out, and their precious souls made white in the blood of the lamb."[85] In effect, the whiteness/purity of their black souls did not rescue black people from the blackness/impurity of their bodies.

That black people were black regardless of the state of their souls also meant that they remained an "ardent" people. Indeed, there were those who protested the "integrated" revival meetings for fear that black men in their emotionally charged state might tempt emotionally charged white women, and thus "violate" white women's "chastity." The pre-Awakening evangelical preacher Cotton Mathers, reminiscent of arguments put forth in the literature of religious racism, went so far as to suggest that the devil ordinarily showed himself on earth as a "small *Black man*."[86]

Again, there were preachers of the Great Awakening who had more equitable views when it came to black people. They likely interpreted the idea of spiritual equality in such a way that it suggested an earthly equality between blacks and whites. Nevertheless, the point remains that such views did not naturally result from this platonized expression of Christianity. As shown above, the focus of platonized Christianity does not compel a concern for black bodies. In fact, it more readily provides for the devaluation of black people and hence vile treatment of black bodies. In many respects the theology of the Great Awakenings and that of religious racism were just different sides of the same coin, the coin of platonized Christianity. Thus, the discourse of evangelical Protestantism and religious racism complemented each other. It can be concluded that whether or not "ordinary" Christians in eighteenth- and nineteenth-century America actually read the literature of religious racism, the theology that they were exposed to was enough to promote and sustain belief in black people's inferiority. Again, this theology of the Great Awakening revered the soul and reproved the body, and accordingly divinized reason and demonized passion; at the same time, it did not challenge white cultural ideology. Consequently, this theology virtually sanctioned the vile depictions and vicious treatment of black women and men. Once again, what we see is that platonized expressions of Christianity partner well with power. In this instance, the theology of the Great Awakening was a natural ally to unjust white power.

The Implications of Evangelical Theology for the Black Body.

What, however, does this suggest for evangelical Protestant theology in general? As said earlier, evangelical Protestantism—even with its "various historical twists" and "theological nuances"—is indisputably a product of these early revivals.[87] As such, it continues to advance the theology of the Great Awakenings. Thus, true to its evangelical moniker, its primary mission is evangelism—that is, converting people to a Christian way of living. The way of living that evangelical Protestantism promotes is a "holy" life free of the bodily temptations of this world. And of course, evangelical Protestantism continues to affirm the Bible as the ultimate authority providing divine truth. Essentially, evangelical Protestantism is a platonized Christian tradition. Consequently, contemporary evangelical Protestantism, even in all of its diverse expressions, carries with it all of the potential problematic tendencies in regard to unjust power.

Yet, it must be remembered that evangelical Protestantism does not invariably lead to white racist treatment of black bodies or to oppressive alliances in general. To reiterate, evangelical theology did in large measure provide the foundation for many antislavery advocates and antilynching activists. Nevertheless, it must be recognized that the substantial platonized character of this theological tradition makes it most susceptible to colluding with inequitable power in such a way that it supports the unjust, if not violent, treatment of various human bodies, especially black bodies (indeed the same can be said for nonwhite bodies in general). Such a collusion does not have to manifest itself in an extreme form such as religious racism. It can be manifested in a more implicit manner, as in the case of the Great Awakening. In its silence on social issues or in its strident defense of the merits of "holy" living, evangelical Protestantism too often finds itself sanctioning the ideological rhetoric of dominating power. Furthermore, platonized/evangelical theology easily accommodates distinctions between evil/un-Godly people and good/Godly people, thus projecting a hostile relationality between groups of people. In addition, platonized/evangelical theology promotes an understanding of sexuality that provides a basis for distinctions to be made between various groups of people. Therefore, simply by putting forth a vigorous public defense of their views on sexuality, evangelical Protestants can easily provide sacred legitimation for oppressive ideology and practices. Though more will be said about

this in the next chapter, it is worth noting now the implications that platonized views on sexuality have for nonheterosexual persons.

Characteristic of patriarchal/heterosexist definitions, sexuality is often erroneously defined in relation to sexual/genital practices. Moreover, socially marginalized people are typically a sexualized people as we have seen in regard to black persons. The same is thus true for nonheterosexual men and women in a heterosexist culture. Hence, nonheterosexuals are characteristically essentialized according to their sexuality, which of course has already been essentialized in respect to genital activity. In short, nonheterosexuals are wrongly defined in relation to their presumed sexual practices. Within a platonized tradition this does not bode well for them. As a result of being characterized as a people categorically engaged in nonprocreative sexual activity, they are deemed unGodly. It is in this way that platonized Christianity—that is, evangelical Protestantism—readily sustains social, political, and ecclesiastical discrimnation against gay, lesbian, and other nonheterosexual persons (again more will be said about this with particular reference to black people).

Finally, in terms of evangelical Christianity, as suggested above, with its primary emphasis on the saving of souls, the actual treatment of human bodies is likely to get insufficient attention, if any at all. It will long be remembered that the justification given by a group of clergy for their lack of support of Martin Luther King Jr. during his fight for black civil rights was that it was the responsibility of ministers to "save souls," not to become involved in controversial issues of social justice. It should come as no surprise, therefore, when various contemporary manifestations of evangelical theological Protestantism get mixed up with the rhetoric and practices of unjust power, whether by silence or direct involvement. In general, inasmuch as evangelical Protestant traditions substantially embrace platonized theology they will continue to be predisposed to troubling connections with unjust power. It is no wonder, then, that there was profound white Christian participation in the lynching of black bodies. For it was an evangelical Protestant theology that significantly shaped the theological consciousness of "everyday" white Christians during that period, as it perhaps continues to do today.

Crucifixion Revisited

With this recognition of white evangelical Protestant involvement in the lynch-style execution of black men and women, we must briefly revisit the centrality of the crucifixion in evangelical thought. Just as it is pivotal to the Christian tradition in general, it is central for evangelical Protestantism in particular. Evangelical Protestants typically proclaim that it is through the death of Jesus that all who believe in him are saved. It is through "his Blood," they often sing, that they are redeemed, that their souls are made "pure." Given the aforementioned parallels between black lynching and Jesus' crucifixion, one must at least continue to question the role that a strong belief in the redemptive nature of Jesus' crucifixion might play in permitting Christian involvement in lynching. To be sure, evangelical Protestant thought allows for the demonization of black people. It is thus not too far a stretch to suggest that in the collective consciousness of white Christians lynching was a way of "saving" the collective souls of white people as they were able to rid their community of evil. In this regard, Orlando Patterson's earlier mentioned observations are borne out: the lynching of black people became a way for many Southern whites to further "redeem" the South. Once again, René Girard's analysis concerning "sacrificial victims" seems fitting in that white society sacrifices black bodies to save itself.[88] At the very least it can be concluded that the confluence of whiteness and a platonized tradition that professes the redeeming power of the crucifixion has troubling connotations for outcast people, particularly for black people. So in many ways the comments of Ida B. Wells and W. E. B. Du Bois were prescient. For when they lamented white Christian acquiescence to the terrorizing of black bodies, they were actually giving voice to the easy accommodation that evangelical Protestantism makes not simply to whiteness but to unjust power in general. With cutting insight Wells put it plainly:

this is a tradition more ready to "save the souls of white Christians from burning in hell-fire [than] to save the lives of black ones from present burning in fires kindled by white Christians."[89] Wells's comments are indeed supported by the observations of the 1933 report on Southern lynching. This reported advised that "the individualistic theology" of a large segment of white Southern churches "leaves intact the views which provide a justification for lynching and other expressions of racial antagonisms."[90]

Repeat

Critical Assessment of Platonized Christianity

What the hell is it?

What, then, can be said about platonized Christianity? First and foremost, we must acknowledge that this tradition is real. It has played a very prominent role in American life and culture. It has indeed found its most comfortable home in evangelical Protestantism. From this context, it has significantly shaped the collective theological consciousness of America and consequently has affected the lives of many people.

Second, it is a platonized Christian tradition that is most responsible for Christianity's explicit and implicit involvement in white terror of black people. This tradition readily accommodates whiteness. As we have seen in our examination of religious racism and the Great Awakenings, the theology of platonized Christianity is compatible with the ideology of white culture. Therefore, platonized Christianity provides a natural sacred covering for white attacks on the black body just as it also allows for Christians to participate in these attacks.

Yet, as made clear in our examination of platonized Christianity's alliance with whiteness, this tradition is heretical. Platonized Christianity is not the whole of the Christian tradition. Nonetheless, this tradition has so insinuated itself into mainstream theological consciousness that it often appears to speak the truth of Christianity. But it does not. Despite its attentiveness to the Bible, it defies the very incarnational identity of the Christian religion because it allows for the degradation of what the incarnation establishes as sacred—the human body. Most particularly, in cooperating with unjust power (i.e., white power), it betrays the existential reality of the incarnation—that is, Jesus' ministry of compassionate solidarity with the oppressed. But especially it actually opposes the revelation of God's power in human history. Again, this is not a power that imposes itself on bodies and destroys them, rather it is one that empowers bodies, particularly those of the abused, in order to foster life.

Finally, regardless of its pervasive historical presence, because of its questionable historical alliances, it must be concluded that platonized Christianity is as dangerous as it is heretical. Of all of its troubling qualities there are two that make platonized Christianity most dangerous: the dualistic divisions it projects between people and its inherent propensity toward unjust power. Because of these two qualities, platonized Christian traditions invariably find themselves providing theological shelter for social, political, and ecclesiastical discrimination and inequality. Just as religion can embolden revolutionary change, so too can it sanction an unjust status quo. To be sure, platonized expressions of Christianity have certainly done this in regard to black people. Without a doubt, platonized Christianity and whiteness portend a blasphemous combination.

They come together in such a way as to provide a formidable witness to that which is anti-Christ. As seen in evangelical Protestantism, it has allowed for Christians to get mixed up in the vilest of human activity, the lynching of black men and women. And so while we may be able to conclude that it is not Christianity itself that is problematic for black people, recognition of platonized Christianity's compliance with whiteness does raise the question of its particular suitability for black people. What does it mean for black people to embrace a theological tradition (namely, evangelical Protestantism) that is significantly a platonized tradition? This question will be taken up in the next chapter.

5

Black Bodies/White Souls

THERE IS PERHAPS NO SONG ever sung that has created a more haunting image of the maimed black body than the song "Strange Fruit" as sung by blues legend Billie Holiday. In what she would call her "personal protest," Holiday sang:

> Southern trees bear a strange fruit.
> Blood on the leaves, blood at the root
> Black bodies swinging in the Southern breeze
> Strange fruit hanging from the poplar trees.[1]

In this stanza alone white cultural contempt for the black body is clear. Perhaps not so clear is the depth of Holiday's "protest." The passion with which she sang "Strange Fruit" was about more than just lynched black bodies. Holiday sang this song in response to the countless deadly humiliations black bodies have suffered in a white racist society. In her autobiography she recounts the time her father was refused hospital care simply because he was black. As a result of this refusal he died from the pneumonia that ravaged his body.[2] It was in part as a response to what happened to her father that she included this song in her repertoire and that she sang it with such arresting poignancy. She recalled that when she was shown the song she "dug it right off [because it] seemed to spell out all of the things that had killed Pop." She went on to recount that even though she became depressed each time she sang the song she had to keep singing it "because twenty years after [her father] died the things that killed him [were] still happening in the South."[3]

For Billie Holiday, "Strange Fruit" was about more than "black

150

bodies swinging in the Southern breeze." Singing "Strange Fruit" was Billie Holiday's strident testimony to the numerous, perhaps even more sinister, ways in which the black body has been put-upon by whiteness. Her singing of "Strange Fruit" indeed signaled the profound deleterious impact of white cultural violence on the black body and the black psyche. The performance of "Strange Fruit" essentially provided a safe medium for Holiday to express the real horror of black living: that while lynching may represent one of the vilest and most visceral forms of white disdain for the black body, the price that black people have paid for their blackness in a society defined by "whiteness" entails far more than the act of lynching. White social, cultural, and even religious destruction of the black body has involved more than "strange fruit hanging from the popular tree." No one was better able to articulate this than literary genius and social critic James Baldwin.

Baldwin's appreciation for the menacing depth of white hatred for the black body is captured in his criticism of the Hollywood version of Billie Holiday's life, *Lady Sings the Blues*. Among other things, he railed against the movie for its interpretation of why Holiday chose to sing "Strange Fruit." The film depicts her as singing the song in response to a particular lynch scene she ostensibly came upon when traveling with her band (an event she never mentions in her autobiography). Baldwin says that to suggest that an actual lynching was the motivation behind Holiday's singing of this song is not only "self-serving," but misses the profound meaning the song held for Holiday and for other black men and women. Again, for Holiday, "Strange Fruit" signified the multiple ways in which black bodies were regularly maligned by whiteness. At the same time that Baldwin recognized that Holiday was "infinitely more complex" than the movie revealed, he also understood that the nature of the white attack on the black body was infinitely more complicated than lynching.[4] In recognizing this, he also understood that Christianity's complicity in maligning the black body involved far more than its sanction of lynching. To him, white social/cultural/religious crimes against the black body are so penetrating as to be virtually "unspeakable." He said, "Yes, it does indeed mean something—something unspeakable—to be born, in a white country, an Anglo-Teutonic, antisexual country, black."[5] But fortunately, Baldwin did speak about the beleaguered black body. He attempted throughout his writings to confront not only white disdain for black flesh but most of all black people's disdain for their own flesh. He eventually resolved that black people's tragic dilemma concerning their own black bodies began with the reality of being "born in a white country, a white Protestant Puritan country."[6] He explained:

> It is very important to remember what it means to be born in a Protestant Puritan country, with all the taboos placed on the flesh, and have at the same time in this country such a vivid example of a decent pagan imagination and the sexual liberty with which white people invest Negroes—and then penalize them for. . . . It's a guilt about flesh. In this country the Negro pays for that guilt which white people have about flesh.[7]

Baldwin's incisive comment properly indicts the troubling interaction between evangelical Protestant theology and white cultural ideology. His observation shrewdly suggests the high price that black people have paid because of this invidious interaction. This *is* a price that goes beyond the reality of lynching. This chapter will explore that price. The premise of this chapter is that this price involves more than white violence against the black body. It also includes black people's own responses to their very own black flesh. Chapter 5 will proceed with an initial look at the evangelical Protestant influence on black people. This section recognizes that evangelical Protestantism is the predominant tradition of [black] Christians and that the prevailing theology of the black faith tradition is a platonized theology. In this regard, the "appropriateness" of black people adopting a faith tradition that demonizes the body/flesh in the same way that they are demonized by white culture will be examined. Specifically, this chapter will explore the interactive effect that platonized theology and white culture has had on black people's attitudes toward their own bodies. James Baldwin's literary insights will provide the foundation for this exploration. The underlying assumption is that these two social-cultural narratives have coalesced in such a way as to alienate black men and women from their sexuality. In so doing, these narratives have not only disrupted black life but also distorted black spirituality. Special attention will be given to the problems of "redemptive suffering" motifs within a platonized black faith tradition. Chapter 5 will conclude by looking at some of the specific ways in which the confluence of a platonized black faith tradition and white culture has interacted with other discourses of power—namely, patriarchal and heterosexist discourse—to further overwhelm black bodies, especially those of women. In the end, chapter 5 maintains that black people's adoption of a platonized Christian tradition (i.e., evangelical Protestantism) has in fact exacted too high a psychological, emotional, spiritual, and physical price, a price that expands the meaning of the black body as "strange fruit." At the conclusion of this chapter, the viability of a black faith tradition and the feasibility of Christianity for a black woman should become clearer. Let us now begin by establishing the evangelical Protestant influence, that is, platonized Christianity, within the black faith tradition.

Evangelical Protestant Theology and the Black Faith Tradition

Evangelical Protestantism, which Baldwin aptly identifies as Protestant Puritanism, has provided prevailing theological influence within the black Christian faith tradition. As noted by numerous black religious scholars, evangelical Protestantism is the predominant tradition of black Christians. This has been the case since the Great Awakenings in America. By most accounts, it was through these eighteenth- and nineteenth-century revivals that most blacks, both enslaved and free, were converted to Christianity. The reasons for the "revivals'" success among blacks suggest an operative *hermeneutic of appropriation* that informs the theological core of the black faith tradition. This hermeneutic will become evident as we examine black people's attraction to the Great Awakenings.

Prior to these revivals there were many barriers to black people's conversion to Christianity, especially for the enslaved population. One of the most uncompromising barriers was slave owners' concern that being a Christian precluded one from being a slave. Obviously aware of the egalitarian themes present throughout the Christian gospels, slaveholders feared that if their "slaves" were "converted" to Christianity, they would have to be set free from bondage. The bishop of London quickly mitigated this fear, however, by issuing a statement that explained that the freedom offered in the gospels was spiritual, not earthly, freedom. To further quell the anxiety of slaveholders, converted "slaves" were made to sign a statement affirming that they understood that their baptism did not imply their emancipation from slavery. Yet even though the slaveholders' fears were addressed, thereby making them generally more receptive to allowing their "slaves" to become Christian, significant numbers of blacks, enslaved and free, were still not attracted to Christianity, at least as offered to them by white missionaries. If nothing else, this fact signaled black people's determination to exercise a measure of agency over what they could in some respect control, their religious/spiritual life (it should also be noted that the emergence of the "invisible institutions" points to the same religious agency).[8] They—not white slavemasters or white people in general—thwarted the efforts to make them Christian. They—black men and women—seized control over their own spirituality by steadfastly rejecting the form and message of Christianity as presented to them by Anglican missionaries.[9]

Before the eruption of the Great Awakenings, Anglican missionaries had the primary responsibility for converting enslaved blacks to Christianity. In 1701 the Church of England established the Society for the Propagation of the Gospel in Foreign Parts (SPG), with one of its primary focuses being the introduction of the Christian gospel to the enslaved population. But this society's efforts went largely unrewarded for two general reasons: because of the manner in which Christianity was offered and because of the notional nature of missionary theology. Let us first examine the way in which the missionaries attempted to introduce blacks to Christianity.

In order to become a Christian, the Anglican missionaries required that the potential convert participate in a tedious process of catechetical instruction. This instruction involved learning the right doctrines, proper practices and rituals of Christianity. Not only did this catechistic way of presenting Christianity take time and demand a level of "literacy" that most of the enslaved black population did not possess; it also did not resonate with black people's African religious heritage.[10]

Black men and women, especially those who were African born, were accustomed to a form of religion and an expression of spirituality that were more empirical than what was presented to them by the Anglican missionaries. Informed by either the survival of ritualistic carryovers from their African religious traditions or first-hand memories, many black women and men maintained that a person's religiosity was defined by more than intellectual assent to certain rules and doctrines. Authentic spirituality—that is, a relationship to divine reality—was not a matter of the mind; it was rather a matter of the soul and body. This meant, then, that a person's spiritual condition—that is, the state of one's soul—and/or one's immediate relationship to divinity should be empirically evident through some form of bodily expression. That the body was considered a means by which "divinity" could manifest itself implied that the body had sacral value. In other words, the body was a potential vehicle for divine witness. Clearly, the staid, formal assent to Christianity required by Anglican missionaries did not accord well with the more spontaneous, empirical expression of African religiosity. It did not readily affirm the sacral quality of the human body. But the Great Awakening revivals did. The "evangelical revivalists succeeded where Anglican missionaries had failed."[11] These revivals resonated with and perhaps awakened both viscerally and intellectually memories of African religiosity.

As previously mentioned, for the revivals, spontaneous emotional responses—conversion—to the preached message was the means by which people became Christian. This phenomenon of empirical conversion was similar to African cultural and religious experiences, especially those involving initiation into spiritual cults and spirit possession. As was the case with conversions, spontaneous bodily expressions of one's spiritual state such as "holy-dancing," rhythmic clapping, shouting, singing, trancelike behavior, or other displays of spiritual enthusiasms typically accompanied African religious experiences. Spontaneous ecstatic bodily expression was a way of witnessing to divine reality. It was in this way that the body achieved sacral meaning. Evangelical conversions seemed to affirm the sacral value of the body. For the conversion was inextricably a full-bodied display of divine presence. The enthusiastic conversions that characterized the Great Awakening revivals therefore conformed to black people's African religious heritage in a way that the Anglican catechisms did not. Consequently, more blacks were attracted to Christianity through the Great Awakenings than through the SPG missionaries' efforts. Albert Raboteau aptly summarizes why the revival style of the Great Awakenings, and not the "learned" methods of the SPG, appealed to black people. He writes:

> The emotionalism of the revivals encouraged the outward expression of religious feeling, and the sight of black and white converts weeping, shouting, fainting, and moving in ecstatic trance became a familiar, if sensationalized, feature of the sacramental and camp meeting seasons. In this heated atmosphere, slaves found a form of Christian worship that resembled the religious celebrations of their African heritage. The analogy between African and Evangelical styles of worship enabled the slaves to reinterpret the new religion by reference to the old, and so made this brand of Christianity seem less foreign than that of the more liturgically sedate Church of England.[12]

The revivals of the Great Awakening appealed to the black population for another, perhaps even more significant, reason than simply its "animated" method of evangelism. Within evangelical Protestant theology black people found an emphasis on "equality" that was not present in the theology of the Anglican missionaries. This emphasis not only resonated with black people's own aspirations for freedom and equality but was also compatible with their African theological heritage.

As mentioned above, even though the message of egalitarianism was apparent in the gospels, the Anglican missionaries found a way to avoid its "earthly" implications. Not only did they stress spiritual equality instead of historical equality, but their very treatment of black people reinforced that, within the missionary theology, the difference between the spiritual and the historical was absolute and unbridgeable. To reiterate, Anglican missionaries typically required that the enslaved population accept the practical difference between the spiritual and the historical realm by making them sign a declaration that in becoming Christian they were not seeking freedom. Once again, the missionary brand of Christianity proved itself unacceptable to black people, both free and enslaved. For what was most clear was that the theology, like the style of missionary Christianity itself, was speculative and not empirical. That is, the determined emphasis on spiritual equality had no concrete application. The lack of a practically oriented theology deterred blacks from accepting Christianity because it did not conform to their dreams for freedom and was not compatible with their understanding of theology. Inasmuch as enslaved and free black men and women were influenced by their African theological heritage, for them, theology had to have practical/historical value. Consonant with the concrete manner in which they expressed their spirituality, the theology with which black people were traditionally familiar was as much empirical as it was speculative. Black ethicist Peter J. Paris explains the African theological heritage:

> Africans are not easily disposed to speculative thought because the latter tends to have little or no empirical basis. Rather, much of African thought, including that of theology and ethics, arises out of the problems of daily experience, and it is pursued for the purpose of discovering solutions for everyday problems. In short, African theology and ethics are practical sciences in the service of the community's well-being.[13]

Even though the evangelical theology of the Great Awakenings also stressed spiritual equality instead of historical equality, within the Great Awakening movement itself, this theological emphasis seemed to have a practical consequence. The revivals themselves suggested a tangible result inherent in the theological emphasis on spiritual equality. (For indeed, blacks and whites participated in the revival gatherings on equal grounds.) They listened together to the fiery preaching of the evangelists and were equally prone to an enthusiastic conversionary response. Winthrop Jordan observed, "Almost by definition a religious revival was inclusive; itinerant preachers aimed at gathering every lost sheep, black as well as white."[14] In addition to the equality of participation that the revivals promoted, they fostered an equality of leadership across the black/white divide. Black preachers were recognized as evangelists and were sometimes permitted to lead revivals that included both black and white participants. As Jordan also noted, "The equalitarian implications in Protestant Christianity were never more apparent; if it was difficult for Negroes to become men of affairs in this world, it became increasingly easy, after the watershed of the Great Awakening, for them to become men of God."[15] Of course, this empirical witness to "spiritual equality" was not acceptable to all whites—including some of the white revivalists. As mentioned earlier, some feared that the integrated revivals would lead to grossly unacceptable interaction between black men and white women. The participation of black preachers in the revivals especially offended one critic of the Great Awakenings, Charles Chauncy. He ranted, "*Negroes*, have taken upon them to do the Business of *Preachers*."[16] That black men were preachers only substantiated for him the nonrational character of the revival tradition. To him, blacks were not capable of the kind of rationality required to be preachers. The "enthusiasm" of the Great Awakenings therefore allowed black people to move beyond their divinely ordered station. Thus, in critique of the emotion-filled Great Awakenings, perhaps with black preachers in mind, he preached:

> 'Tis not therefore the pretence of being moved by the SPIRIT, that will justify *private christians* in quiting [*sic*] their own proper station, to act in that which belongs to

another. Such a practice as this naturally tends to destroy the order, GOD has constituted in the church, and may be followed with mischiefs greater than we may be aware of.[17]

No doubt, one of the mischievous acts Chauncy imagined was "lustful" interaction between black men and white women. Nevertheless, regardless of whatever opposition there may have been, black people were attracted to the Great Awakenings theological emphasis on spiritual equality because of its apparent practical consequences. Seemingly, evangelical theology as advanced during the Great Awakenings was not entirely speculative. Whether or not it was the conscious intention of the white evangelists was less significant than the fact that, apparently caught up in their own revivalistic enthusiasm, the evangelists permitted the perhaps inexorable consequence of a movement thoroughly committed to the theological notion of spiritual equality: an earthly expression of that equality. To repeat, a theology that gave way to concrete practice resonated with African understandings concerning the nature of theology. But black people were no doubt attracted to the theology of the Great Awakening for yet another reason—it was consistent with certain core concepts within their African theological heritage.

Unquestionably, the African theological heritage of the early black converts to Christianity was rich and diverse. This heritage consisted of various religious and theological systems. Despite this rich diversity, however, there are certain theological affirmations that are generally upheld as true across the various religious systems. One such affirmation involves the understanding of divine reality and the implications for the human community. It is this understanding with which evangelical theology complied.

While West African theologies bear witness to a pantheon of divine realities, West African religions are foundationally monotheistic.[18] A core theological belief is the existence of a "Great High God" or supreme deity. This Great High God does not directly interact with the human realm. It is believed, in fact, that "by maintaining distance from nature and humanity the [Great High God] manifests divine care."[19] Otherwise, human

beings as well as nature would be overwhelmed and possibly
destroyed by the very power and presence of the supreme deity.
Thus, the remoteness of the Great High God is perceived as an act
of divine kindness. Yet human beings are not without access to the
Great High God. Within the divine realm are a pantheon of lesser
divinities that interact in the earthly realm and to which human
beings have access. In addition, there are "ancestral spirits" who
also occupy a space within the divine realm, and they too provide
a link between the Great High God and humanity. It is important
to note that all of these "divinities" and "spirits" come from and
are thoroughly dependent upon the Great High God. Essentially,
everything that is owes its existence to the Great High God. In
this respect, all of creation, divine and human, has sacred value
because it is intrinsically connected to God. It is perhaps for this
reason that all of reality in the African experience is considered
"sacred reality." This belief accords well with the sacral value the
body is given in religious rites and rituals. Essentially, as has been
well documented, "secularity has no reality" in African life.²⁹ It
cannot be stressed enough that according to the African theological consciousness, everything is connected to the Great High
God; therefore, everything is sacred. The importance of this particular theological affirmation will become clearer later in this discussion. Significant to understand for now is the organizing
principle of this pantheon of beings because it is here that we dis-
cover the practical implications of African theology.

The principle that holds all of these beings together is "harmony." Every level of creation is to exist in harmony with the
other levels. Every being, divine and human, is responsible for
nurturing harmony within and between the various levels of created existence and hence with the Great High God. The manifestation of disharmony is considered evil and not reflective of the
Great High God. All that is of God bespeaks a sense of equilib-
rium, unity, and concord. Peter J. Paris states:

> The African understanding of the supreme deity as creator
> and preserver of all that is implies divine order and harmony
> both in and among the realms of spirit, nature, and history.

In the realm of spirit that hierarchical relationship among the supreme deity, the subdivinities, and the ancestral spirits is the paramount exemplar of order and harmony, and African peoples seek to emulate it in their familial and tribal communities.[21]

Clearly then, as Paris points out, there is a practical, ethical obligation intrinsic to the African theological affirmation of divine harmony—that is, that human beings are to mirror divine harmony in their own living. In the collective African theological consciousness, the well-being of the community is of utmost concern. It is the task of each member of the community to promote harmonious relationality. Any discord or imbalance of relationship is a reflection not of God but of evil and subsequently can have a devastating impact on the whole community. *between tribes*

With this summary understanding of a core African theological affirmation, the compatibility between it and evangelical theology becomes clear. The evangelical theological emphasis on a spiritual equality, especially as it was reflected in revival practices, no doubt awakened the African theological consciousness of many enslaved and freed blacks as it reverberated with two core African principles the idea that everything that exists is connected to God and the notion of harmony.

First, the emphasis on spiritual equality in the very least implies that God values all human beings (even if people do not). Every man and woman, regardless of race, has sacred value. Again, the very acceptance of black women and men in the Great Awakening movement bore practical witness to this theological affirmation. Moreover, this affirmation cohered with the African theological claim that all of creation is connected to God and thus all of creation, including every single human being, is sacred. But most importantly, this claim defied notions that black people were intrinsically inferior beings, created to be slaves. This leads to the second aspect of spiritual equality that resonated with African theology.

To repeat, all that was created was meant to live in harmonious relationship. Enslavement of human beings was therefore inherently inconsistent not only with African theological concepts but with the evangelical emphasis on spiritual equality. Granted, the Great Awakenings were not characterized by a forthright commitment to abolish slavery, and there were prominent evangelists who stressed the compatibility between "conversion" and slavery. However, regardless of how the issue of slavery was or was not addressed, that the Great Awakenings theologized about spiritual equality and also maintained equality of participation within the revivals themselves no doubt appealed to the religious/theological consciousness of many blacks—if for no other reason than the revivals were an exemplar of that which was pleasing to God. They were a model of harmonious relationality, thereby inviting hope in the possibility that such a spirit of harmony might be maintained beyond the revival gatherings. Jordan captures this sense of hope as he recognizes the importance of revivals for black life.

> The effects of the Great Awakening on American feelings about the Negro rippled slowly through colonial society. By clearing an avenue down which Negroes could crowd into an important sector of the white man's community, the Awakening gradually forced the colonists to face more squarely the fact that Negroes were going to participate in the American experience.[22]

Ironically, however, the hope that blacks placed in the "enthusiasm" of the Great Awakening for equality did not come to fruition. Indeed, evangelical Protestantism would itself become a tradition "divided" by race.[23] Yet during the times of the Great Awakenings the black converts seemed to maintain the capacity to tolerate the discrepancy between their "revival" experience and societal experience. To be sure, irrespective of their status in American society, black people were visible and equal participants in the Great Awakenings. They were converted to Christianity in what then were record numbers. While the logic of white cultural ideology would conclude that black people were attracted to the Great Awakenings because the revivals were characterized by emotion and passion as opposed to intellect and reason, black people's attraction to the Awakening revivals actually reveals a more discerning response to evangelical religiosity and theology. Their attraction to the evangelical version of Christianity as opposed to the Anglican missionary version exposes their use, whether deliberately or not, of a *hermeneutic of appropriation* that was grounded in their own theocultural heritage. This was a heritage that allowed them not simply to survive but perhaps most importantly to affirm their sacred humanity, even as that humanity was being viciously defiled. In this regard, black men and women accepted Christianity only inasmuch as it too, both ritualistically and theologically, was consonant with their theo-cultural heritage and thus affirmed the sanctity of their very humanity. The Great Awakening's version of Christianity, evangelical Protestantism, seemed to do just that. To reiterate, it affirmed the sacral value of the body with its stress on the importance of the conversion experience, and it affirmed the sacredness of black humanity through its practical theological regard for "spiritual equality." Evangelical Protestantism was thus appropriated into the black faith tradition, thereby becoming for black Christians a prevailing theological influence. Before looking at the implications of this influence, it is important to highlight the significance of this hermeneutic of appropriation.

Clearly, a hermeneutic of appropriation was operative in the formation of the black faith tradition. This hermeneutic provided a tool for black people to fashion a Christian tradition that spoke to their own unique experiences of being black in a society generally hostile to their blackness. This hermeneutic involved more than speculative judgments concerning the appropriateness of a particular religious belief or practice. That is, whether or not something was appropriated into the black faith tradition was determined by more than simply intellectual assent. It involved the assent of the ethical/aesthetic imagination as well. A particular religious belief or practice had to also correspond to, and in fact awaken, black people's own vision concerning the sacred reverence of their own black bodies for them to appropriate that belief of practice as a part of their faith tradition. In other words, as suggested above, the normative measure of this hermeneutic of appropriation was whether or not a particular belief or practice was consistent with black people's own desires that their bodies be free and regarded with dignity. That black people employed a hermeneutic of appropriation, whether systematically or not, is again made obvious by the very fact that they did not accept unconditionally what the missionaries or evangelists told them was Christianity. Black men and women—even as they were enslaved—were not passive recipients of the Christian religion. Moreover, the early black converts to Christianity clearly did not grant the religion infallible, sacred authority. Rather, they scrupulously appropriated Christianity only as it conformed to their own theo-cultural affirmations of their black humanity. What was of utmost importance to them was the preservation of harmonious relationships between themselves and their God(s) and hence harmonious relationality within the community. Again, this meant that who they were as sacred human beings had to be protected both ritualistically and theologically. If a particular tradition or aspect of Christianity did not do that, they rejected it or denied its authority. This hermeneutic of appropriation underscores what has been argued by numerous scholars of black religion; that from the very beginning of their introduction to Christianity in America, black people "made it truly their own." There are two other factors to note in this regard.

First, a hermeneutic of appropriation was also employed in black people's approach to the biblical witness. While the authority of the Bible has always been central to the black faith tradition, a hermeneutic of appropriation has been fundamental to black people's approach to the Bible. Again, what did not accord with black people's own aspirations regarding the treatment of their black bodies was not appropriated as authoritative within the black faith tradition. This means that not everything written in the Bible was granted authority. For instance, as has been well established by biblical and other scholars of black religion, the exodus saga concerning God's liberation of the Israelites from bondage was given normative authoritative status, while the Pauline Epistles, particularly with their directives for "slaves to submit to their masters," were not.[24] The point is, and this will become germane in our later discussion, a selective appropriation of the Bible has been fundamental to the black faith tradition. The fact that a belief or practice is affirmed in the Bible did not necessitate the acceptance of that belief or practice into the black faith tradition. It was accepted only insofar as it passed the scrutiny of the definite hermeneutic of appropriation.

Second, a hermeneutic of appropriation has been instrumental in shaping the theological core of the black faith tradition. In effect, by utilizing a hermeneutic of appropriation, black people were able to establish for themselves core theological themes. These themes have tended to reflect the influence of an African theological heritage in that they are compatible with a commitment to maintaining harmony with God and community. These are themes such as equality, justice, and love. At the same time, the meaning of these theological ideas within the black faith tradition is also consistent with the African notion of theology. For they implied something about both God's actions and human's actions. Central to the black faith tradition is the theological affirmation that God stands for equality, justice, and love and thus acts accordingly in history, particularly in regard to black people. Correspondingly, black people are expected to act in the same manner with special regard for their own community. In effect, there are core themes that define the black faith tradition that do not merely mirror the theological claims of others (i.e., white Christians) but reflect black people's African theological heritage and experience of blackness in a white society. More will be said in the next chapter about these core themes, but important to note for now is that an operative hermeneutic of appropriation helped to shape the theological core of the black faith tradition.

In summary, because of a decisive process of discernment early black converts to Christianity in America were significantly attracted to the Great Awakening's version of Christianity, evangelical Protestantism. Thus it is the case that evangelical Protestantism has had a dominant influence on black people's religious and theological consciousness, and this influence continues today. According to recent statistics, 57 percent of black Americans say they are "born-again Christians."[25] The majority of those who are churchgoing belong to Baptist, Methodist, or Pentecostal denominations—all denominations significantly influenced by evangelical

Protestant theology. Thus, that the Great Awakenings provided the route through which significant numbers of blacks became Christian portended the pervasive impact that a platonized theology would have upon the black Christian community. In the main, the black faith tradition is a platonized Christian tradition.

In recognizing the platonized character of the black faith tradition, a seemingly fundamental contradiction becomes apparent for a people who have traditionally affirmed the sacredness of their bodies. To reiterate, platonized theology characteristically promotes a dualistic dynamic between the soul and body in which the body is demonized. Consequently, platonized Christianity does not have the same sacred regard for the human body that is typical of African religious and cultural traditions. Thus, in accepting a platonized version of Christianity the early black converts were accepting a theology that contradicted claims central to their African theological heritage and seemingly contrary to the value they assigned to their black bodies. How, then, are we to understand the adoption of a platonized theological paradigm in the black faith tradition?

Ironically, a platonized view of the body, and concomitantly sexuality, served a very practical purpose in the lives of these early black converts' lives (later discussion will show that it continues to do so). In so doing, it paradoxically cohered with their theological commitment to "equality." As earlier mentioned, the African theological heritage perceives theology as that which is not simply speculative in nature but also practical. Recalling the words of Peter Paris, African theology "arises out of the problems of daily experience, and it is pursued for the purpose of discovering solutions for everyday problems."[26] A platonized view of the body/sexuality in fact responded to a problem in black life and ostensibly provided a solution to that problem.

As earlier discussed, one of the primary justifications for the dehumanizing treatment of black people, and hence violent attacks on their bodies, was the white cultural portrayal of black people as hypersexual. The image of black people as incorrigibly oversexualized presented a significant barrier to their acceptance as equals to whites or even as human beings. If, however, black men and women could show that they were not given to bestial sexuality, then perhaps they would be one step closer to being accepted as equal human persons. By adopting the chaste, pure lifestyle advanced by evangelical theology they could at least challenge the white cultural claim that they were irredeemably driven by the passions of their black bodies. That black men and women actually believed that the adoption of a chaste life might actually affect white people's perceptions of them is evident in the words of prominent activist thinkers such as Maria Stewart and Ida B. Wells. In an 1830 tract addressed to "people of color" Maria Stewart wrote:

> It is not the color of the skin that makes the man, but it is the principles formed within the soul. . . . Never, no, never will the chains of slavery and ignorance burst, till we become united as one, and cultivate among ourselves the pure principles of piety, morality and virtue.[27]

Ida B. Wells believed similarly to Stewart that for the "uplift of the race" black people had to refrain from bodily excesses like "drinking, gambling and fornication."[28] Wells called upon black women in particular "to refute" charges of black people's lascivious nature by leading a "stainless life."[29] In effect, then, despite the fact that platonized theology at first glance seemed to contradict black people's belief in the sacredness of the human body, it actually corresponded to their concern to protect the very sanctity of their black bodies. It provided an avenue for black people to show their equal humanity and hence possibly ward off the vile maltreatment of their bodies. Thus, what on the surface appears contradictory to a core theme in the black faith tradition, and concomitantly in the African theological heritage, was not—at least for the early black architects of the black faith tradition. Platonized notions of the body/sexuality complemented the theological claim of equality at the same time that it supported black people's own aspirations for freedom and respect. Therefore, it can once again be concluded that the early black Christians' acceptance of a platonized Christian tradition with its views about the body was not a passive compliance with white evangelical thought. Rather, it bespoke their reliance on a hermeneutic of appropriation in making judgments about what was suitable for them.

Yet even though there may be positive value in a platonized theology for black lives put-upon by white cultural violence, black people have also paid a "heavy" price for their adherence to platonized views about the body/sexuality. The value of a platonized Christian tradition for black people is thus a complex matter. While platonized theological thinking has certainly benefited black people in their struggle to protect the sanctity of their black bodies, it has also impaired black people in their acceptance of their own black body selves and the bodies of others. As earlier suggested, no one has done more to expose the complex and troubling reality of a platonized tradition for black people than James Baldwin. In works such as the novel *Go Tell It on the Mountain* and the drama *Amen Corner*, Baldwin, shaped by his personal experience with the rich and creative complexity of the black faith tradition, passionately reveals how cultural and religious convictions have anathematized the black body/sexuality, thus impinging on black people's power to celebrate their full black humanity. Baldwin skillfully exposes the subtle interplay between white cultural ideology and platonized theology as the culprit in denigrating black sexuality to such a degree as to disrupt black life and well-being, if not to distort black spirituality. Thus, he stridently proclaims, "The Negro pays for that guilt which white people have about the flesh."[30] Given the perceptiveness of his literary insights, Baldwin's work will provide the foundation for our examination of a platonized black faith tradition.[31]

Platonized Theology and the Black Faith Tradition

In *Go Tell It on the Mountain*, James Baldwin provides a revealing literary look into the complex interactive cultural-religious assault on the black body, specifically black sexuality. In this novel, Baldwin tells the story of the Grimes family primarily through the eyes of fourteen-year-old John Grimes. The story opens with John, on the morning of his fourteenth birthday, awakening from a wet dream and wrestling with his salvation. He is troubled by the thought that salvation may not be a possibility for him given his emerging sexuality. The depth of John's struggle is brought to light as Baldwin recounts the journeys to salvation of various members of the Grimes family, most notably John's stepfather, Gabriel, and John's mother, Elizabeth. He insightfully reveals how the "brutality" of white male patriarchy has variously impacted the faith of each of the Grimeses. In the end, John finds himself on the "threshing floor," experiencing a historically, emotionally, and physically cathartic conversion. It is, in fact, through the intricate lives and relationships of the Grimes family that Baldwin so skillfully examines the complex connection between black faith and the black sexual body. He effectively does this through the portrait of one black female character, Gabriel's first wife. He describes her in this way:

> When [black] men looked at Deborah they saw no further than her unlovely and violated body. In their eyes lived perpetually a lewd, uneasy wonder concerning the night she had been taken into the fields. That night had robbed her of her right to be considered a woman. No man would approach her in honor because she was a living reproach, to her herself and to all black women and to all black men. . . . Since she could not be considered a woman, she could only be looked on as a harlot, a source of delight more bestial and mysteries more shaking than any a proper woman could provide. Lust stirred in the eyes of men when they looked at Deborah, lust that could not be endured because it was so impersonal, limiting communion to the area of her shame. . . . Reinforced in Deborah [was] the terrible belief against which no evidence had ever presented itself: that all men were like this, their thoughts rose no higher, and they lived only to gratify on the bodies of [black] women their brutal and humiliating needs.[32]

Deborah was raped by a group of white men. The fact of her rape highlights white cultural assumptions about black people in general and black women in particular. The consequences of her rape disclose the profound multilevel impact these assumptions have had on black people's relationships to their own black bodies and sexuality.

Deborah's rape witnesses to the history of black women's violation at the hands of white men. It points to the aforementioned white cultural ideology that fosters such violation. Because white culture labels black women as promiscuous seductresses—in short, Jezebels—white men have been allowed to rape them with legal, if not moral, impunity. In a society governed by a racially sexualized discourse of power, it was essentially impossible for black women to be seen as rape victims. "White power became indistinguishable from sexual dominance."[33] In the illogic of white cultural ideology, white men were considered the victims of black women's seductive wiles. Indeed, the literature of religious racism revealed just how dangerous to white purity black women were considered. It should be recalled that they were at times portrayed as the one seducing Eve to disobey the commands of God, thus changing the course of humanity's relationship to their bodies and to God.[34] Essentially, through Deborah's rape, Baldwin accurately exposes the historical reality of black women as they have been left to navigate the danger of being cast as Jezebels. Unfortunately, the fictional Deborah, like so many actual black women, was not able to avoid the sexual violence associated with being black and female in a society governed by white cultural ideology. She subsequently suffered the debilitating stigma of white culture's sexualized violence against the black female body. She felt guilty about the rape. She became ashamed of her own black female body. She became alienated from her own female sexuality. Eventually, she was able to see herself only through the prism of white culture, as a sexual object. This self-image subsequently impacted her relationships with black men. She viewed them as lustful predators—unwittingly agreeing with white culture's sexualized image of the black male. At the same time, black men looked upon Deborah as a harlot—again a view consistent with that of white culture.

Baldwin's portrayal of Deborah's reaction to her rape is consistent with the testimony of various enslaved black females following similar rapes. Despite the fact that their rapes were the unavoidable reality of white sexualized power, they often experienced profound personal shame, as if the rapes were their fault. In her narrative on her life as a slave, Linda Brent speaks of the deep disgrace she felt over becoming impregnated by a white man. Brent became involved with the white Mr. Sands by her own choice. She made this choice, however, only in an effort to avoid her master's rapacious desires. Thus, even though her pregnancy was not the result of an actual rape, it was the inexorable consequence of white culture's sexualized exploitation of black women's bodies. Yet even in recognizing the perilous extreme circumstances that forced her to make the choice to become pregnant, Brent felt deeply blameworthy. She confesses, "My self-respect was gone! I had resolved that I would be virtuous, though I was a slave. I had said, 'Let the storm beat! I will brave it till I die.' And now, how humiliated I felt!"[35] Linda Brent's testimony, along with Baldwin's portrayal of Deborah, suggests a perhaps unique sense of shame experienced by black female victims of racially sexualized violence. Certainly these women experienced the same misplaced shame felt by most rape victims, as their personhood had been so brutally violated. In her perceptive, comprehensive study of violence against black women, womanist ethicist Traci West highlights the multifaceted "shame" all women experience as a result of the "intimate violence" perpetrated against them. The reality of shame is so prevalent that West identifies it as "a crucial ingredient in women's responses to intimate violence."[36] Yet the racialized nature of the abuse against black women's bodies adds another dimension of humiliation that complicates black women's responses to the attacks against their bodies. No doubt, as Brent's testimony clearly witnesses, given black women's precarious reality, they constructed various means to protect themselves and exert agency over their bodies. In the midst of being characterized as wanton promiscuous creatures, with resourceful ingenuity and indomitable standards, they diligently tried to safeguard their virtue. They mustered their physical, intellectual, instinctual, and especially spiritual resources—all in their attempts to escape the immoral privilege that white men claimed over their bodies. An appreciation for the role of their spirituality in maintaining agency over their bodies is key to an understanding of the depth of the shame women like Brent and Deborah felt after their racialized rapes.

Historically a *spirituality of resistance* has been central to black people's survival and wholeness in a society that demeans their very black humanity. Such spirituality is characterized by a sense of connection to one's own heritage as well as to the divine. As such, it provides black men and women with a buffer of defense against white cultural characterizations of them as beings unworthy of freedom, dignity, even life.[37] At the same time, a spirituality of resistance grants them, especially black women, a sense of control over their own bodies. For, just as it connects them to their God and to cultural history, it also affirms the sacred value of their bodies. In so doing, a spirituality of resistance has uniquely empowered black women to claim agency over their sexuality. They have viewed their bodies as sacred vessels that should not be violated. Moreover, reflective of platonized theological thinking, maintaining their "chastity" has been an essential element to their spirituality, for it is a key factor in enjoying a "right" relationship with God. Black religious scholar Marla Frederick recognizes the constancy of this vital connection between spirituality and sexuality for black women in her recent study of the spirituality of a group of black women in North Carolina. She says of them: "Because sex is seen as both a physical and a spiritual act, 'proper sex' influences one's access to God and one's intimacy with God. Women's experiences of sexuality, thus, have been key to their expression of spirituality."[38]

Throughout their history, a platonized view of sexuality has supplied many black women with the spiritual resolve to resist the racialized sexual indecency fostered by white culture. For it was not simply a matter of protecting their bodies, but also a matter of protecting their souls and hence their relationship to God. For them, the treatment of their bodies was inextricably connected to the state of their souls. Such an understanding is reminiscent of black women's African theological heritage, in which the body itself is seen to have sacred meaning. Unfortunately, given the oppressive social-cultural conditions to which black women have been subjected, especially during the antebellum and postbellum periods, a spiritual resolve is often not enough. Presumed spiritual agency over their sexuality did not guarantee them actual agency over their bodies. So in the end, the very spirituality that was key to their resistance and positive sense of self became potentially damning when their efforts to resist the sexual violence of white men failed. Hence, they were left to experience an almost impenetrable level of shame. For not only had black women's bodies been violated but so too had their souls. Subsequently, their relationship with God had been disrupted. It is for this reason that Deborah became virtually "sexless" after her rape, leading a life of Bible reading and prayer while bearing a "shame" from which only a "miracle of human love" could deliver her.[39] It is also for this reason that Brent confessed, "I have sinned against God and myself."[40] West provides further insight into the profound shame of Deborah and Brent in her observation that "restrictive" Christian notions concerning women's sexuality (what I have identified as a platonized sexual ethic) "can accentuate the feeling of shame and self-blame particularly for victim-survivors of sexual violence who depend upon their Christian faith as an important resource in moments of crisis."[41] all raped women

The shame seen in Deborah and Brent in fact signifies the complex insidious interactive impact of white cultural ideology and platonized theology on black lives. James Baldwin illuminates the complex nature of this impact in another description of Deborah, this time through the thoughts of Gabriel:

What better woman could be found? *She* was not like the mincing daughters of Zion! She was not to be seen prancing lewdly through the streets, eyes sleepy and mouth half-open with lust, or to be found mewing under mid-night fences, uncovered, uncovering some black boy's hanging curse! No, their married bed would be holy, and their children would continue the line of the faithful, royal line. And, fired with this, a baser fire stirred in him also, rousing a slumbering fear, and he remembered . . . that Paul had written: "It is better to marry than to burn."[42]

This description of Deborah represents the thoughts of the afore-mentioned Gabriel, also a black preacher, as he contemplates the merits of marrying Deborah and making her his first wife. In Gabriel's mind, Deborah is redeemed from the "disgrace" of her rape because she has remained sexually inactive since that attack in the woods. She is "pure and holy" as long as she denies any sex-ual impulses she may have. A sexually repressed Deborah is, thus, suitable for marriage. Gabriel further reasons that marriage is a redemptive act for him as well as for Deborah. Just as it would free Deborah to *properly* express her sexuality for reproductive pur-poses, it would allow him to act on his very present sexual urgings without jeopardizing his soul's salvation.

Needless to say, Gabriel's thoughts about Deborah are trou-bling on many levels, not the least of which is that they imply both his condemnation of Deborah for being raped and his image of her as wanton because of the rape. Interestingly, Deborah, fully aware of Gabriel's past life of lustful sin, never condemns him. At the same time, Gabriel's thoughts show no self-condemnation for his once willful unrestrained lifestyle. To be sure, a patriarchal nar-rative is also operative in Deborah and Gabriel's relationship. More will be said later about this narrative. For the current dis-cussion it is important to note what Gabriel's reflections clearly do indicate—a platonized Christian influence. It bears repeating that within this tradition sexuality is seen as evil.[43] "Sexuality and spir-ituality are viewed as opposites. . . . Persons can be either sexual or spiritual, but not both in any meaningful, integrated way."[44] For Gabriel, the way to integrate sexuality and spirituality was within the bounds of marriage, a view consistent with a platonized Christian tradition. Thus, Gabriel did resolve to marry Deborah, presumably saving himself even as he redeemed her. Ironically, in the end, Gabriel's marriage to Deborah would prove destructive for both of them because it denied Gabriel the kind of sexual plea-sure his body craved. At the same time, it did not free Deborah to experience the vibrancy of her own sexuality. Baldwin describes the destructive tragedy of Gabriel and Deborah's marriage this way:

> [Gabriel] was made to remember that though he was holy he was yet young; the women who had wanted him wanted him still; he had but to stretch out his hand and take what he wanted—even sisters in the church. He struggled to wear out his visions in the marriage bed, he struggled to awaken Deborah, for whom daily his hatred grew.[45]

Throughout Baldwin's novel, his characters wage war against their sexual bodies in an effort to safeguard their souls and hence to secure their relationship with God. They struggle with the temptations of masturbation, intimate pleasure, adolescent desire, and homoerotic passions. They believe that giving in to their sexual desires, for purposes other than procreation within wedlock, might please their body but jeopardize their souls. Baldwin goes on, however, to uncover the debilitating truth surrounding this kind of platonized black faith spirituality: the "price of the 'redeeming' ticket" is far too costly. He dramatically points out that to safeguard one's spirituality/soul by denying the fullness of one's sexuality is to forfeit personal and intimate relationality, and hence happiness and well-being. He explicitly shows this in a dialogue between two characters in his play *Amen Corner* about the ministry of a black female evangelist:

> Luke: Margaret, once you told me you loved me and then you jumped up and ran off from me like you couldn't stand the smell of me. What you think *that* done to my soul?
> Margaret: I had to go. The Lord told me to go. We'd been living like—like two animals, like children, never thought of nothing but their own pleasure. In my heart, I always knew we couldn't go on like that—we was too happy. . . . We hadn't never thought of nothing but ourselves. We hadn't never thought on God![46]

What Baldwin captures in the struggles of his fictional characters, as illustrated by this dialogue, is a significant part of the black faith tradition, the part most influenced by platonized theology. It is the belief that things of the "flesh" are evil, antithetical to God, and detrimental to one's very soul. Such a belief has certainly, as we have documented, served a positive function in the lives of both black women and men. It has been the theological impetus for black people to adopt a lifestyle potentially demonstrative of their humanity. It has provided the theological underpinning of black women's spiritual agency over their own sexuality. Marla Frederick, in the above-mentioned study, has shown the continued importance of a platonized theology for the lives of black women in their "everyday struggles of faith." As spiritual power historically gave black women agency over their sexuality in their efforts to thwart white male violence, it has done the same in their daily attempts to claim control over their sexual bodies. A commitment to platonized notions of sexuality were, for the women of Frederick's study, "not just about the physical consequences of sexual engagement, but about what their sexual engagement says about their commitment to God and their willingness to submit to God's desires." Frederick insightfully concludes that protecting their bodies was a matter of "protecting sacred space."[47] Such a belief is reminiscent of an African theological heritage. Basically, a commitment to platonized notions of sexuality has provided these black women, and no doubt others like them, with the divine right to "negotiate their own set of body politics," in the various relationships of which they are a part.[48] Platonized theology, in effect, sanctioned their right to make decisions about the way their body should be engaged. Such a right is most important for black women, given the ways in which their bodies have consistently been violated by white sexualized power. So once more, platonized notions of lustful sexual behavior as an anathema to God have at times functioned in a positive manner within the black faith tradition. Even Baldwin realizes the practical value of a platonized notion of sexuality for black lives. In *Go Tell It on the Mountain*, though the main protagonist, John, is uneasy with the "holy living" that his father tries to impose upon his brother and him, he still acknowledges that it is perhaps the one thing that stands between him (John) and a life filled with crime and lustful waste. John recognizes the truth in his mother's words, "there ain't no safety except you walk humble before the Lord."[49] Baldwin affirmed a similar truth for his own life. In speaking of childhood friends he said, "Some went on wine or whisky or the needle, and are still on it. And others, like me, fled into the church."[50] Clearly, then, a platonized faith tradition has been key for black people's well-being. It has promoted a certain standard of living that has enhanced black people's self-regard and no doubt saved black lives. It must never be forgotten that inasmuch as black people are viewed as sexualized beasts, they are vulnerable to violent attack. Yet the platonized influence on black lives has not been without negative consequences. Even as it has empowered black people in their struggle against the brutal injustices of sexualized racist ideology, for lives already put-upon by white culture, it joins with this culture in such a way as to disable black health and well-being. Thus, the reality of a platonized tradition for black lives is not so straightforward. This becomes clear with an appreciation for how platonized theology and white cultural ideology influence one another. Before moving forward in this discussion, therefore, the confluence between white cultural ideology and platonized Christianity bears repeating.

As earlier stated, platonized Christianity argues that sexuality is virtually a cauldron of evil and opposes the human connection to God. By arguing the "evilness" of sexuality, Christianity implicitly provides a theological justification for any claims that a people governed by sexual desires are innately evil. Christianity, especially when it does not challenge the sexualized depictions, in effect vindicates white culture's vilification of black people. Platonized Christianity and white culture become de facto allies in demonizing an entire race of people. It is also important to recall that just as platonized Christianity essentializes sexuality—characterizing it as a sexual/genital activity—it also sexualizes the body. That is, the body is seen only as a cauldron of sexual activity. Again, while a platonized notion of sexuality has had practical value for black women and men, there is a more indistinct, less obvious manner in which platonized Christianity has functioned in black lives. It is on this subtle level that its detrimental implications for black people can be seen.

What we too often find in relation to black people is, in fact, a twofold sexualized condemnation of their humanity. In this regard, the interaction between white culture and platonized Christianity is almost lethal. With this interaction, the resulting image is not simply the sinfulness of the sexualized body but also the vileness of blackness. In other words, black people are left to find ways to protect not only the integrity of their soul but also the dignity of their blackness. This double burden fundamentally compels black men and women to develop fairly intransigent attitudes toward sexuality, all in an effort to at least sever the dehumanizing link made between it and blackness. Practically speaking, black people's hope for soul salvation and social acceptance rests on one pivotal requirement: the adoption of a *hyper-proper sexuality*. Offsetting white cultural hyper-sexualization of them, black people adopt a hyper-proper sexuality primarily defined and legitimated by a platonized theology. With a singular commitment to a hyper-proper sexuality, black people can at once affirm their humanity and redeem their souls. Such an approach to sexuality potentially disproves white cultural characterizations and promises a "saved" soul. This hyper-proper sexual attitude is characterized by a determination to engage sexuality in a "proper" manner. While what it means to be proper is primarily shaped by a platonized sexual ethic, social-cultural narratives of power also influence it. Accordingly, black people's commitment to a hyper-proper sexuality has significant social as well as interpersonal implications. It suggests the way black males and females might relate to themselves and others. Let us now turn to the implications of this hyper-proper sexuality.

The commitment to a hyper-proper sexuality potentially leaves black men and women vulnerable to a profoundly disturbing rejection of their very black selves. All too often this commitment is manifested as a rejection or denial of one's own sexuality. That is, black people can become so focused on refraining from lustful, nonprocreative sex that they practically reject their very expressive sexuality. In regard to their intimate relationships, "proper" expression of sexuality is reproductive, not ardent. Black people thus vigorously adopt a platonized approach to sexuality that labels sexual pleasure as lustfully sinful. As earlier stated, within a platonized Christian tradition sexuality is seen as either reproductively good or lustfully bad. The value of sexuality in the nurturing of a loving relationship is dismissed. The tenacity with which black women and men so often commit themselves to a hyper-proper sexuality must be understood not simply as their acceptance of a platonized Christian tradition, that is, evangelical Protestantism, but also as a result of their history of being sexualized by white culture. Their commitment reflects the thrust of a *theo-historical* dynamic. That is, platonized theology and white cultural ideology come together with such force in the lives of black people that together they generate a dedication to sexual propriety that becomes an almost impregnable denial of sexuality. James Baldwin understood this troubling theo-historical dynamic.

In *Go Tell It on the Mountain,* Baldwin effectively depicts how black people's history of white degradation and faith interact to create a severe commitment to a hyper-proper sexuality. As earlier mentioned, throughout his recounting of each character's spiritual journey, Baldwin weaves the story of black people's history of oppression. As he specifically unpacks the spiritual life of each character, he relates the ways in which white racist society has affected their particular life. Baldwin thus presents each character's acceptance (or in the case of Gabriel's sister Florence, nonacceptance) of a "holy-life" defined by hyper-proper sexuality as inextricably connected to their personal struggles of being black in a society hostile to their blackness. For Baldwin's characters, their faithfulness to a platonized notion of sexuality signals not just the burden of sin carried in their human flesh, but also the burden of history borne by their black bodies. We saw this in our earlier discussion of Deborah. It is certainly this double theo-historical burden that leads Gabriel to adopt a hyper-proper sexuality. It is, in fact, through Gabriel that Baldwin points to the potential disquieting consequence of such a sexual attitude. Gabriel's radical com-

mitment to such a holy way of living, which for all practical purposes meant a denial of his sexual body, effectively alienated him
from his family and community. The more he was unable to affirm
the fullness of his body, the more harshly he seemed to treat the
bodies of those around him. For just as he accepted platonized
notions of the body as essentially sexualized, he sexualized the
bodies of others. Therefore, as he came to resent his own sexualized body with its unremitting desires, he resented the sexualized
bodies of others, especially women, because of their seemingly
unrelenting temptation. The harsher he acted toward himself, the
harsher he became in his treatment of others. The source of this
harsh reality was the interactive impact of his platonized faith and
history as a black man. To say the least, Gabriel was miserable and
made those around him miserable. Again, through characters such
as Gabriel, Baldwin exposes a troubling truth of a platonized black
faith tradition.

To the extent that the interplay between platonized theology
and white cultural ideology generates a virtually unassailable
hyper-proper sexual attitude, it invariably interferes with black
men and women's ability to enjoy healthy relationships with themselves and others. If sexuality is that aspect of the human person
that allows for and prompts one's "communion and community"
with themselves and others, then to virtually reject one's sexuality
(based on a platonized essentialization of it) is to reject that which
cultivates healthy relationships. This issue of rejection is even more
compounded for black people.

There is a penetrating and perhaps more difficult to discern
form of rejection nurtured by the collusion of platonized Christianity and white culture in the black faith tradition. It occurs
through black people's inevitable attempts to escape the sexualized stereotype associated with being black. Such attempts can
result in not merely a rejection of sexuality, but an unwitting rejection of one's very blackness. In effect, black men and women
acquiesce to the white depiction of blackness. They do this as they
try to separate themselves from the sexualized depiction by adopting a platonized sexual ethic. This adoption has at least two detrimental implications. First, it sets hyper-proper sexual black people

apart from those black people who perhaps foster the sexual stereotype by unabashedly finding pleasure in nonprocreative sexual expressions. Such persons become a part of the "unsaved," the "unredeemed," and the "unholy," while those who follow a platonized ethic are a part of the "saved," "redeemed," and "holy." Black people potentially fall prey to placing a judgment on one another similar to the way that white culture judges them, only in this instance the defining categories are holy versus nonholy as opposed to white versus black. Such a judgment is hauntingly similar in nature to the judgment white culture places on black people. For the sacred hyper-proper sexuality of the saved is contrasted with the demonized improper sexuality of the unsaved. As white culture demonizes black people on the basis of their sexuality, a platonized black faith tradition does the same.

The second implication of a platonized black faith tradition is perhaps even more unsettling. The adoption of this faith tradition lends itself to black men and women, in effect, rebuffing their own black selves. That is, they try to offset their "blackness" by adopting a platonized model of sexual purity. They atone for their black body by acquiring a "white" soul. While not actually denying their racial identity, their holiness, not their blackness, becomes the mark of their very humanity and thus the gateway to their salvation. Their blackness is at best downplayed and at worst overcome. "Holiness," therefore, does not necessarily signal spiritual health. Instead, it may portend a sexually racialized self-loathing. In effect, the "robes" of holiness cover the flesh of blackness. Baldwin points to this racialized shame in *Go Tell It on the Mountain* as he poignantly juxtaposes blackness with the garments of whiteness.

John, the young protagonist, comes across a photograph of himself with his family. In this photograph John is the only one naked. We learn that John experiences profound shame every time he looks at this photograph. Baldwin casts John's shame, however, as being about more than just modesty. Rather, it is about the raw reality of his blackness. Essentially, Baldwin suggests that John has been made to feel ashamed of the very blackness of his body. This point is enunciated as Baldwin contrasts John's black nakedness against the backdrop of whiteness and with the bodies of two of the children in the picture who are outfitted in white:

> John in his photograph lay naked on a white counterpane. . . . But John could never look at it without feeling shame and anger that his nakedness should be here so unkindly revealed. None of the other children was naked; no, Roy lay in his crib in a white gown . . . and Sarah . . . wore a white bonnet.[51]

Baldwin recognized that his own father had covered his racialized self-loathing with a holy life. He said of his father, "he was defeated long before he died because, at the bottom of his heart, he really believed what white people said about him. This is one of the reasons that he became so holy."[52] This insidious dynamic of sanctified self-loathing is reflected also in an evangelical hymn very popular in the black faith tradition:

> Oh! Precious is the flow
> that *makes me white as snow*
> no other fount I know
> nothing but the blood of Jesus! (emphasis mine)

Ironically, a version of this very song was most likely what informed the white evangelist referred to in the previous chapter as he tried to make clear that regardless of the state of a black person's soul, the person was still black.[53] So, while in the minds of many early white revivalist preachers the whiteness of a black person's soul did not rescue one from the blackness of one's body, it potentially does for black people. To be made "as white as snow" is to be cleansed from the sexualized stain of blackness.

It is also interesting to note at this point the implications of redemptive models of Jesus' crucifixion. As suggested in the song above, as well as addressed in chapter 3, a belief in the redeeming power of Jesus' blood characterizes the black faith tradition.[54] When redemptive theological motifs are viewed in relation to black people's attitudes toward their sexual bodies, another troubling aspect of this theology within a black faith tradition emerges. Essentially, there is an implicit parallel drawn between Jesus' sacrifice of his body and black people's sacrifice of their sexual bodies. In this instance, as Jesus was willing to sacrifice his body even unto death for the sake of human salvation, black people are moved to sacrifice their black bodies for the sake of their particular salvation. In effect, redemptive approaches to Jesus' crucifixion potentially sanction black people's rejection of their sexuality, subsequently provides theological shelter for a sexually racialized self-loathing. The sacrifice of the black body is considered crucial to attaining a white soul. Once again, therefore, the imperative to rethink the centrality of Jesus' crucifixion within the black faith tradition becomes clear.

The centrality of the cross within the black faith tradition is fitting since Jesus' crucifixion unmistakably establishes his compassionate solidarity with black people. That his body was so viciously assailed vindicates black people's faithful testimony that he empathizes with the suffering they experience as a result of the white attack upon their bodies. What is not befitting the black faith tradition, however, is any suggestion that God sanctioned the crucifixion. At the same time that the resurrection asserts the very sanctity of Jesus' body, it makes clear that there is no redeeming value in Jesus' crucified body. Through the crucifixion-resurrection event, God clarified the power not of Jesus' blood but of his life. Hence, the redemptive power displayed on the cross is not one that denies or defiles the sacredness of the human body; rather it is one that substantiates that sacredness. Furthermore, God's redemptive power repudiates any force that acts to violate the sacred body. The parallel that should be made between Jesus' crucified body and the black body is, therefore, in regard not to what was done to it by oppressive power but how God redeemed it. To suggest that there is redeeming power in the blood of Jesus is to suggest God's sanction of the white attack on the black body. Such a suggestion, as we have earlier argued, is itself anti-Christ. As the resurrection makes clear that the crucifixion was wrong, it also suggests that to believe a rejection of the black body is necessary for one's soul salvation is theologically misguided. A hyper-proper sexuality that lends itself to a tacit rejection of blackness belies the central meaning of Jesus' compassionate solidarity with the oppressed, that is, black people. The meaning of his solidarity is found not in the sacrifice of his body but in redemptive reclamation of it. Inasmuch as a platonized black faith tradition foils black people in their attempts to take pleasure in and thus affirm the divine goodness of their own black bodies it betrays the meaning of Jesus' crucifixion and is subsequently detrimental to black lives.

The overall truth that Baldwin attempts to capture in his literary look into the black faith tradition is that, given the white cultural attack on black bodies, a platonized black faith tradition can too easily become a means by which black people denounce their very selves. The stark reality is that the white cultural characterizations of black people as hypersexual remain a part of the collective black consciousness. It is a palpable fact of the black experience in America. Therefore, whether with conscious intent or not, black women and men must find ways to negotiate this racially sexualized identity. The adoption of a platonized sexual ethic is one way to do that. The problem with such an adoption, however, is that it readily lends itself to self-rejection. Being "born-again" with a white soul can too easily become an antidote for being born into a black body. As long as one's identity is so tied to whiteness, even if it is a spiritual whiteness, then one is hindered in one's ability to affirm one's very blackness. Baldwin states, "People who cannot escape thinking of themselves as white are poorly equipped, if equipped at all, to consider the meaning of black."[55]

Unfortunately, insofar as the black faith tradition is platonized, it poses a potential threat to black well-being. The platonized quality of black faith virtually ensures the dubious interplay between black faith and white culture. As we have just seen, it is this interplay that produces the kind of hyper-proper sexuality that breeds a subtle self-opposition. Ironically, then, the very faith that black people have crafted to sustain and empower them in their struggle against imposing white power potentially turns against them. With the promise of achieving a spiritual whiteness, it not only masks the actual iniquity of whiteness, but it also diverts black people from investigating the divine virtue of their own blackness. That black faith does this is consistent with its platonized nature. Reflective of a platonized tradition, black faith is prone to unsettling connections with inequitable power. To reiterate an earlier point, platonized Christianity's demonization of sexuality aids and abets inequitable power's dehumanization of the people it exploits; therefore, platonized traditions and inequitable power have a natural affinity. And so it is that platonized black faith unwittingly aligns with white cultural ideology. This collusion, even if it is tacit, is almost unavoidable, since both impugn black sexuality. The tragic irony of a platonized black faith tradition is, therefore, that the faith of a powerless people invariably finds itself cooperating with various narratives of power. While such cooperation may be inadvertent and obscure when it comes to white cultural discourse, it is often more intentional and overt in relation to patriarchal and heterosexual discourses of power. Let us thus briefly examine the interaction of black faith with each of these two oppressive discourses—this is particularly important because each interaction redoubles the injury to certain black bodies.

Black Faith and Patriarchal Discourse

Once again, Baldwin's novel is helpful in exposing the alarming, and perhaps inevitable, interaction between a platonized black faith tradition with a patriarchal discourse of power. Specifically, Baldwin reveals the dangerously precarious predicament in which this interaction places black women. He does this through his character Gabriel. In *Go Tell It on the Mountain*, Gabriel's relationship to black women is defined by the fact that he violently abuses them. We read specifically of his abuse toward his second wife, Elizabeth. This abuse is dramatically revealed when Gabriel, blaming Elizabeth for the harm that has come to their son Roy, viciously slaps her. "Then, with all of his might," Baldwin writes, "[Gabriel] reached out and slapped [Elizabeth] across the face."[56] Roy's reaction to the slap and Elizabeth's reaction to Gabriel even before the slap, make it clear that this assault is not the only instance of Gabriel's physical abuse toward Elizabeth. There are undoubtedly many reasons for Gabriel's violence toward her. However, throughout the novel, Baldwin points toward the matter of Gabriel's sexuality. Time and again, Baldwin tells of Gabriel's discomfort with Elizabeth's sexuality. Just as Gabriel's relationship with his first wife, Deborah, was distorted by her rape, his relationship with Elizabeth was marred by the child (John) she bore out of wedlock. As images of Deborah being sexually violated interfered with his intimate bond with her, images of Elizabeth in a loving sexual relationship with another man compromised his marriage to her. Gabriel consistently doubted the sincerity of Elizabeth's dedication to a hyper-proper sexuality. And for Gabriel, a wanton Elizabeth was completely unacceptable. She threatened his very pious commitment, since to him she was an ever-present sexual temptation. Her very presence seemed to seduce Gabriel back to a past of lustful living. Baldwin makes this clear in a scene where Gabriel asks a pregnant Elizabeth "if she had truly repented of her sin." When Elizabeth equivocates in her response, Gabriel begins to question his own piety. He wonders if the son that he and Elizabeth produced would be any different from the son she gave birth to out of wedlock. Gabriel apparently cannot bear the thought that his male heir would be a product of "unholy" sex, as was the son he fathered with Esther, a woman with whom he had an affair during his marriage to Deborah. In Gabriel's mind, Elizabeth's perceived shameless sensual nature jeopardizes his very soul, if not also the soul of his then unborn heir, Roy. We see this as Gabriel's questioning of Elizabeth culminates with Gabriel thinking about the lustful relationship he had with Esther. Baldwin writes, "And his mind, dwelling bitterly on Elizabeth, yet moved backward to consider once again Esther, who had been the mother of the first Royal."[57] As the connection is made between Elizabeth and Esther, one thing becomes clear: just as Gabriel refused to allow Esther to drag him "right on down to Hell with her" (thus he did not marry her), he certainly was not going to let the one he did marry drag him there either.[58]

It is in recognizing the force of Gabriel's mistrust of Elizabeth's sexuality that the reason for his blame and physical abuse of her becomes clearer. He blames her for Roy's injury for reasons not of maternal neglect but because of her female sexuality. Gabriel, in effect, accuses Elizabeth of cursing Roy in the womb with her wanton sexual nature. Because he believes that she was not truly repentant of her "unholy" living, Roy has been destined to live an unholy, reckless life, just as the son Gabriel fathered with Esther did. Thus, Gabriel slaps Elizabeth. What Baldwin seems to suggest through the perilous interaction between Elizabeth and Gabriel is the complicity of a platonized black faith tradition in suborning violence against black women. The reality of this complicity is evident as we consider the way in which the patriarchal narrative intersects with white cultural ideology to place black women in an almost unbearable situation.

Patriarchy, as is typical of inequitable power, sexualizes its victims. Patriarchal power is sustained by and secretes a discourse that sexualizes women.[59] As noted by West, feminist theories make clear that "the reproduction of violence against women stems from male dominance that is inscribed throughout the social order."[60] What this implies for black women is daunting. Black women are sexualized both because of their race and because of their gender. Black women's bodies carry the double burden of racially gendered sexualization. The end result is that to be black and female in a society shaped by white patriarchal discourse is to be a symbol of intoxicating sexuality. This means that black women are virtually sitting ducks for violent attack and abuse because, according to Girard's aforementioned study, sexuality itself arouses violent response.[61] That black women are doubly sexualized means that their bodies are extraordinarily exposed to violent exploitation. If, as West asserts, "the meaning of womanhood can signify an *invitation* to violate," then the meaning of black womanhood voices a plea to be violated.[62]

This present analysis is consistent with the ways in which various womanist scholars have framed black women's peculiar vulnerability to violent attacks. These scholars have identified multilayered and interactive social-cultural constructions as instigators in assaults against black women's bodies and psyches. Sociologist Cheryl Townsend Gilkes has paid particular attention to the way in which black people's "history of racial oppression" has been sexualized to the extent that it has undermined black people's ability to love their black embodied selves. This, she argues, has been particularly problematic for black women, because black women are assaulted not only by a "sexualized racism" but also by a "racialized sexism." She says:

> [Black people] find that our history of racial oppression has always been sexualized. And that all sexism is racialized. . . . Racialized sexism, particularly in the form of specialized sexism that assaults African-American women, compounds our community's ambivalence about the meaning of being Black and female in America. This ambivalence is a source of the "multiple jeopardy" that characterizes our experience of oppression.[63]

Toinette Eugene, like Gilkes, draws attention to the violence that black women incur as a result of "racist/sexist" assaults on their psyches. These assaults are most pronounced, Eugene says, when black women "internalize the judgments made by others and become convinced of their own inferiority."[64] While Gilkes and Eugene emphasize the psychological violence that black women have endured, Delores Williams points to the reality of domestic violence. She argues that in order to appreciate the complexity of this violence, one must consider the history of black women's violation in three different contexts: national, work, and home.[65] In the study to which I have already referred, West provides the most compelling and comprehensive examination of violence against black women. Consonant with the arguments of other womanist scholars, she maintains that any reliable interrogation of this violence must take seriously black women's "richly varied, complexly textured reality."[66]

One of the cruelest aspects of black female reality is pointed out by Baldwin: the complicity of the black faith tradition in instigating and perpetuating black male violence against the bodies of black women. The very tradition that black women especially have relied on to protect their virtue facilitates their violation by male members of their own community. This occurs in large measure because of the way in which a platonized black faith gives way to a hyper-proper sexuality in conjunction with the patriarchal character of the faith context. The institutional context of black women's faith is typically the black church.

Before proceeding with this discussion it is important to clarify the meaning of the black church. The black church is essentially a disparate grouping of churches that reflect the diversity of the black community itself. These churches may be within white denominational structures or independent of them. They reflect congregational, connectional, and episcopal systems. They can be urban, suburban, or rural. They range in size from storefronts to mega-churches. They are middle class, working class, and poor. They reflect both highly rapturous and very restrained forms of spiritual expression. As diversified as black churches are, however, they do share a common history and play a unique role in black life, which attests to their collective identity as the black church.

Any discussion of the black church in general, however, must appreciate black churches in particular. For example, while there are prevailing attitudes that characterize the black church community, such as patriarchal and heterosexist attitudes, there are also noteworthy exceptions to these attitudes. Thus, while this particular discussion of the black church expressly focuses on the prevalent patriarchal and heterosexist disposition of the black church, it implicitly acknowledges that there are various black churches with more equitable views and practices. With that said, let us now examine the intricate relationship between the platonized black faith tradition and patriarchal discourse as it creates a context that assails the black woman's body.

The black church is characteristically patriarchal. Womanist ethicist Marcia Riggs makes it plain; she says that the black church "has developed a normative patriarchal institutional ethos" thereby becoming a "'protected space' for sexual-gender transgressions."[67] It is because of the black church's prevailing patriarchal character that a platonized faith becomes especially troubling for black women.

Inasmuch as the black church is patriarchal, black women are unable to escape the image of being oversexualized beings. Black women's theo-historically induced commitment to a hyper-proper sexuality does not free them from their gender-based sexualization. In a patriarchal context, the "whiteness" of black women's souls does not overcome the femaleness of their bodies. The patriarchal disposition of the black church thereby precludes black women's commitment to holy living from being taken seriously or respected by black men, even by black male preachers. What this implies for the way that black women's bodies are treated and regarded—even within the walls of the church—is, to say the least, unsettling.

Black women's bodies are fundamentally viewed as a source of temptation. As such, they become targets for unwanted sexually exploitative attention and behavior. Riggs points to this in a scenario she constructs in which a black male preacher—even as he warns that "you certainly can't find salvation in sex"—is eager to be fixed up with the "woman with those big breasts who was sitting on third aisle to [the] left," that he noticed while he was preaching this very admonition.[68] The truth that this scenario exposes is that the patriarchal culture of the black church confers on black men the privilege to disregard black women's sincere commitment to "holy living" and the privilege to ignore the hypocrisy of their own lifestyle. Accordingly, black women are held accountable for any sexual lapses that "holy" black men may experience. The logic of the black church's patriarchy suggests that black womanhood seduces black men into sinfully sexual behavior. The rhetoric of eighteenth-century religious racism is virtually played out in the black church. For black women are, in effect, regarded as the tempting serpent, bringing not only themselves down but also black men. There is an even more disconcerting outcome of this platonized/patriarchal interplay in the black church as it relates to black people's adoption of a hyper-proper sexuality.

When the commitment to a hyper-proper sexuality that a platonized black faith tradition nurtures in response to white cultural ideology is transgressed in any way, the response to the transgression is as severe as the commitment is hyper. The breach of hyper-proper sexuality prompts a hyper-reactive response. We have seen this in black women. The violation of their virtue produces an inordinate amount of self-blame. Even more problematic for black women, however, is when the hyper-proper sexuality of black men is transgressed. The patriarchal narrative of the black church exonerates men from responsibility for their sexual behavior in relation to black women. At the same time, it encourages them to project blame onto their black female victims. The black woman is therefore not only judged for violating her commitment to "holy living" but also blamed for trying to drag the man "right on down to Hell with her." The end result is that as long as the black church is a "protected space" for black men to enjoy patriarchal privilege, it will be a hazardous location for black women. Not only will the bodies of black women remain vulnerable to sexual exploitation, but black women will also be constant victims of harsh recriminations. In effect, as long as the black church provides sanctuary for patriarchal discourse, and thus projects black women as sexualized beings, black women will continue to be sexually mistreated and castigated for that mistreatment. Worst of all, insofar as this patriarchal institution advances the adoption of a platonized hyper-proper sexuality as essential to salvation, black women will be seen as deserving some of the most vile, even violent, treatment. This intricate interplay between the patriarchal narrative and platonized black faith no doubt contributes to the ineffectiveness of the black church when dealing with issues of violence against black women.

Conversations with black women consistently relate how their churches have not provided adequate spiritual or emotional support for women who have been victims of sexual or domestic violence. These women speak of how their male pastors have been insensitive to violence perpetrated against women. Far too often black women have reported that one of the first questions put to them by their black male pastors in response to an act of male violence is, "What did you do to cause it?"[69] Womanist religious scholars have pointed to the same problem. Frances Wood, for instance, stridently indicts the black church for creating an atmosphere and perpetuating myths that allow for black men to view violence against women as "simply a hazard of being female, as opposed to a consequence of the behavior of men who choose to victimize women."[70] Wood further says that violence against black women too often go "unchallenged" in the black church and when black women report such violence to their pastors they are frequently insulted. She says, "To add insult to injury, when a battered woman approaches her pastor for assistance, she is frequently advised either to become a better wife; bear her cross in faith; or pray for her husband."[71]

Traci West's study reveals how the combination of certain "restrictive" faith claims within "androcentric"/patriarchal Christian traditions nurtures dynamics where violence against women is accommodated and shame and self-blame of female victims is common. West thus rightly concludes that "Churches must be engaged in a continual self-critique that focuses on eliminating acts of violence among its members and ferreting out messages that reinforce the acceptability of violence against women within its traditions and practices."[72] Such a self-critique of the black church must involve more than just the recognition of the patriarchal narrative and platonized faith that characterize the church. It must also include the way in which white cultural ideology intersects with both of these restrictive systems of belief to create a complexly threatening situation for black women. What we find when trying to discern the dynamics that perpetuate the denigration of black women's bodies within the black church is the convoluted but inevitable interplay between a platonized black faith tradition and a patriarchal narrative that is fueled and shaped by white cultural depictions of black people. This invidious interplay of religious, social, and cultural discourses overwhelms the sexuality of both black women and men to such an extent that it devastates their mutual relationships as it wreaks abusive emotional, spiritual, and physical havoc on black women.

The situation for black bodies is even more complicated and devastating when we consider what happens when a heterosexist discourse is added to this religious-social-cultural mix. Let us now examine briefly the implication of a heterosexist discourse in conjunction with a platonized black faith.

Black Faith and Heterosexist Discourse

Baldwin again becomes helpful in understanding this problematic interaction. In *Go Tell It on the Mountain* the spiritual journey of the young protagonist, John, is complicated by his homoerotic desires. Early in the novel, Baldwin reveals these desires when John wakes up from a wet dream that causes him to remember a sin he committed even more sinister than the sin of a wet dream. John recalls:

> he had sinned with his hands a sin that was hard to forgive. In the school lavatory, alone, thinking of the boys, older, bigger, braver, who made bets with each other as to whose urine could arch higher, he had watched in himself a transformation of which he would never dare to speak.[73]

Adding to John's sin is his attraction to Elisha, the young male musician at his church. This attraction is made clear in a playful wrestling match between him and Elisha. Also revealed in this match is Elisha's attraction for John. Their wrestling ends with each boy taking in the scent and body of the other as if recovering from a passionate sexual encounter:

> And so they turned, battling in the narrow room, and the odor of Elisha's sweat was heavy in John's nostrils. He saw the viens rise on Elisha's forehead and in his neck; his breath became jagged and harsh, and the grimace on his face became more cruel; and John, watching these manifestations of his power, was filled with a wild delight. They stumbled against the folding-chairs, and Elisha's foot slipped and his hold broke. They stared at each other, half grinning. John slumped to the floor, holding his head between his hands.[74]

Even though John and Elisha's mutual attraction becomes clearer throughout the novel, by the novel's end it becomes obvious that this attraction is not likely to culminate in an intimate loving relationship. Such male love will simply not be tolerated within their black church community. So in the end, John, despite whatever ambivalence he may feel, is converted to a platonized faith and Elisha presumably moves forward in his relationship with a young woman in the church. Through this uneasy and furtive attraction between John and Elisha, Baldwin points to the complexity of the heterosexist/homophobic dynamic of the black faith community.

In *Sexuality and the Black Church*, I establish how white cultural ideology comes together with black faith to produce passionate homophobic sentiment and practices within the black church. This present discussion will not revisit that. What will be examined is how a hyper-proper sexuality overlayed with both patriarchal and heterosexist discourse contributes to a recently recognized phenomenon within the black community—that is, life on the "down low," commonly known as the "DL."

Life on the "DL" within the black community has been the recent focus of significant attention. The "DL" life refers to black men who proclaim to be "straight," thereby leading a heterosexual lifestyle, yet they sleep with men. One self-professed DL man, J. L. King, says that men on the down low, "are so undercover, so in denial, so 'on the low' that they are *behind* the closet."[75] Benoit Denizet-Lewis, in his study of the DL lifestyle, says: "There have always been men—black and white—who have had secret sexual lives with men. But the creation of an organized, underground subculture largely made up of black men who otherwise live straight lives is a phenomenon of the last decade."[76] King further observes that concern over the DL lifestyle in the black community has led the "HIV-prevention industry" to create specific nomenclature to describe the DL man: non-ID MSM, or "non-identified men who sleep with men."[77] King also points out that the DL lifestyle was a source of such concern that at the 2002 International AIDS Conference in Barcelona, Spain, the focus of a panel discussion was "Confronting Challenges of Prevention Outreach to Non-Identified MSM of Color."[78]

The DL lifestyle was recognized as a particular problem within the black community when health officials began to discern contributing factors to the startling HIV/AIDS demographics. The Centers for Disease Control (CDC) reports that 68 percent of all new AIDS cases in the United States are black women. Seventy-five percent of these women reported having contracted the disease from heterosexual sex. For many black women, "the Down-Low Brother . . . has emerged as public enemy No. 1."[79] According to King, a 2000 CDC study in fact revealed that of the 8,780 HIV-positive men who said that they were infected through same-sex sexual encounters, 25 percent of the black men identified themselves as heterosexual. Recent CDC statistics indeed suggest that the leading cause of HIV infection among black men is sexual contact with other men.[80] Data such as these forced the "DL" phenomenon into public discourse. Clearly, for whatever reasons black men live on the DL, this lifestyle is a source of concern not only in terms of the community's overall well-being but also in terms of the persons who have been forced into such a life of secrecy. To be sure, life on the DL cannot be easy. While prevailing heterosexist narratives of power tend to make villains out of DL men, to do so only ignores the social-cultural realities that make it virtually impossible for these men to live open, self-affirming lives. If nothing else, the DL way of living challenges the black community to examine the ways in which its social, cultural, and religious narratives are complicit in fomenting life on the DL. Through the struggles of John and Elisha, Baldwin in fact connects John and Elisha's inability to celebrate the richness of their sexuality with the black faith tradition. Let us now explore what Baldwin perceived of black faith in relation to black male homoeroticism to thus gain insight into the cultural-religious tradition that perhaps spawns a DL life.

Within the black church community, hyper-proper sexuality, while grounded in a platonized sexual ethic, is informed by at least two dominant social narratives: the patriarchal narrative and the heterosexist narrative. The confluence of these two narratives with a hyper-proper sexuality creates an almost absolute intolerance for black male homosexuality. Again, it must always be kept in mind that black hyper-proper sexuality is in large measure a response to white cultural sexualization of black people. Hence, in efforts to sever the link between "abnormal" sexuality and blackness, the black community typically conforms to white social-cultural norms of sexuality. This means conforming to heterosexist standards of sexual expression and patriarchal standards of male sexuality. Such standards are theologically sanctioned by the black faith tradition since they conform to the platonized notion that only procreative sex is "holy" sex. When patriarchal and heterosexist notions of sexuality thus combine with a platonized faith to shape black hyper-proper sexuality, a sense of hyper-masculinity emerges. That is, black men are expected to model the white social-cultural "idea" of manhood, which is defined by dominant relationships with women. This model of manhood receives sacred validation within a platonized faith. Again, complying with white cultural sexual norms is imperative as black people try to escape sexualized stereotypes and thus safeguard their bodies. Clearly, then, not only is heterosexual intimacy unacceptable, but homoerotic male love becomes unforgivably intolerable. It is that about which one "never dares to speak" and in which one never dares to participate. In effect, male homoeroticism breaches two norms of sexuality that have been made sacrosanct in the black faith tradition: that it is male-centered and that it is heterosexual. The end result is that there is virtually no room for black male homoerotic intimacy within the black church community. In order to be granted all the privileges of power that men in the black church community accrue, black men must be patriarchally, heterosexually masculinized males. Otherwise, they are relegated to what some have described as "open closets": they may be musicians or in the pews, but not in the pulpit or on the boards of power.[81] The hyper-proper sexuality that is characteristic of the black church practically compels black men into patriarchally masculinized relationships with women. This is what Baldwin points to as his character Elisha clandestinely flirts with John but openly dates Ella Mae. Baldwin insightfully recognizes the troubling results of a platonized black faith tradition intersecting with patriarchal and heterosexual discourse. Such an intersection forces nonheterosexual black males to live lives "behind the closet." Benoit Denizet-Lewis's study revealed that "[m]ost DL men identify themselves not as gay or bisexual but first and foremost as black. To them, as to many blacks, that equates to being inherently masculine."[82] Regardless of the social, cultural, and religious pressures that may generate life on the DL, this lifestyle obviously has detrimental implications for black bodies.

First, as already mentioned, it does not permit nonheterosexual black men to experience the life-affirming richness of their sexual bodies. At the very least, it projects on these men a sense of shame that serves to alienate them from their sexual selves even as it drives them into a clandestine life. Moreover, such a lifestyle of "secreted" sexual behavior mitigates the possibility for loving relationships of mutuality, whether they are heterosexually or nonheterosexually defined. Finally, profoundly hidden sexual intimacy lends itself to the type of sexual activity that jeopardizes the very bodies of both men and women as suggested by the HIV/AIDS statistics within the black community. To be sure, it has been easy to blame the DL man for the alarming numbers of black women who have become HIV infected. While the DL lifestyle is no doubt a contributing factor, many rightly point out that one has to be careful in imputing responsibility to these men without looking at the wider social, cultural, and religious practices that contribute not simply to DL living but also to the spread of HIV/AIDS within the black community.[83] It is in this way that the DL life is a matter for the black faith tradition to reckon with, not in terms of condemnation of DL men, but rather in terms of theological self-critique. For, insofar as the black faith tradition provides theological shelter for patriarchal heterosexuality while it theologically condemns other patterns of intimate relationality, it will prompt men and women to express their sexuality in ways that may have devastating consequences for black bodies.

What then can be said about the viability of a platonized black faith tradition for black people? When considering how white cultural ideology intersects with platonized faith to produce a hyper-proper sexuality, which combines with patriarchal and heterosexist discourse in a manner that threatens black bodies, one must affirm James Baldwin's earlier observation: black people's tragic dilemma in regard to their bodies does begin with being "born in a white country, a white Protestant Puritan country." White culture and platonized faith do come together in a way that creates "guilt" about the black flesh. The enormity of this guilt, however, goes beyond blackness. For to be black is to be at least redeemable, but to be black and female, or black, male, and nonheterosexual, is to be, for all intents and purposes, irreparably flawed. Within a platonized black faith tradition, the black body is saved by a white soul; there is, however, no saving "holy" space for the female or nonheterosexual male body. Both of these latter two bodies are at best disrespected and at worst vilified. What happens to these two bodies *is* something virtually "unspeakable." Clearly then, a platonized black faith tradition fosters discord within the black church community as it values certain black bodies and scorns others. The passionate truth behind Billie Holiday's singing of "Strange Fruit" is borne out in a platonized black faith context. For a platonized black faith tradition does make strange fruit of black bodies even when they are not swinging from Southern trees.

Yet the dilemma that Baldwin's insightful comments point us to is about more than how a platonized tradition comes together with white culture to beset the black body. Indeed, a platonized tradition has provided an invaluable spiritual resource for black people's survival and dignity in a society defined by a white cultural disdain for blackness. There is no doubt that without a platonized faith tradition even more black bodies would have been swinging from Southern trees. Herein lies the heart of the dilemma: What are we to say about a tradition that at once helps and hurts the black body? How are we to view a platonized black faith? How are we to navigate its profound influence on black lives? How are we to at once affirm yet disavow this tradition? These are the questions to be taken up in next chapter as we come to our final conclusions concerning the viability of the black faith tradition.

6

Black Faith Reexamined

So well put!

IN HIS ESSAY "Of the Faith of the Fathers," W. E. B. Du Bois, trying to understand what seemed to be the ambivalent character of black faith, pointed to the "double life" as a "Negro" and an "American" that black people must live. He stated, "Such a double life, with double thoughts, double duties, and double social classes, must give rise to double words and double ideals, and tempt the mind to pretence or to revolt, to hypocrisy or radicalism."[1] Du Bois's discerning comments admit two truths of black living. First, black people's persistent historical struggle is complex. Black men and women have had to find ways to sustain both life and dignity in a society hostile to their very blackness. One of the tools that they fashioned to navigate their experience of struggle was faith. This brings us to the second truth of black living suggested by Du Bois. The black faith tradition is as complicated as the black struggle is complex. Even as the black faith tradition was born out of and speaks to the black experience of struggle, it has been both a bane and a blessing for black people. While on the one hand black faith has provided a sacred canopy of protection for black bodies, on the other hand it has offered theological justification for the denigration of black bodies. This tradition has at once affirmed and relinquished blackness. It has simultaneously esteemed certain black bodies and damned others. This is the "double" speak that Du Bois tries to understand when it comes to the faith of black people. Du Bois connects the "double" speak of the black faith tradition to the complex reality of black life. Du Bois is in part correct in making this connection.

Because black men and women have crafted a culture to respond to the intricate and wide-ranging nuances of black living, the faith of that culture has been correspondingly nuanced and dynamic. There are aspects of the black faith tradition that are more predisposed toward "pretence"—that is, survival—and other aspects more fitting of "revolt"—that is, freedom. The apparent contradictory nature and disposition of the black faith tradition likewise reflects the ebbing and flowing challenges of the historical black experience. During those times when the wider society seems more accepting of black people, black faith is more likely to project an accommodating/integrationist tone. At those times when white society is more hostile, black faith is liable to nurture a revolutionary/nationalist spirit. Essentially, the black faith tradition is as dynamic as the black experience is volatile. There is, however, another reason for the black faith tradition's seemingly ambivalent disposition. The uncertain impact of black faith upon black lives reflects two features integral to the tradition itself: its black cultural-historical identity and its platonized theological character. The black faith tradition is at once black and platonized. And, as we have demonstrated in the previous chapter, these two defining aspects sometimes conflict with each other. The platonized nature of the faith, even though it provides a foundation for protecting black lives, at times opposes the blackness of the tradition. The question thus becomes, how are we to reconcile the relationship between blackness and a platonized theology within a singular faith tradition? How are we to consider the black faith tradition in order to affirm its indispensable value in the black struggle for life and well-being, while also disavowing its complicity in the devastation of black bodies? Is it possible, in other words, to conceive of a platonized black faith tradition that reliably preserves and respects the sacred dignity of all black people? These are the controlling questions of this chapter as it moves toward conclusions concerning the suitability of a platonized black faith tradition and hence the feasibility of being at once black and Christian. This chapter will proceed by first discerning the theological core of the black faith tradition, then highlighting the importance of a hermeneutic of appropriation in establishing that core, before finally making determinations about the possibilities of a black faith tradition. Given the womanist theological commitment to the "survival and wholeness" of entire people, special reference will be made to a womanist response to the platonized black faith tradition. At the same time, it is from a womanist perspective that I will finally be able to answer the question, How can I, a black female, be Christian?

Core Theological Themes

As mentioned in the previous chapter, the black faith tradition is distinguished by core theological themes.[2] These themes are very enduring. They were not derived from speculative ideas about God, about good and evil, or about right and wrong. Rather, they came forth from black people's own concrete experiences as they navigated life in a society antagonistic to their very blackness. As black women and men carved out a spirituality of resistance during their earliest encounters with white racist terror and accordingly identified what was crucial to the assertion of their embodied black humanity, core theological themes emerged. What became a part of black faith's theological core abided by the following standards: it empowered and sustained black bodies under antagonistic social-historical conditions; it resonated with black people's deepest aspirations for life and dignity; and it reflected the continued presence of God in black people's lives as informed by the biblical witness to God and their African theological heritage. The African theological influence on the black faith tradition is perhaps most seen in the significant metaprinciple implicit in all of the core themes: harmony. *idealized*

As noted in chapter 5, the concept of harmony was integral to the African theological worldview. According to African theological thinking, every member of created reality had to maintain a harmonious relationship with the rest of the created realm so that all of creation could remain in harmony with its creator, the Great High God. Considered befitting God were practices or beliefs that projected harmonious relationality. It was in part for this reason that enslaved Africans were resolute in their faith testimony that God did not sanction slavery. Slavery fundamentally defied any notions of harmony. — *no — human worth in God's eyes*

When one considers the core themes of black faith, one thing
stands out—they all bespeak harmonious relationality. These are
themes such as equality, love, justice, and hope. These particular
themes have persisted in the black faith tradition. Black theologian
James Cone acknowledges the perseverance "from slavery to the
present" of "major" black faith themes. He similarly identifies
them as "justice, hope, and love." Cone explains, "The black religious themes of justice, hope, and love are the product of black
people's search for meaning in a white society that did not
acknowledge their humanity."[3]

Black men and women have given voice to the core theological
themes of their faith in their songs, prayers, and testimony to and
about God. For instance, enslaved blacks crafted the spiritual that
continues to be sung in black churches today:

Didn't my Lord deliver Daniel, deliver Daniel, deliver
    Daniel,
Didn't my Lord deliver Daniel,
An' why not every man.[4]

Relying on the biblical witness to God delivering Daniel from the
lion's den (Dan. 6:16), this spiritual plainly testifies not only to the
equality and justice of God but also to a people's hope, because it
suggests that just as God saved Daniel from undue suffering, God
will do the same for them. The black faith tradition essentially
asserts that God is inherently just and responds to historical injustice. More particularly, God acts to empower and liberate black
people in their struggle with white oppression and to put down
the inequitable power of whiteness. It is the justice of God that
gives black people hope that their beleaguered situation will
change. In effect, black faith in the justice of God makes clear that
God affirms the sacred value of the black body. Again, the implied
unifying principle of all of these core theological themes is harmony. Each theme signifies a certain harmonious relationship that
God maintains with all of creation and that God advances within
created history itself. The core themes of the black faith tradition

suggest a corresponding harmonious relationality to be maintained within the black community. They project, in other words, a community where all black bodies are to be respected as the sacred bodies that they are, and are to be accorded just, equal, and loving treatment. In sum, the core themes of the black faith tradition suggest a reverence for the black body as they uphold the life and dignity of black men and women. It is, most significantly, the core themes of the black faith tradition that connote its very blackness.

There is, as mentioned earlier, another defining feature of the black faith tradition—its platonized theological character. To reiterate, given the general evangelical Protestant nature of the black faith tradition, the prevailing theological influence on this tradition is platonized. In this respect, the black faith tradition characteristically espouses a platonized sexual ethic that is grounded in a dualistic split between the soul and body. The soul is revered while the body is devalued. The body is viewed as a harbinger of sin, namely, sexual lust. According to a platonized ethic, only procreative sex is "holy" sex. This platonized theological sexual ethic most regularly manifests itself in various *contingent theological beliefs* that also constitute the black faith tradition.

These contingent beliefs are more transitory than the core theological themes. They emerge in response to particular social and historical challenges. They reflect what is seen as crucial for the black community's well-being at any given time. While these contingent beliefs are given theological legitimacy within the black faith tradition, they are not necessarily inviolable. They are often a source of discussion within the black faith community itself. Not all black churches, for instance, maintain the same contingent theological beliefs. These beliefs, unlike the core claims, may be shaped by social-economic factors in relation to a particular denomination. Views on engagement with "worldly culture" (e.g., secular music, popular entertainment); on proper attire, especially for women; on the role of women in the church and ministry; or on the theological propriety of nonheterosexuality and hence the proper place for nonheterosexual persons within the church are examples of contingent theological beliefs. Though these beliefs are contingent, in that they are predominantly determined by more specific life circumstances and emerge out of particular faith communities, they are no less tenacious than the core theological themes. For just as the core themes are a response to the complex realities of historical black life, the contingent claims are a response to the complex realities of today's black life. In addition, just as the core claims are grounded in the biblical witness, the contingent beliefs are likewise grounded (e.g., platonized claims found within the Pauline epistles). *Evil Paul!* :-)

Interestingly, however, these contingent beliefs do at times conflict with the core theological themes of the black faith tradition. The core themes reflect the black faith tradition's most profound and enduring claims. They represent the identifying character of this tradition—what it stands for and what it believes about God. Again, the core themes reflect the *black* identity of the faith tradition. The contingent beliefs, while presumably they derive from the core themes, are not always commensurate with them. They are more context driven. Perhaps most significantly, they are routinely shaped by a platonized theological influence. In this respect, the contingent beliefs of the black faith tradition bespeak the platonized character of the tradition. It is this influence that creates the conflict between the core and contingent claims. For, reflective of a platonized influence, these contingent beliefs not only typically regard the body as a source of sin, but also reflect platonized theology's inclination toward power. The contingent beliefs, therefore, generally reverberate with the values of patriarchal and/or heterosexual discourses of power. What we find then, is that the platonized theological character of black faith lends itself to contingent beliefs that easily betray the values projected by the core themes (i.e., equality and justice) and in so doing, oppose the very blackness of the tradition.

That platonized theology can serve as a contesting force within the *black* faith tradition is consistent with its compatibility with a particular discourse of power, that is, white cultural ideology. In many respects, platonized theology more naturally coincides with whiteness than it does with blackness. For again, just as white ideology distorts sexuality to assail black bodies, platonized theology's restrictive notions of sexuality virtually do the same. In the end, both lead to a sexualized disrespect of black bodies—white ideology does so absolutely, while platonized theology does so conditionally, depending on its connections with various other discourses of inequitable power. The fact remains, however, that platonized theology does allow for certain black bodies to be condemned at the same time that it subtly repudiates blackness in general. Nevertheless, regardless of platonized theology's theoretical connections to white cultural ideology and its complicity in the disregard of black bodies, platonized theology remains a pervasive aspect of the black faith tradition. Insofar as it has beneficial value by spawning contingent beliefs that have seemingly safeguarded black bodies, then platonized theological thinking will be persistent in the black faith tradition. James Baldwin's own ambivalence toward the black faith tradition (namely, its platonized theological character) points to the attractiveness of platonized thinking for the black faith community. For even though platonized views about sexuality condemned him as a nonheterosexual man, he still equivocated concerning its role in his life because he realized that such thinking kept him from a deadly life of "wine, whiskey, the needle," and anonymous sex. In general then, as long as platonized theology continues to produce positive outcomes for black lives, it will be a tenacious part of the black faith tradition. For this reason, the platonized theology of the black faith tradition cannot simply be dismissed and condemned as being antithetical to blackness, even though it may be. Instead, its relationship to the black faith tradition must be carefully analyzed. Let us now explore how this might occur and thus examine the possibilities for a tradition at once platonized and black.

Reconciling a Platonized Theology with a Black Faith

When considering the black faith tradition two things stand out in regard to its formation: a hermeneutic of appropriation and theo-

logical historicity. A hermeneutic of appropriation has been operative throughout the development of this tradition. It has functioned to determine black people's responses to Christianity and
to establish the black faith tradition's theological core. As the
black faith tradition has evolved, the normative measure of its
hermeneutic has become clear. That which is sanctioned within
this faith tradition advances the life, freedom, and dignity of the
black body. In so doing, the core themes of this tradition ostensibly foster spiritual, communal, and interpersonal harmony. Adherence to the themes that characterize the black faith tradition
presumably provides for a "saving" relationship with God and cultivates harmonious relationality within the black community both
communally and interpersonally.

This brings us to the second significant feature of the black faith
tradition, theological historicity. Reminiscent of its African theological heritage, the black faith tradition is not first and foremost
speculative. It is not given to theological abstractions that have no
bearing on black living. The black faith tradition is marked by *the-*
ological historicity, which is defined by two interrelated presuppo-
sitions. First, theological affirmations are not based on conceptual
theorizing but derive from God's revelation in human history. As
mentioned above, core black faith claims about God are grounded
in black people's own experiences of God as well as the biblical
witness to God in human history.

The second presupposition of theological historicity is that the
meaning of God in black faith always has implications for black life.
God-talk within the black faith tradition is inherently theo-ethical.
There is no knowledge of God that is not also a prescription for
black living. For instance, to affirm the justice, equality, and love of
God is also to affirm the necessity for black people to maintain and
build just, equitable, and loving relationships. The black faith tradition emerges out of the complex realities of black living and provides guiding principles for navigating those realities. In short, it
evolves out of black life and speaks to black life. It is this interde-
pendent relationship to black life that ensures the very black identity of the tradition. This leads to assumptions about the meaning
of blackness implied in the hermeneutic of appropriation.

Blackness refers not simply to a historical racial identity but also to a morally active commitment. In effect, racial historical identity is not the sole determinate of one's blackness and hence not the sole determinate of the faith tradition's black identity. Blackness also significantly involves a morally active commitment to advancing life, freedom, and dignity for all black bodies. It is not enough simply to be black; one must also act morally black. That is, one must act in a way that serves the well-being of all black people. Such an understanding of blackness accords with the meaning of God in the black faith tradition. For God *is* black as God enters into the black historical struggle, thus identifying with black people and acting against anything that would deny them life, dignity, and freedom. Indeed, the effectiveness and importance of the hermeneutic of appropriation in the black faith tradition are seen in the preservation of blackness within that tradition. This faith tradition is black not only as it emerges out of the black historical experience, but also as it serves to protect and to empower black men and women. Essentially, it is the operative presence of a hermeneutic of appropriation that ensures a relevant black faith tradition—that is, one that is usefully and morally connected to black life. In short, it is a tradition that remains true to its core theological themes. This brings us to the implications for platonized theology. What does a hermeneutic of appropriation suggest about the influence of platonized theology within the black faith tradition?

On a conceptual theological level, platonized theology is easy to dismiss from any religious tradition that claims to be Christian. As has been demonstrated throughout this discussion, platonized theology is inherently heretical. Its dualistic approach to the soul and the body, and thus the diminution of the body, defies the defining incarnational center of Christianity. Platonized theology's innate tendency toward inequitable power reveals it as potentially anti-Christ. In recognizing the heretical/anti-Christ qualities of platonized theological thinking, it would seem almost a given that it should be exorcised from the black faith tradition. However, a black faith hermeneutic of appropriation reminds us that the black faith tradition is based not solely, and not even primarily, on con-

ceptual theological analysis. The concrete/practical veracity of theological thinking is just as important as, if not more than, the conceptual veracity. Thus, the blasphemous thinking of platonized
theology is not enough to warrant dismissing it from the black faith
tradition. Within the black faith community the truth of platonized
theological thinking is found not in theological abstractions but in
concrete practices. Therefore, in order for platonized theology to
have less influence on the black faith tradition or be expunged from
black faith, its detrimental value to black lives will have to be
demonstrated. This becomes the task of the theologians of the
black faith tradition.

Karl Barth was right to proclaim that theology is the "self-test"
for the church.[5] Not only must theology reflect what a community believes, but, most importantly, it must hold faith communities accountable to their own professed claims. In this respect, it is
the task of the black church's theologians to hold the black faith
community accountable to its very *black* faith tradition. This is of
special concern for womanist theology. Womanist theology, as it
comes forth from the particular struggles of black women, professes to be invested not simply in the welfare of black women but
also in the "survival and wholeness of entire people." If indeed
this is the case, then womanist theology must concern itself especially with that which allows black bodies, particularly those of
black women, to be maligned. This means that womanist theology
is compelled to confront the troubling platonized theological
influence within the black faith tradition. Let us thus explore the
possibilities for a womanist approach to platonized theology in
our efforts to move closer to final conclusions concerning the propriety of platonized theology for black faith. This approach should
indeed be instructive for any theology that professes to be inter-
ested in the life, freedom, and dignity of all black men and women.

A Womanist Critique of Platonized Theology

A womanist theological approach to a platonized black faith tradition must be guided by that very tradition. Specifically, womanist

theology must adopt the hermeneutic of appropriation that helped to shape the black faith tradition even as it engages that tradition. In this way, it should employ this hermeneutic not only in its critical approach to the black faith tradition but also in relation to its own theological discourse. To do so would help womanist theology to challenge more effectively and authentically the platonized theological influence on the black faith tradition. Let us now see how this is the case.

First, a hermeneutic of appropriation would oblige womanist theology to push beyond racialized notions of blackness. A hermeneutic of appropriation as described above would prompt womanist discourse to go beyond racial constructs in its responses to the consistency of the black faith tradition. Womanist theology would thus question the black faith community's inability to respond to issues of suffering and injustice that seem to reach beyond what is typically regarded as a historically or culturally "black" concern. It is interesting to note, for instance, that it was not until the issue of HIV/AIDS became racially coded—that is, when the disease began disproportionately to impact black men and women—that the black faith community became more actively involved in addressing it. As long as it was viewed as a disease that primarily ravished homosexual bodies—even if some of those bodies were black—the black faith community was notably and notoriously negligent in dealing with this health crisis.[6] Womanist theological discourse is constrained by a hermeneutic of appropriation as well as by its own mission to critique and rise above restrictive notions of black identity that prevent the black faith and theological community from responding to the suffering of human bodies, especially black bodies, simply because that suffering is not racially coded. Again, the operative hermeneutic within the black faith tradition locates the meaning of blackness not simply in racial-historical identity but also in a morally active commitment to all black bodies. An expansion of the meaning of blackness is essential if womanist theology is to challenge effectively the status of platonized theology within the black faith tradition and hold the black faith community accountable for its own core theological themes.

white also.

Theological themes are tied directly to biblical relatives for all cultures. The interplay of how biblical ideas are played out is relevant to every race and culture

Second, a hermenuetuic of appropriation is essential to womanist theology if this theology is to maintain its relevance to black lives, especially the lives of "ordinary" black women who sit in the pews. Essentially, the hermeneutic of appropriation of the black faith defines theological truth in relationship to black reality. The integration of this hermeneutic essentially holds womanist theology accountable to its own community. It serves to remind womanist theologians that the truth of their theological claims does not depend on their conformity to scholarly, conceptual standards of thinking—particularly because those standards are disinterested in the life and well-being of black women and men. Rather, womanist theological credibility is measured by its practical value in the lives of black men and women. Inasmuch as womanist theological claims make possible the life and dignity of all black bodies, they have credibility. When they do not, they must lose credibility. Even when womanist theology remains silent on issues that affect the well-being of black people, it loses credibility. By not confronting issues that impinge upon the body of any black person, womanist theology belies the very faith tradition to which it is beholden. It tacitly betrays the meaning of blackness intrinsic to that tradition. This brings us now to the womanist challenge of platonized theology.

If womanist theology is to foster a sacred regard for all black bodies, men and women, heterosexual and nonheterosexual, then it must forthrightly engage those beliefs and practices within the black faith community that terrorize and diminish the worth of particular black bodies, namely, female and nonheterosexual bodies. This is where its theological truth and credibility are measured. It cannot be said enough that womanist theology cannot refrain from taking on these difficult issues. It must move beyond the boundaries of race and gender to confront issues that involve the life, dignity, and freedom of black women and men in particular and other humans in general. This means confronting the ways in which platonized theology has aligned with patriarchal and heterosexual discourse to create dehumanizing, demoralizing and threatening conditions for women and nonheterosexual persons within the black faith community. Issues of heterosexual intimacy, the sexual objectification and exploitation of black women, as well as violence against black women must absolutely be addressed. But most importantly, the complicity of platonized theology in generating contingent beliefs and concomitant behavior that disregards and disrespects black bodies must be exposed.

Although womanist theology has to push the black faith community beyond strictly racially coded understandings of blackness, it must also recognize that the key to dismantling the influence of platonized theology within the black faith tradition is in revealing its practical connections to white racist practices. In this regard, womanist theology must not simply clarify platonized theology's historical connections to a religiously racist tradition; it must also make clear how platonized thinking has continued to compel the black community into alliances that are detrimental to the community's very blackness as this theology generates contingent beliefs commensurate with the maintenance of white power. One of the more obvious ways in which this development has occurred involves the issue of heterosexual intimacy and marriage.

Although there are definitely significant black church leaders who support same-sex marriages, in general the black faith community has been vociferously opposed to the idea. The Reverend Doctor Fred Shuttlesworth has said, for instance, "Despite what many of this world may argue, I cannot waiver from the God-established principle that marriage is a union meant to be shared between a man and a woman."[7] The Honorable Reverend Walter Fauntroy provides an elaborate and (as we will soon see) telling argument against same-sex marriages. He says:

There are two functions for which civil society rewards a man and a woman with the title "marriage" and certain financial benefits that we call tax exemptions. Civil society cannot survive without men and women perpetuating the species. Same-sex unions cannot provide civil society with that service. Secondly, civil society cannot function without its children becoming bonded to both a man and a woman in their

questionable! — at least

formative years. . . . These two functions—procreation and socialization—cannot be performed by same-sex couples and, therefore, same-sex couples should not be rewarded with tax benefits for something they cannot do.[8]

Interestingly, the intense opposition within the black faith community to same-sex unions has created disturbing alliances. For instance, it was reported recently that a black preacher proclaimed from his pulpit, "If the KKK opposes gay marriage, I would ride with them."[9] Needless to say, such an overt alliance with white racist power is not characteristic of the black faith community. What is characteristic, however, is the more subtle alliance that is unavoidable in light of homophobic/heterosexist beliefs.

c.r.a.z

It must be understood that white attacks on black sexuality and on same-sex sexuality are intricately connected.[10] Both black sexuality and same-sex sexuality ostensibly threaten the very supremacy of whiteness. Black sexuality does so because it may lead to the production of an impure race; hence, white cultural discourse is characteristically hostile to black-white intimacy and marriages. Same-sex sexuality jeopardizes white supremacy because it is not reproductive; thus, white discourses of power typically oppose same-sex intimacy and marriage. In this regard, opposition to same-sex marriage parallels the opposition to black-white marriage, as both marriages are seen as a threat to the continued existence of white society. What black faith leaders must be made aware of is how in their opposition to same-sex unions they coincide with those who find their blackness as much as of a threat to white society as homosexuality. Intriguingly, the above-quoted comments by Reverend Walter Fauntroy make this point; for all one needs to do is to replace his words "civil society" with "white society," and the point becomes clear. Again, even though the black faith community may not wittingly align itself with the social-historical agenda of white racism, it must be made to recognize that uncritical allegiance to a platonized theology predisposes it to such an alliance. This alliance typically manifests itself in the very beliefs and behaviors generated by platonized thinking—that is, heterosexist views. A platonized approach to sexuality inexorably lends itself to sheltering and being taken up by inequitable power at the same time that it sets black people against one another. Poet and scholar Nikki Giovanni astutely recognizes this possibility as she observes, "I think the so-called notorious homophobia of some Black people is playing right into the hands of the right wing. Because once you find out what a people dislike you can use that against them to divide them."[11]

Womanist theology is compelled to make explicit the dubious connections between platonized theology and unjust power. If it does so, it will be able to show how platonized theology defies the very identity of the black faith tradition, especially as it is intrinsically connected to white cultural discourse in regard to its approach to sexuality. Essentially, the task of womanist theology is to help the black faith community recognize that platonized theology characteristically spawns systems and structures of oppression. It generates contingent beliefs that serve to dehumanize and disrespect human bodies, especially black bodies. It is for this reason that it must be deemed sinful and not given authoritative theological privilege within the black faith tradition.

It is only as black faith communities abandon their allegiance to platonized thinking that they can remain reliably true to their *black* faith identity and, moreover, that the black faith tradition can reliably preserve and protect black life. However, even in recognizing the sinful, detrimental character of platonized theology within black faith, its positive value cannot be forgotten, especially by womanist theology. For again, platonized views about the body/sexuality have enabled black women to exercise agency over their own bodies. If womanist theology is to challenge the black faith community to abandon its commitment to platonized theology, then it must address the positive theological void that is left when this is done. Hence, in appreciating the practical value of platonized theology in black lives, womanist theology must also be constructive and therefore advance a theological view toward sexuality that empowers black women and is consistent with the black faith tradition. Let us now examine what this might look like.

A Womanist Approach to Sexuality

Clearly, the most problematic aspect of platonized theology is its defining aspect—its view toward sexuality. Platonized theology presents a dualistic perspective on sexuality. To reemphasize an earlier point, sexuality is viewed as either procreatively good or lustfully bad. There is no third sexual option in a platonized tradition. Sexuality is not granted the theological space to be relationally right. It is disconnected from intimate relationality and thus is not seen as an expression of loving relationships. In this respect, platonized theology objectifies sexuality; thus, it provides for the sexually objectified exploitation and/or denigration of various human bodies. This has certainly been the case in regard to black female bodies. Platonized theology's collusion with white ideology legitimated the sexually objectified exploitation of black women by white men. Likewise, platonized theology's collusion with patriarchal ideology has sheltered similar treatment of black women by black men. What needs to be retrieved is what platonized theology abandons—the connection between sexuality and loving relationships. It is that connection that black women have historically tried to preserve and protect in terms of their own bodies. It is ironic, then, that they have relied on a platonized theology to help them protect their virtue, while indeed a platonized sexual ethic does not even acknowledge loving sexual intimacy. However, the black faith tradition itself does suggest a view of the body/sexuality that would consistently contest the sexually objectified mistreatment of various human bodies, especially black women's, while also affirming the sacredness of sexuality.

The defining core theological themes of the black faith tradition cohere around the principle of harmony. Once again, essential to the black identity of the black faith tradition is its role in preserving harmonious spiritual, communal, and interpersonal relationality. In this regard, anything that would obstruct the development of harmony as it involves black people's relationship to God, to their community, and to one another must be abandoned and, indeed, deemed sinful. The implication for a sexual ethic is clear. When sexuality is expressed in a way that provides for

and nurtures harmonious relationships—that is, those that are loving, just, and equal—then it is sacred. Only when sexual expression is objectified and thus disconnected from harmonious
relationships is it sinful. The measure of what is sinful has to do
with whether or not it contributes to right/harmonious relationships with God, community, and others. Thus, it is not the
body/sexuality itself that is seen as sinful or a cauldron of evil.
That which is sinful and thus evil has to do with the way that the
body/sexuality is regarded. As we have seen, reflective of its
African theological heritage, the black faith tradition demands that
the body/sexuality be revered, accorded sacral value, and treated
and regarded as giving witness to God. Such a view of the
body/sexuality is also in keeping with the incarnational identity of
Christianity. It is the reverence for the body/sexuality and the
commitment to harmonious relationality that womanist theology
must uphold in providing the black faith community with a sexual
ethic that at once empowers black women and is consistent with
its own black identity. At the same time, such a sexual ethic provides space for same-sex relationships. In sum, womanist theology
would affirm the necessity for sexual expression to be relationally
right—that is, an intimate expression of loving/harmonious relationality. It is when sexual expression is not relationally right that
it becomes problematic, if not sinful. With this, let us now discern
the suitability of a platonized black faith tradition in particular and
black Christianity in general.

Concluding Assessments

Platonized theological thinking is anathema to the black faith tradition. It generates contingent beliefs and subsequent practices
that contradict the core theological themes of black faith and thus
contravenes spiritual, communal, and interpersonal harmony
within the black community. For this reason, it must be
unabashedly renounced. There is virtually no possibility for a reliable faith tradition that is at once platonized and black. However,
to abandon platonized theology is not to abandon Christianity.

For while platonized theology does not readily accord with blackness, blackness and Christianity are compatible. To reiterate, it is a platonized Christian tradition that is damaging for black people, not Christianity itself. It was a platonized tradition that allowed for the lynching of black bodies, even as it was Christianity that supplied black people with the spiritual resources to endure, if not overcome, such vicious attacks.

Most specifically, the core themes of the black faith tradition are consistent with Christianity's incarnational reality. These themes comply with Jesus' revelation of a God who enters into history in compassionate solidarity with the oppressed, thus affirming the value of their very embodied lives. Christianity thereby opposes whiteness, inasmuch as whiteness signifies oppressive power. Christianity affirms blackness, inasmuch as blackness signals black people's struggle against white tyranny and movement toward a just, loving, and equitable community. It must be concluded in no uncertain terms that it is whiteness and Christianity that do not go together, for indeed whiteness, like platonized theology, belies Christianity's very defining incarnational character. So, the black faith tradition, when remaining true to its very black identity, provides one of the most potent witnesses to the truth of Christianity. The question of how one can be black and Christian gives rise to an affirmation of black Christianity. It is blackness that reveals the authentic character of Christianity. It *is* the black faith tradition that exposes the heresy of white Christianity, which is characteristically a platonized Christianity. Even as W. E. B. Du Bois struggled to understand the ambivalent character of the black faith tradition, he understood why black people were Christian. He recognized, as did many black thinkers before him, that the truth of Christianity, as it is revealed through Jesus, affirmed the hypocrisy of white Christianity and the value of black lives.[12] Du Bois in fact recognized the very blackness of Christianity as he recognized the essential blackness of the incarnate God. He said, "Who can doubt that if Christ came to Georgia today one of his first deeds would be to sit down and take supper with black men, and who can doubt the outcome if He did?"[13] The truth of Christianity is found in the integrity of blackness.

Returning to the question asked by my student Gabrielle that began my journey in this book, "How come black people adopted the religion of their oppressors?" My response to Gabrielle remains as it did when I first answered her: black people did not adopt the white Christianity of their white oppressors. Instead, they developed a black faith tradition that exposes the "hypocrisy" of white Christianity and affirms the very sacred value of the black body. *But did they?*

A Womanist's Postscript

How Can I Be a Christian?

THIS BOOK BEGAN with Gabrielle's penetrating question, "How could you, a black woman, possibly be a Christian?" How, she wanted to know, could one who is a self-proclaimed womanist be a part of a tradition with a legacy of complicity in attacks against black and female bodies? This book thus far has addressed one level of Gabrielle's concern—the nature of Christianity itself. She wanted to know if there was something about Christianity that deemed it unsuitable for those who were subjugated and accordingly made it most suitable for those who wield brutal power. Essentially, she wondered if Christianity was too fundamentally white ever to be a fitting religion for black people. This book has demonstrated that while there has been a legacy of terror carried forth under a Christian banner, this legacy is indeed anathema to Christianity itself, as is the theology that has sustained it. Platonized Christianity represents a theological perversion of Christianity's incarnational identity both ontologically and existentially. It negates the sacredness of the body attested to by the incarnate divine–human encounter. It defies, if not treats with contempt, Jesus' ministry of compassionate solidarity with the poor and oppressed. In short, white Christianity represents a theological abomination and, hence, a perversion of Christianity itself. And so, to Gabrielle I can still answer that I am a Christian because it *is* the faith of my grandmothers. The integrity of Christianity is embodied in the lives of black women as they quest for life, freedom, and dignity among the harsh realities of a society that disdains their very black female bodies.

There was, however, another level of Gabrielle's question that

218

posed a greater personal challenge. Even though the tradition of Christian tyranny represents a fundamental distortion of Christian theology, the fact remains that Christianity's monotheistic and christological core has made it vulnerable to being exploited by unscrupulous power. Furthermore, it has provided even those who have been victimized by a terrorizing Christian tradition with the theological justification necessary to victimize others. Particularly, the black faith tradition, whose very existence witnesses to the hypocrisy of white Christianity, has mirrored white Christianity in its treatment of women and nonheterosexual persons. In effect, the troubling legacy of "Christianity" suggests that it is a religion in which imposing discriminatory power can find theological cover. Hence, the truth of Christianity is that it has generated at least two prevailing legacies: one that terrorizes and oppresses and another that empowers and liberates; the first is most defined by whiteness and the second is most defined by blackness.

Clearly, as has been demonstrated throughout this discussion, the fact of my cultural/historical blackness does not exempt me from the possibility of advancing a "white" Christianity, just as it has not exempted the black church community from doing so. In other words, my history of oppression as a black woman, even as that has been sustained by a distorted Christian tradition, does not preclude my distorting Christianity to devalue others. It is with this recognition in mind that Gabrielle's question of how I, a black female, could be Christian takes on a different meaning. It becomes not just a question about my allegiance to a particular religion but also a question concerning my faithfulness to a certain faith tradition. It is, in other words, a question of accountability. How do I enter into the Christian story? To whom am I accountable? And so, how is it that I am a Christian? What difference does my being black, female, and a womanist make to my Christian theological witness?

That I am black, female, and a womanist means that I am accountable to my grandmothers and their faith. It is from women like them, those everyday women who sit in the pews of black churches on Sunday mornings, that I learn. These are the women who provide me with the substance of my womanist work. Their faith is the resource for knowledge about God and the meaning of God for black women and men in struggle. It is their faith that provides the foundation for my womanist theological claims. It is from their experiences of crafting a life for themselves and their families that my womanist theological questions and answers must come. But most importantly, that I am accountable to these women indicates that my theological claims must ring true to their struggles and aspirations for life, freedom, and dignity. This means that the priority of my theological work is to challenge the social, cultural, and theological discourses that prevent black women and men from enjoying harmonious relationality with their bodies, their communities, and those they love. I am thus obliged to raise what my grandmothers would perhaps not dare to raise or even know how to raise—the difficult issues of faith, scripture, and theology that have suborned the unfair treatment of black women as well as nonheterosexual persons. In effect, in answering the question of how I can be a Christian, I must discern the Christian legacy to which I belong. For me, it is the legacy of black women like my grandmothers, whose Christian faith sustained them in their fight to safeguard their bodies as well as the bodies of those they loved.

At the same time that my grandmothers' faith informs my theological discourse, it also informs the meaning of my faith. For the meaning of their faith was found in the way in which it affirmed them and allowed them to be a part of a wider community of faith. Their faith thus checks my faith, keeping me from using faith as a divisive weapon against others.

In the end, one must conclude that the Christian story is a complicated and sometimes troubling story. Regardless of how social, cultural, philosophical, and theological factors have coalesced to distort what might be considered the "truth" of the Christian religion, Christianity has supported and even spawned a disturbing tradition of tyranny and terror against black bodies, male and female. And it must also be admitted that it is easy to use

Christianity to terrorize. Yet, for me, as long as there continues to be a Christian story that has protected, empowered, and advanced the sacred dignity of human bodies—especially those of black women—then I can continue to be a Christian. For in the long run, the question that (I and other black people of faith must answer is not how we can be Christian but to which Christian legacy we belong.)Inasmuch as we who are black and Christian utilize our faith to prevent anyone from enjoying free and loving harmonious relationality, then we have become a part of the same Christian legacy that denigrated and derided our very black bodies; and it is then that we betray our own *black* faith story.

Ten years ago, in my book *The Black Christ*, I began a journey to try to understand my maternal grandmother's faith. I indeed wanted to know how she could be a part of a religious tradition, and particularly a black faith community, that often discriminated against women. During that part of my journey, I discovered the power of Christ's presence in her life. (To her, Christ was One who understood her pains, her sorrows, her needs, and her desires. Christ was the One to whom she prayed each night and talked to throughout the day. I concluded then that the meaning of Christ was found "inside of my grandmother and other Black men and women as they fight for freedom and wholeness."[1] Ironically, ten years later my journey has come full circle. Regardless of the many theological twists and turns that my journey has taken over the years, I have returned to my grandmother's faith. For it is in her faith story about a God who values and cherishes her black female body that the truth of Christianity is found. I have come even more to understand that Jesus was the center of her faith because he revealed God's compassionate solidarity with the oppressed and, thus, God's compassionate solidarity with her.

This book has attempted to answer the question of how I can be Christian against the backdrop of Christian involvement in the lynchings of black bodies. My grandmothers grew up in the South during a time when lynchings were a part of the Southern land-scape. Yet, even as they were no doubt aware of the "good" white Christians who participated in these vile attacks against black bodies like theirs, they clung to their Christian faith. Somehow they knew that the faith of the lynchers was not the faith of Jesus Christ, was not really Christian, and thus was not the faith that they proclaimed. And so it is, I can continue confidently to declare that I am a Christian because the faith of my grandmothers *is* Christianity.

Notes

Introduction

1. Gayraud Wilmore, *Black Religion and Black Radicalism: An Interpretation of the Religious History of African Americans*, 3rd ed. (Maryknoll, N.Y.: Orbis Books, 1998), 22.

2. Paraphrase of Mary Daly in her discussion of Christianity's central symbol, Christ, in *Beyond God the Father: Toward a Philosophy of Women's Liberation* (Boston: Beacon Press, 1973), 72.

1. A Platonized Tradition

1. *New York World*, December 7, 1899, quoted in *100 Years of Lynchings: The Shocking Record behind Today's Black Militancy*, ed. Ralph Ginzburg (New York: Lancer Books, 1969), 24-25 (emphasis mine).

2. *Chicago Record-Herald*, June 24, 1903, quoted in *100 Years of Lynchings*, 53.

3. W. E. B. Du Bois quoted in Orlando Patterson, *Rituals of Blood: Consequences of Slavery in Two American Centuries* (Washington, D.C.: Civitas/Counterpoint, 1998), 173.

4. The news reports of Sam Hose's lynching wrongly identified him as Sam Holt. This misnaming points to the disregard of the lynch victims. In this book I will maintain Sam Hose's correct name, indicating the mistakes in the quotations of news stories.

5. Editorial from the *Springfield* (Mass.) *Weekly Republican*, April 28, 1899, quoted in *100 Years of Lynchings*, 19-20.

6. For more on the phenomenon and rituals of lynching, see the very comprehensive study by Philip Dray, *At the Hands of Persons Unknown: The Lynching of Black America* (New York: Random House, 2002).

7. Patterson, *Rituals of Blood*, 232. More will be said about this later in part 1 of this book.

8. James Carroll, *Constantine's Sword: The Church and the Jews* (Boston: Houghton Mifflin, 2001), 171.

9. Carter Heyward, "Jesus of Nazareth/Christ of Faith: Founda-
tions of a Reactive Christology" in *Lift Every Voice: Constructing Christian Theologies from the Underside*, ed. Susan Brooks Thistlethwaite and
Mary Potter Engel (New York: Harper & Row, 1990), 191-200.

10. The following discussion revisits an argument I previously made
(see my *Sexuality and the Black Church: A Womanist Perspective* [Mary-
knoll, N.Y.: Orbis Books, 1999], 19-23), as it is germane to this current
analysis.

11. Michel Foucault, *The History of Sexuality*, trans. Robert Hurley, 3
vols. (New York: Vintage Books, 1990), 101.

12. More will be said about religious racism in chapter 4 below.

13. Various interpreters of this early period in Christian history argue
that there was a popular trend toward monotheism. See, e.g., Henry
Chadwick, *The Early Church* (New York: Penguin Books, 1967); J. N. D.
Kelly, *Early Christian Doctrines*, rev. ed. (New York: Harper & Row,
1978); Elaine Pagels, *The Origin of Satan* (New York: Vintage Books,
1995).

14. Chadwick, *Early Church*, 72.

15. For more on early Jewish theology, see, e.g., Bernhard W. Ander-
son, *Understanding the Old Testament*, 3rd ed. (Englewood Cliffs, N.J.:
Prentice-Hall, 1975); Gerhard von Rad, *Old Testament Theology*, with an
introduction by Walter Bruggemann (Louisville: Westminster John Knox
Press, 2001).

16. All biblical quotations are taken from New International Version
unless otherwise designated.

17. This Christian self-understanding as the "new/true Israel" is discussed in Elaine Pagels, *Adam, Eve, and the Serpent* (New York: Vintage
Books, 1988), especially chapter 1, 7ff.

18. See Justin Martyr, *First Apology* 1.5-6 in *The New Eusebius: Documents Illustrative of the History of the Church to A.D. 337*, ed. J. Stevenson (London: SPCK, 1957), 62.

19. Ignatius, *Letter to the Magnesians*, VIII, IX, X in *New Eusebius*,46.

20. It has been pointed out on numerous occasions that monotheistic traditions indeed have problems explaining evil, and therefore often
stretch the bounds of monotheism by positing a lesser evil being.

21. William James, "The One and the Many," in *The Writings of
William James*, ed. John J. McDermott (Chicago: University of Chicago
Press, 1977), 264-65.

22. Gregory Nyssenus, *Contra Eunomium*, quoted in Jaroslav
Pelikan, *Christianity and Classical Culture: The Metamorphosis of Natural
Theology in the Christian Encounter with Hellenism* (New Haven: Yale
University Press, 1993), 75.

23. "An Anonymous Brief for Christianity Presented to Diognetus," in *Early Christian Fathers,* ed. Cyril C. Richardson (New York: Macmillan, 1970), 214.

24. It is interesting to note, as pointed out by Elaine Pagels, that the English word "demons" evolves from the Greek word *daimones,* which meant "spiritual energies" originally having no intrinsic evil connotation. Early Christian writings eventually transformed this word to signal an evil reality—hence the word "demons." For a more thorough discussion of this, see Pagels, *Origin of Satan,* 120ff.

25. Ibid., 130-31.

26. See Justin Martyr, *Second Apology,* especially chapter 13, in which he speaks of the "spermatic word." Although he suggests that there is some seed of wisdom planted in others, the fullness of wisdom and reason is reflected in Jesus Christ; thus Christianity is again deemed superior to any other religions or systems of belief.

27. Though I was drawn to this particular quotation by Elaine Pagels's citation of it (*Origin of Satan,* 120) this particular translation is taken from "The First Apology of Justin, The Martyr" in *Early Christian Fathers,* 257-58.

28. Quotation from Chadwick, *Early Church,* 69. See also Pagels's discussion of early Jewish attitudes toward the stranger (*Origin of Satan,* especially chapter 2, "The Social History of Satan").

29. Chadwick, *Early Church,* 69ff.

30. What is at issue in the christological settlement is not Jesus' own self-understanding. How he viewed himself has been a matter of debate since his ministry, as evidenced by the various Gospel interpretations of him. Important to this particular discussion is the christological tradition/settlements that have shaped the Christian tradition.

31. Taken from Chalcedon settlement excerpted in Kelly, *Early Christian Doctrines,* 339-40.

32. A thorough discussion of the christological controversies leading to the Nicene and Chalcedon confessions is provided by Kelly, *Early Christian Doctrines.*

33. Ibid.

34. See the discussion of theism in G. L. Prestige, *God in Patristic Thought* (London: SPCK, 1952).

35. *The Christological Controversy,* ed. and trans. Richard A. Norris, Jr. (Philadelphia: Fortress Press, 1980), 2.

36. We will later see how Jesus clarified that the life required of God's kingdom resists a dehumanizing Christian tradition. For now, it is important to discern how his ministry contributed to a problematic theological core.

37. This definition relies on *The American Heritage College Dictionary*, 3rd ed. (Boston: Houghton Mifflin, 1997).

38. See above, pp. 6-7.

39. This particular understanding and interpretation of Philo are taken from Justo L. González, *The Story of Christianity*, volume 1, *The Early Church to the Dawn of the Reformation* (New York: Harper & Row, 1971), 13.

40. There are many discussions of this meeting in early church history texts; see e.g., González, *Story of Christianity*, vol. 1; for a thorough discussion of the apostle Paul's participation in this assembly, see Günther Bornkamm, *Paul=Paulus*, trans. D. M. G. Stalker (New York: Harper & Row, 1971).

41. Plato's *Timaeus* in *Plato: The Collected Dialogues*, ed. Edith Hamilton and Huntington Cairns (Princeton, N.J.: Princeton University Press, 1961), 1161.

42. Ibid., 1166.

43. J. N. D. Kelly provides a good discussion of Platonic and Neoplatonic thought in *Early Christian Doctrines*, 14-22.

44. The reader should be reminded that this will be taken up more fully in chapter 3.

45. See Elaine Pagels's comprehensive discussion of the meaning of *gnosis* in *Origin of Satan*.

46. For a thorough discussion of both religions, see Kelly, *Early Christian Doctrines*.

47. Mark D. Jordan describes Jesus' view toward marriage and celibacy as "severe" in *The Ethics of Sex* (Oxford: Blackwell, 2002), 48.

48. Jordan's interpretation of Jesus' ethic at this point helps to inform this particular discussion; ibid., 49-50, as well as Pagels's *Adam, Eve, and the Serpent*, 13-15.

49. On this notion of an "urgent" ethic, see Elaine Pagels's consistent reference to Jesus' and Paul's "urgent concern for the practical work of proclaiming the gospel" (*Adam, Eve, and the Serpent*, 17).

50. Pagels, *Adam, Eve, and the Serpent*, 15. I am indebted to Pagels's discussion of Jesus' focus on the coming of God's kingdom for this interpretation of Jesus' ethic. See her discussion in chapter 1, "The Kingdom of God is at Hand."

51. Bornkamm, *Paul*, 72.

52. Again, Pagels's interpretation of Paul at this point provides the foundation for this particular discussion; see *Adam, Eve, and the Serpent*, 16ff.

53. Pagels, *Adam, Eve, and the Serpent* , 17; see also Jordan's discussion of both Jesus' and Paul's sexual ethic (*Ethics of Sex*).

54. See above, pp. 6-7.

55. The influence of Paul's teachings in early Christian literature can be seen in writings such as the *Stromata* of Clement of Alexandria and the *First Apology* of Justin Marytr.

56. Jordan, *Ethics of Sex*, 109.

57. Augustine, *Confessions* 2.2., trans. R. S. Pine-Coffin (New York: Penguin Books, 1961), 43.

58. This particular version of Rom. 13:14 is taken directly from Augustine's *Confessions* 8.12, trans. Pine-Coffin, 178.

59. Augustine, *City of God* 8.13, trans. Henry Bettenson, with an introduction by John O'Meara (New York: Penguin Books, 1972), 522.

60. Augustine, *City of God* 14:16, trans. Bettenson, 577.

61. Ibid.

2. Christianity and Power

1. *100 Years of Lynchings: The Shocking Record behind Today's Black Militancy*, ed. Ralph Ginzburg (New York: Lancer Books, 1969), 24-25 (emphasis mine).

2. See above pp. 6-7. James Carroll suggests that after Constantine's conversion Christianity "became an entity so different from what had preceded it as to be almost unrecognizable" (*Constantine's Sword: The Church and the Jews* [Boston: Houghton Mifflin, 2001]).

3. From Eusebius, *The Conversion of Constantine* (ca. 338) excerpted in *A New Eusebius: Documents Illustrative of the History of the Church to A.D. 337*, ed. J. Stevenson (London: SPCK, 1957), 299-300.

4. See, for instance, the early interpreter Lactantius's version of events as summarized in *New Eusebius*, 299. There are many discussions of the events surrounding Constantine's conversion. See, e.g., James Carroll, *Constantine's Sword*, esp. chap. 17; see also Justo L. González, *The Story of Christianity*, vol. 1, *The Early Church to the Dawn of the Reformation* (San Francisco: Harper & Row, 1984), esp. chap. 12.

5. Though these conclusions were arrived at independently, they are supported and informed by Jacob Neusner's understanding of these events as they have been highlighted in Carroll, *Constantine's Sword*, 176. See Jacob Neusner, *Judaism and Christianity in the Age of Constantine: History, Messiah, Israel, and the Initial Confrontation.* (Chicago: University of Chicago Press, 1987).

6. Carroll, *Constantine's Sword*, 176.

7. González, *Story of Christianity*, 1:134.

8. From St. John Chrysostom, *A Demonstration Against the Pagans that Christ is God; From The Saying Concerning Him in Many Places in*

the Prophets, in *Apologist, John Chrysostom*, trans. Margaret A. Schatkin and Paul W. Harkins, *Fathers of the Church* 73 (Washington, D.C.: Catholic University of America Press, 1985), 249-50.

9. Carroll, *Constantine's Sword*, 189.

10. This concept derives from Sigmund Freud's concept of "identification with the aggressor." Sandor Ferenezi develops this further. See Ferenezi's discussion in "The Confusion of Tongues between Adults and Children: The Language of Tenders and Passion," in *Final Contribution to the Problems and Methods of Psychoanalysis*, ed. M. Blaint, trans. E. Mosbacker (London: Karmac Books, 1980), 156-67.

11. René Girard, *I See Satan Fall like Lightning* (Marykoll, N.Y.: Orbis Books, 2001), esp. chap. 2, "The Cycle of Mimetic Violence."

12. From Eusebius, *Oration on the Tricennalia of Constantine* (A.D. 336), excerpted in *New Eusebius*, 391-92.

13. In *The Origin of Satan* (New York: Vintage Books, 1995), Elaine Pagels refers to Israelite conflicts with those outside of the Jewish faith community as "foreign or alien enemies." She refers to the intracommunal conflicts as conflicts with "intimate enemies." It is from her that I borrow the term.

14. Carroll, *Constantine's Sword*, 177.

15. Ibid.

16. Rosemary Radford Ruether provides a thorough discussion of the *Adversus Judeaos* tradition in *Faith and Fratricide: The Theological Roots of Anti-Semitism* (New York: Seabury Press, 1974), esp. chap. 3, "The Negation of the Jews in the Church Fathers."

17. Justin Martyr, *The Dialogue with Trypho* in *Saint Justin Martyr*, trans. Thomas B. Falls, *Fathers of the Church* 6 (Washington, D.C.: Catholic University of American Press, 1948), 353.

18. Reuther, *Faith and Fratricide*, 173.

19. St. John Chrysostom, "Eight Homilies against the Jews," in *The Writings of Saint John of Chrysostom*, Homily 5, 5:1, www.chrysostom. org/writings.html (accessed November 2003).

20. Quoted in Carroll, *Constantine's Sword*, 295.

21. Clearly this antisemitic theological sentiment spawned a deadly legacy for the Jews. Throughout history, various Christian theologians would justify Jewish suffering with some version of "retributive suffering." For more on the theological underpinnings of Christian antisemitism, see Ruether, *Faith and Fratricide*.

22. René Girard, *Violence and the Sacred*, trans. Patrick Gregory (Baltimore: Johns Hopkins University Press, 1979), 14.

23. Ruether, *Faith and Fratricide*, 180-81.

24. "1805 Oration of Red Jacket," in *Literature, Race, and Ethnicity: Contesting American Identities,* ed. Joseph T. Skerrett, Jr. (New York: Addison Wesley Longman, 2002), 54.

25. Studs Terkel interview with Frank Chin in *Literature, Race, and Ethnicity,* 391.

26. I have made this argument in other places and so will not elaborate on it here. Instead I reiterate the argument I made in *Sexuality and the Black Church: A Womanist Perspective* (Maryknoll, N.Y.: Orbis Books, 1999), esp. 19-22.

27. Quoted in James Miller, *The Passion of Michel Foucault* (New York: Doubleday, 1993), 293.

28. One should recall Justin Martyr's portrait of pagans as well as their gods as passionate beings "who did things which it is disgraceful even to speak of . . ." See chap. 1, n. 27 above.

29. Carroll, *Constantine's Sword,* 175.

30. For my understanding of the role of the cross after Constantine's conversion I am most indebted to James Carroll's discussion in *Constantine's Sword,* 174ff.

31. Translation taken from *The Christological Controversy,* trans. and ed. Richard A. Norris, Jr. (Philadelphia: Fortress, 1980), 157.

32. See the discussion of platonized Christianity and the earthly realm in chapter 1 above.

33. See my discussion of this in *The Black Christ,* Bishop Henry McNeal Turner/Sojourner Truth Series in Black Religion (Maryknoll, N.Y.: Orbis Books, 1994), 110ff.

34. See Carroll, *Constantine's Sword,* 190-91.

35. Note, for instance, Anselm's treatise *Cur Deus homo* as well as St. Thomas Aquinas's theory of atonement as "satisfaction" and Peter Abelard's understanding of Jesus' death on the cross as a sign of God's love. Central to all of these theories is Jesus' suffering and death on the cross. Each of these theories variously attempts to explain the significance of the cross to human salvation. I will say more about these theories later in this chapter. One can find a concise yet thorough discussion of each of these atonement theories in Alister E. McGrath, *Historical Theology: An Introduction to the History of Christian Thought* (Malden, Mass.: Blackwell, 1998).

36. In making this argument about the place of the cross in the Nicene Creed I rely on and extend an argument I previously made in *The Black Christ,* though this particular rendering of events is guided by Carroll's interpretation in *Constantine's Sword.*

37. See Eusebius's account of Constantine's conversion in *New Eusebius,* 299-300.

38. St. John Chrysostom, "Eight Homilies Against the Jews," Homily 6, 2:10.

39. Ruether, *Faith and Fratricide*, 181.

40. Girard, *I See Satan Fall like Lightning*, xi.

41. Ibid., 62.

42. Girard, *Violence and the Sacred*, 4.

43. Girard provides examples of various sacrificial mythologies; see *I See Satan Fall like Lightning*, chapter 5, "Mythology."

44. Girard, *Violence and the Sacred*, 6.

45. Ibid., 14.

46. See the discussion of patristic atonement theories in McGrath, *Historical Theology*, 133ff.

47. See Anselm of Canterbury, *Cur Deus Homo*, ed. and trans. Jasper Hopkins and Herbert Richardson (New York: Edwin Mellen Press, 1975-76).

48. See St. Thomas Aquinas, *Summa Theologiae*, 2.2.1 in *Summa Theologiae*, trans. Richard T. A. Murphy, O.P. (New York: McGraw-Hill, 1964).

49. For more on Abelard's "moral influence" theory of atonement, see especially Peter Abelard, "Commentary on St. Paul's Letter to the Romans," in *A Scholastic Miscellany*, ed. E. R. Fairweather (Louisville: Westminster John Knox Press, 1982).

50. See Calvin, *Institutes of the Christian Religion*, book 2, chapter 16, section 5.

51. Girard, *I See Satan Fall like Lightning*, 21.

52. See Girard's reference to this saying. One should keep in mind that for Girard it is a scandal that eventuates into the need for a sacrifice (*I See Satan Fall like Lightning*, 24ff).

53. Ibid., 23.

54. It should be noted that it took the Roman authorities as well as the great Jewish council of the Sanhedrin to make the crucifixion possible.

55. Quoted in James H. Smylie, "Countee Cullen's 'The Black Christ,'" *Theology Today* 38, no. 2 (July 1981): 164.

56. Countee Cullen, *On These I Stand: An Anthology of the Best Poems of Countee Cullen* (New York: Harper & Row, 1947), 104. For an in-depth analysis of *The Black Christ*, see Smylie "Countee Cullen's 'The Black Christ.'"

57. Cullen, *On These I Stand*, 137.

58. Claude McKay, "The Lynching," in Nathan Irvin Huggins, *Voices from the Harlem Renaissance* (New York: Oxford University Press, 1976), 354-55.

59. From Langston Hughes, *The Panther and The Lash: Poems of Our Times* (New York: Alfred A. Knopf, 1967, repr., 1987), 37.

60. W. E. B. Du Bois, *Darkwater: Voices from within the Veil* (1920; reprinted with introduction by David Levering Lewis, New York: Washington Square Press, 2004), 19.

61. Ibid., 195.

62. See discussion in Orlando Patterson, *Rituals of Blood: Consequences of Slavery in Two American Centuries* (Washington, D.C.: Civitas/Counterpoint, 1998), 221-22.

63. Ibid., 215.

64. Ibid., 217.

65. See my detailed discussion of this in *Sexuality and the Black Church*.

66. See reference to this in Carroll, *Sword of Constantine*, 217ff.

67. John D'Emilio and Estelle Freedman, *Intimate Matters: A History of Sexuality in America* (New York: Harper & Row, 1988), 86ff.

68. It is in fact the case that the most common reason given for the lynching of a black, particularly a black man, was that he had committed a sex crime against a white woman.

69. Girard, *Violence and the Sacred*, 35.

70. For the reasons for black lynchings one of the best accounts remains Ida B. Wells, *On Lynchings: Southern Horrors, A Red Record, Mob Rule in New Orleans* (1892; reprint, New York: Arno, 1969).

71. James Weldon Johnson, *The Autobiography of an Ex-Coloured Man*, with an introduction by Arna Bontemps (New York: Hill & Wang; 1960), 187-88.

72. Ibid., 189 (emphasis mine).

3. A Heretical Tradition

1. Reported in *100 Years of Lynchings: The Shocking Record behind Today's Black Militancy,* ed. Ralph Ginzburg (New York: Lancer Books, 1969), 11 (emphasis mine). Again it should be noted that while the media reported that the victim's name was Holt, it was actually Hose. Such failure to get the name right further emphasizes the gross disregard that white society had for the humanity of black people. Moreover, just as easily as they misnamed the victims of lynching, so too did white society wrongly accuse them of "lynchable" crimes.

2. Reported in *100 Years of Lynchings,* 152.

3. Reported in Grace Elizabeth Hale, *Making Whiteness: The Culture of Segregation in the South, 1890-1940* (New York: Pantheon Books,

1998) esp. chap. 5, "Deadly Amusements: Spectacle Lynchings and the Contradictions of Segregation as Culture," 213.

4. This is a tradition, as noted in chapter 2, set into motion by Augustine, Anselm, and Abelard. See pp. 58-59 above.

5. See both the Matthean and Lukan accounts of Jesus' conception.

6. See my discussion of this in *Sexuality and the Black Church: A Womanist Perspective* (Maryknoll, N.Y.: Orbis Books, 1999), 116ff.

7. For more on the trinitarian settlement and the controversies leading to them—Docetism and Arianism—see Alister E. McGrath, *Historical Theology: An Introduction to the History of Christian Thought* (Malden, Mass.: Blackwell, 1998), 65ff.

8. For more on the concept of *perichoresis*, see ibid., 65ff.

9. For more on the Council of Nicaea, see Justo L. González, *The Story of Christianity,* volume 1, *The Early Church to the Dawn of the Reformation* (New York: Harper & Row, 1971).

10. See reference to Heyward in chapter 1, p. 6.

11. Note what is commonly referred to as the Prologue, John 1:1-18.

12. This conference, sponsored by the World Council of Churches (WCC), took place in Minneapolis, Minnesota (November 4-7). It was an ecumenical international gathering of women participating in the WCC's ecumenical debate in solidarity with women. This particular quotation comes from a session entitled "Re-Imagining Jesus" held on November 5 of that conference.

13. Remarks in session entitled "Re-Imagining Jesus."

14. See Delores Williams's identification of black oppression as a demonarchy in "The Color of Feminism," *Christianity and Crisis*, April 29, 1985, esp. 164-65.

15. Williams, *Sisters in the Wilderness: The Challenge of Womanist God-Talk* (Maryknoll, N.Y.: Orbis Books, 1993), 166.

16. Ibid., 165.

17. Ibid., 167.

18. JoAnne Marie Terrell, *Power in the Blood: The Cross in the African American Experience* (Maryknoll, N.Y.: Orbis Books, 1998), 120-21.

19. Ibid., 124-25.

20. Williams suggests that for black women to believe that human sin was overcome by Jesus' death on the cross as opposed to his ministerial vision for life belies their intelligence. See Williams, *Sisters in the Wilderness,* 165.

21. Terrell, *Power in the Blood,* 142, 124-25.

22. Ibid., 140.

23. See, e.g., James Cone, *The Spirituals and the Blues: An Interpretation* (New York: Seabury Press, 1972; reprint Maryknoll, N.Y.:Orbis

Books, 1991); Howard Thurman, *Deep River and the Negro Spiritual Speaks of Life and Death* (Richmond, Ind.: Friends United Press, 1975).

24. See, e.g., Gustavo Gutiérrez, *The Power of the Poor in History: Selected Writings,* trans. Robert R. Barr (Maryknoll, N.Y.: Orbis Books, 1983).

25. René Girard, *I See Satan Fall like Lightning* (Maryknoll, N.Y.: Orbis Books, 2001), 189.

26. Ibid., xix.

27. See p. 64 above.

28. "The Son of God" was originally published in *Crisis* (1933), and "The Gospel According to Mary Brown" in *Crisis* (1919). They are reprinted in *Du Bois on Religion,* ed. Phil Zuckerman (Walnut Creek, Calif.: AltaMira Press, 2000), 181-85 and 143-46, respectively.

29. This and other citations from "Gospel According to Mary Brown," in *Du Bois on Religion,* 145.

4. Christian Theology and White Ideology

1. Quoted in Ida B. Wells, *Crusade for Justice: The Autobiography of Ida B. Wells,* ed. Alfreda M. Duster (Chicago: University of Chicago Press, 1970), 65-66.

2. Ibid., 71.

3. W. E. B. Du Bois, *The Crisis* (1932) reprinted in *W.E.B. Du Bois: A Reader,* ed. David Levering Lewis (New York: Henry Holt and Company, 1995), 478.

4. Wells, *Crusade for Justice,* 154-55.

5. W. E. B. Du Bois, *Darkwater: Voices from within the Veil* (1920; reprinted with introduction by David Levering Lewis, New York: Washington Square Press, 2004), 26.

6. I have discussed the advent and nuances of white culture more fully in *Sexuality and the Black Church: A Womanist Perspective* (Maryknoll, N.Y.: Orbis Books, 1999), 113-19.

7. For a good discussion of the social and racial activism spawned within the evangelical tradition, see Ralph E. Luker, *The Social Gospel in Black and White: American Racial Reform, 1885-1912* (Chapel Hill: University of North Carolina Press, 1991).

8. See discussion of this in chapter 3 above, pp. 81ff.

9. Forrest G. Wood, *The Arrogance of Faith: Christianity and Race in America from the Colonial Era to the Twentieth Century* (New York: Alfred A. Knopf, 1990), 238.

10. Reference taken from Mason Stokes, *The Color of Sex: Whiteness,*

234 NOTES TO CHAPTER 4

Heterosexuality, and the Fictions of White Supremacy (Durham, N.C.: Duke University Press, 2001), 83.

11. For more on Christianity and slavery, see H. Shelton Smith, *In His Image But: Racism in Southern Religion 1780-1910* (Durham, N.C.: Duke University Press, 1972); Albert Raboteau, *Slave Religion: The "Invisible Institution" in the Antebellum South* (New York: Oxford University Press, 1978); Kelly Brown Douglas, *The Black Christ*, Bishop Henry McNeal Turner/Sojourner Truth Series in Black Religion (Maryknoll, N.Y.: Orbis Books, 1994), esp. chapter 1; and Wood, *Arrogance of Faith.*

12. Winthrop D. Jordan, *White over Black: American Attitudes Toward the Negro, 1550-1812* (Chapel Hill: University of North Carolina Press, 1968; reprint, New York: W. W. Norton, 1977), 429.

13. Thomas Jefferson, "Notes on the State of Virginia," in *The Life and Selected Writings of Thomas Jefferson*, ed. Adrienne Koch and William Peden (New York: Modern Library, 1998), 258. Here Jefferson says, "Indeed, I tremble for my country when I reflect that God is just. . . ."

14. Ibid., 238, 239.

15. Ibid., 239-40.

16. Ibid., 242, 243, 239 (emphasis mine).

17. Jordan, *White over Black*, 455.

18. Naomi Zack, "The American Sexualization of Race," in *Race/Sex: Their Sameness, Difference and Interplay*, ed. Naomi Zack (New York: Routledge, 1997), 150.

19. See, e.g., *Sexuality and the Black Church;* and Jordan, *White over Black.*

20. Immanuel Kant, "What Is Enlightenment?" (1784), in *The Portable Enlightenment Reader*, ed. Isaac Kramnick (New York: Penguin Books, 1995), 1.

21. John Locke, *An Essay Concerning Human Understanding*, ed. Peter H. Nidditch (Oxford: Clarendon Press, 1975), 704, book IV.19, 20.

22. It is interesting to note Charles W. Mills's argument concerning the development of a "racial contract." He suggests that it was during this period that a "racial contract" began to fully evolve in Europe and America. This contract of course was in large measure based on "eurocentric" norms of rationality, thus allowing for "non-europeans" to be cateogorized as non-persons (*The Racial Contract* [Ithaca, N.Y.: Cornell University Press, 1997]).

23. Peter Gay, *The Enlightenment: An Interpretation*, vol. 2, *the Science of Freedom* (New York: W. W. Norton, 1969), 560.

24. Locke, *Essay Concerning Human Understanding*, 105, book II.1.3.

25. Ibid., 105, 108, book II.I.4, 8.

26. For a thorough and succinct presentation of Jefferson's views concerning black people and the controversy they created, see Jordan, *White over Black*, chapter 12, pp. 429-81. My own interpretation of Jefferson has been greatly enriched by this discussion.

27. Locke, *Essay Concerning Human Understanding*, 43, book I.1.1. It should be noted that Locke's belief in the natural freedom and equality of all individuals prompted him to believe that slavery was "vile" and ought not be practiced. He wrote that the "natural liberty" of individuals precluded them from becoming subject to any other man. Thus, that Locke's ideas concerning speculation and reflection could be taken to support the enslavement of black people perhaps contradicts his own beliefs. At the same time, however, it must be kept in mind that when Locke spoke of the individual he meant free, propertied men. See Locke, "The Second Treatise of Civil Government," in *Portable Enlightenment Reader*, 396f. Moreover, his beliefs did not preclude his own involvement in the slave-trading industry. See Gay, *Enlightenment*, 409-10.

28. Frederick Douglass, "The Claims of the Negro Ethnologically Considered: An Address Before the Literary Societies of Western Reserve College at Commencement, July 12, 1850" (Library of Congress: The Frederick Douglass Papers internet access Manuscript Division, http://memory.loc.gove/amem/doughtml/doughome.html 9.

29. For more on these specious sciences in terms of racism, see George M. Fredrickson, *The Black Image in the White Mind: The Debate on Afro-American Character and Destiny, 1817-1914* (1971; reprint with introduction, Middletown, Conn.: Wesleyan University Press, 1987), esp. chapter 3, "Science, Polygenesis and the Proslavery Argument."

30. Jordan, *White over Black*, 284.

31. See pp. 113-14 above.

32. Jefferson, "Notes on the State of Virginia," 240.

33. This characterization is taken from *Portable Enlightenment Reader*, xii.

34. Gay, *Enlightenment*, 2:174.

35. Kant, "What Is Enlightenment?" 5.

36. This characterization is taken from *Portable Enlightenment Reader*, xii.

37. Locke, *Essay Concerning Human Understanding*, 619, 621, book IV.10.1, 6.

38. Martin Marty, *Pilgrims in Their Own Land: 500 Years of Religion in America* (New York: Penguin Books, 1984), 155.

39. See Marty's characterization of the religion needed for this time of Enlightenment in ibid., 157.

40. Benjamin Franklin, "Something of My Religion . . .," in *Portable Enlightenment Reader*, 166, 167.

41. See Jefferson, "Notes on the State of Virginia," 255ff. The reference to the Trinity as "gibberish" is taken from Marty, *Pilgrims in Their Own Land*, 160.

42. See Thomas Jefferson, "Syllabus of an Estimate of the Doctrine of Jesus, Compared with Those of Others," in *Portable Enlightenment Reader*, 164-65.

43. See, e.g., Peter Gay's interpretation, *Enlightenment*, vol. 2, esp. chapter 3, "The Spirit of the Age."

44. Quoted in Wood, *Arrogance of Faith*, 99. Wood also notes that as Harvard professor Louis Agassiz put forth these views before a Literary Society of Charleston in 1847 many of the listeners were "surprised and dismayed."

45. Jefferson, "Notes on the State of Virginia," 194.

46. William J. Wilson, "What Shall We Do with the White People?" (1860), quoted in Stokes, *Color of Sex*, 85. I am indebted to Mason Stokes's interpretation of this anti-black literature and the response to it in my own rendering and appreciation of the interaction between science and religion on the matter of race.

47. Frederick Douglass, "Claims of the Negro Ethnologically Considered," 20.

48. Ariel, *The Negro: What Is His Ethnological Status?* (Cincinnati: Published by the Proprietor, 1967). See Web site of Library of Congress: The African American Pamphlet Collection, 1824-1909, 3.

49. Ibid., 4. Payne a.k.a. Ariel speaks of the difference between the "white and black race."

50. Ibid., 21, 23, 44.

51. Charles Carroll, *The Negro a Beast* (1901; reprint, New York: Books for Libraries Press, 1980), 10.

52. Ibid., 11.

53. For illustration and captions, see ibid., 8. It should be noted that Carroll includes numerous illustrations throughout both books in his effort to reinforce his position of religious racism.

54. Carroll, *Negro a Beast*, 116.

55. Ibid., 339. The motivating force of Carroll's argument is to show how "the amalgamation between Whites and Negroes is 'a violation of natural law" (p. 116).

56. My understanding of *The Tempter of Eve* is significantly informed by Mason Stokes's rendering of this text in his essay "Someone's in the

Garden with Eve: Race, Religion, and the American Fall," in his *Color of Sex;* quotation from p. 97.

57. Not only did Buckner Payne's 1867 publication, *The Negro: What Is His Ethnological Status?* put forth a similar argument, but so too did William Campbell's *Anthropology for the People: A Refutation of the Theory of Adamic Race Origin of All Races, by a Caucasian* (1891); and Alexander Harvey Shannon's *Racial Integrity and Other Features of the Negro Population* (1907). For a thorough overview and discussion of the significant literature characteristic of religious racism see Wood, *Arrogance of Faith.*

58. W. S. Armistead, *The Negro Is A Man: A Reply To Professor Charles Carroll's Book "The Negro Is a Beast or In the Image of God"* (Tifton, Ga.: Armistead & Vickers, 1903).

59. Stokes, *Color of Sex*, 96.

60. In his aforementioned 1850 commencement address at Western Reserve College, Douglass commented that the 1839 publication of Dr. Samuel George Morton that argued for black people's inferiority on the basis of brain size and shape was "widely read in the country" (p. 16).

61. D. G. Hart, *That Old-Time Religion in Modern America: Evangelical Protestantism in the Twentieth Century* (Chicago: Ivan R. Dee Publisher, 2002), 6.

62. William Martin, *With God on Our Side: The Rise of the Religious Right in America* (New York: Broadway Books, 1996), 4.

63. Marty, *Pilgrims in Their Own Land*, 108.

64. See Wood's discussion of Finney in *Arrogance of Faith.*

65. Martin, *With God on Our Side*, 4.

66. Quoted in Marty, *Pilgrims in Their Own Land*, 117-18.

67. Ibid., 111.

68. Ibid., 110.

69. Ibid., 113.

70. Jonathan Edwards, "The Distinguishing Marks of a Work of the Spirit of God," in *Sermons in American History: Selected Issues in the American Pulpit 1630-1967,* ed. Dewitte Holland (Nashville: Abingdon Press, 1971), 88.

71. Ibid., 88-89.

72. George Whitefield, "Marks of A True Conversion," Sermon 23, www.reformed.org/documents/whitefield.html.

73. Referred to in Wood, *Arrogance of Faith*, 194.

74. Ibid.

75. Jonathan Edwards, "The Heinous Sin of Drunkenness," Sermon 52, www.reformed.org/documents/whitefield.html.

76. Jonathan Edwards, "Divine and Supernatural Light," in *Ameri-*

can Sermons: Pilgrims to Martin Luther King, Jr. (New York: Library of America, 1999), 328.

77. Referred to in Marty, *Pilgrims in their Own Land*, 114.

78. Ibid., 109.

79. *Portable Enlightenment Reader*, xv. I am beholden to the interpretation of the Enlightenment emphasis on individualism and the importance of Descartes as presented in the *Portable Enlightenment Reader*, xvff.

80. John Locke, "A Letter Concerning Toleration," in *Portable Enlightenment Reader*, 83.

81. Hart, *That Old-Time Religion in Modern America*, 10f.

82. From George Whitefield's journals, quoted in Smith, *In His Image But*, 12.

83. Whitefield quoted in Michael O. Emerson and Christian Smith, *Divided by Faith: Evangelical Religions and the Problem of Race in America* (New York: Oxford University Press, 2000), 26.

84. Jordan, *White over Black*, 215.

85. Ibid., 215.

86. Cotton Mather, "The Wonders of the Invisible World: Observations as well Historical and Theological, upon the Nature, the Number, and the Operations of the DEVILS," in *American Sermons*, 196.

87. Hart, *That Old-Time Religion in Modern America*, 9.

88. See discussion of sacrifice in chapter 2 above, pp. 56-58.

89. See pp. 110-11 above.

90. Arthur F. Raper, *The Tragedy of Lynching* (Chapel Hill: University of North Carolina Press, 1933; reprint, Mineola, N.Y.: Dover, 2003), 23.

5. Black Bodies/White Souls

1. See *billie holiday lady in autumn: the best of the verve years,* compact disc, Polygram Records, Inc., 1991, disc 1, track 2.

2. Billie Holiday with William Dufty, *Lady Sings the Blues* (1956; reprinted with a revised discography, New York: Penguin Books, 1992), 65ff.

3. Ibid., 84.

4. For Baldwin's discussion of this movie, see his essay "Where the Grapes of Wrath are Stored," in *The Devil Finds Work* (New York: Delta Books, 1976), 103ff.

5. James Baldwin, "Down at the Cross: Letter from a Region in My Mind," in *The Fire Next Time* (1963; reprint, New York: First Vintage International Books, 1993), 30.

6. Studs Terkel Interview 1961, in *Conversations with James Baldwin*, ed. Fred L. Standley and Louis H. Pratt (Jackson: University Press of Mississippi, 1989), 5.

7. Ibid., 8-9.

8. For more on the emergence and significance of the "invisible institution" during slavery, see Albert Raboteau, *Slave Religion: The "Invisible Institution" in the Antebellum South* (New York: Oxford University Press, 1978).

9. For a more thorough discussion of attempts to Christianize the enslaved blacks as well as the bishop of London's exact response and an example of the statement converted slaves were required to sign, see Raboteau, *Slave Religion,* chapter 3.

10. It is important to note that West Africa was the origin of most enslaved blacks in America. In this regard, unless otherwise designated, when speaking of African traditions the focus is West Africa.

11. Albert Raboteau, *A Fire in the Bones: Reflections on African-American Religious History* (Boston: Beacon Press, 1995), 21.

12. Ibid., 21-22.

13. Peter J. Paris, *The Spirituality of African Peoples: The Search for a Common Moral Discourse* (Minneapolis: Augsburg Fortress Press, 1995), 132.

14. Winthrop D. Jordan, *White over Black: American Attitudes Toward the Negro, 1550-1812* (Chapel Hill: University of North Carolina Press, 1968; reprint, New York: W. W. Norton, 1977), 212.

15. Ibid., 213.

16. Charles Chauncy, *Seasonable Thoughts on the State of Religion in New England* (Boston, 1743), quoted in Jordan, *White over Black*, 212.

17. Charles Chauncy, *Enthusiasm Described and Cautioned Against* (Boston: J. Draper, 1742), in *Sermons in American History: Selected Issues in the American Pulpit 1630-1967*, ed. Dewitte Holland (New York: Abingdon Press, 1971), 113. It should also be noted that Chauncy believed that the Great Awakenings permitted women to move beyond their proper station.

18. The reader should again be reminded that in my discussions of black people's African heritage I am referring to West Africa unless otherwise designated, because it was in West Africa that most of the enslaved Africans were captured.

19. Paris, *Spirituality of African Peoples*, 30. I am indeed indebted to Peter Paris's precise and thorough discussion of African religions and theology for providing the substance of this particular presentation.

20. Ibid., 27.

21. Ibid., 42.

22. Jordan, *White over Black*, 214.

23. For a discussion of the evangelical Protestant tradition and the issue of race from the Great Awakenings forward see Michael O. Emerson and Christian Smith, *Divided by Faith: Evangelical Religion and the Problem of Race in America* (New York: Oxford University Press, 2000).

24. Because I have elaborated on this in other places I will not do so here. For more detailed discussion of how black people approach the biblical witness, see essays in *Stony the Road We Trod: African American Biblical Interpretation,* ed. Cain Hope Felder (Minneapolis: Fortress Press, 1991).

25. 2001 statistics provided by research done by The Barna Group found on Web page http://www.barna.org/FlexPage.aspx.

26. Paris, *Spirituality of African Peoples*, 132.

27. Maria W. Stewart, "Religion and the Pure Principles of Morality: The Sure Foundation On Which We Must Build" (1831), in *Maria W. Stewart: America's First Black Woman Political Writer, Essays and Speeches* ed. Marilyn Richardson (Bloomington: Indiana University Press, 1987), 29-30.

28. See *The Memphis Diary of Ida B. Wells: An Intimate Portrait of the Activist as a Young Woman,* ed. Miriam DeCosta-Willis (Boston: Beacon Press, 1995); see particularly her letters written under the pen name Iola.

29. Quoted in Philip Dray, *At the Hands of Persons Unknown: The Lynching of Black America* (New York: Random House, 2002), 55.

30. Studs Terkel Interview 1961, in *Conversations with James Baldwin,* 8-9.

31. This discussion focuses on Baldwin's first novel, *Go Tell It on the Mountain,* because it provides a comprehensive fictionalized autobiographical look into the black faith tradition especially as it impacts the black body. As it does this, it sets the stage for how he explores this issue in later works. Examination of those later works goes beyond the scope of this discussion. For a fine comprehensive study of Baldwin's views on the black faith tradition as expressed in his literary corpus, see Clarence Hardy III, *James Baldwin's God: Sex, Hope, and Crisis in Black Holiness Culture* (Knoxville: University of Tennessee Press, 2003).

32. James Baldwin, *Go Tell It on The Mountain* (1952; New York: Modern Library Edition, 1995), 86-87.

33. Paraphrase from James Baldwin, "Who Saw Him Die? I, Said the Fly," in *Devil Finds Work,* 71.

34. See discussion in chapter 4 above, p. 131.

35. Linda Brent, *Incidents in the Life of a Slave Girl* (1861), in *The Classic Slave Narratives,* ed. Henry Louis Gates, Jr. (New York: Penguin

Books, 1987), 386-87. It should be noted that Linda Brent was the pseudonym for Harriet Jacobs.

36. Traci C. West, *Wounds of the Spirit: Black Women, Violence, and Resistance Ethics* (New York: New York University Press, 1999), 67.

37. I first spoke of a *spirituality of resistance* in *The Black Christ*, Bishop Henry McNeal Turner/Sojourner Truth Series in Black Religion (Maryknoll, N.Y.: Orbis Books, 1994). There I argued that "if Black people have a pride in their own cultural and historical heritage, as well as a knowledge that they are children of God, then they will not be as vulnerable to the oppressive structures, systems and ideologies that attempt to convince them that they are nobody and their lives are not worth living." I have since discerned another important aspect of this spirituality of resistance that involves black peoples' agency over their sexuality.

38. Marla F. Frederick, *Between Sundays: Black Women and Everyday Struggles of Faith* (Berkeley and Los Angeles: University of California Press, 2003), 186.

39. Baldwin, *Go Tell It on the Mountain*, 120.

40. Brent, *Incidents in the Life of a Slave Girl*, 389.

41. West, *Wounds of the Spirit*, 74.

42. Baldwin, *Go Tell It on the Mountain*, 135.

43. One should be reminded that while sexuality certainly involves more than intimate interactions, given the manner in which platonized Christianity tends to essentialize it as intimate interactions, this is what is intended when referred to in this text unless otherwise indicated.

44. *Presbyterians and Human Sexuality 1991* (Louisville: Presbyterian Church [U.S.A.], 1991), 1.

45. Baldwin, *Go Tell It on the Mountain*, 161.

46. James Baldwin, *The Amen Corner* (New York: Dial Press, 1968; reprint, New York: First Vintage International Books, 1998), 59-60.

47. Frederick, *Between Sundays*, 190.

48. Ibid., 194.

49. Baldwin, *Go Tell It on the Mountain*, 23.

50. James Baldwin, "Down at the Cross: Letter from a Region in My Mind," in *Fire Next Time*, 20.

51. Baldwin, *Go Tell It on the Mountain*, 27-28.

52. James Baldwin, "My Dungeon Shook: Letter to My Nephew on the One Hundredth Anniversary of the Emancipation," in *Fire Next Time*, 4.

53. See p. 143 above.

54. See pp. 90ff.

55. Baldwin, "Who Saw Him Die? I, Said the Fly," 59.

56. Baldwin, *Go Tell It on the Mountain*, 54.

57. Ibid., 144.
58. Ibid., 190.
59. For a succinct definition of patriarchy, see *Dictionary of Feminist Theologies*, ed. Letty M. Russell and J. Shannon Clarkson (Louisville: Westminster John Knox, 1996), 205f.
60. West, *Wounds of the Spirit*, 111.
61. See pp. 67-68 above.
62. West, *Wounds of the Spirit*, 111 (emphasis mine).
63. Cheryl Townsend Gilkes, "The 'Loves' and 'Troubles' of African-American Women's Bodies: The Womanist Challenge to Cultural Humiliation and Community Ambivalence," in *A Troubling in My Soul: Womanist Perspectives on Evil and Suffering*, ed. Emilie M. Townes (Maryknoll, N.Y.: Orbis Books, 1993), 235.
64. Toinette Eugene, "While Love Is Unfashionable: Ethical Implications of Black Spirituality and Sexuality," in *Sexuality and the Sacred: Sources for Theological Reflection*, ed. James B. Nelson and Sandra P. Longfellow (Louisville: Westminster John Knox, 1994), 109.
65. See Delores S. Williams, "African-American Women in Three Contexts of Domestic Violence," in *Violence Against Women, Concilium*, ed. Elisabeth Schüssler Fiorenza and M. Shawn Copeland (Maryknoll, N.Y.: Orbis Books, 1994), 34-43.
66. West, *Wounds of the Spirit*, 6.
67. Marcia Y. Riggs, *Plenty Good Room: Women versus Male Power in the Black Church* (Cleveland: Pilgrim Press, 2003), 86.
68. Ibid., 71-74.
69. These observations are a compilation of numerous conversations I have had with black women throughout the twenty-one years of my ordained ministry as I have preached, lectured, and/or conducted workshops at numerous black churches.
70. Frances E. Wood, "Take My Yoke upon You': The Role of the Church in the Oppression of African-American Women," in *A Troubling in My Soul*, 40.
71. Ibid., 40.
72. West, *Wounds of the Spirit*, 199.
73. Baldwin, *Go Tell It on the Mountain*, 14.
74. Ibid., 62.
75. J. L. King with Karen Hunter, *On the Down Low: A Journey into the Lives of "Straight" Black Men Who Sleep with Men* (New York: Broadway Books, 2004), 20.
76. Benoit Denizet-Lewis, "Double Lives on the Down Low," in *New York Times Magazine*, August 3, 2003, 30.
77. King with Hunter, *On the Down Low*, 20.

78. Ibid., 27.

79. Zondra Hughes, "Why Sisters Are the No. 1 Victims of HIV," in *Ebony Magazine,* July 2004, 64.

80. For data on HIV/AIDs in the black community, see the Center for Disease Control Web site, www.CDC.gov/hiv/pubs/facts/afam.htm.

81. See Mindy Thompson Fullilove and Robert E. Fullilove III, "Stigma as an Obstacle to AIDS Action: The Case of the African American Community," in *American Behavorial Scientist* 42 (1999): 1117-29.

82. Denizet-Lewis, "Double Lives on the Down Low," 30.

83. Ibid.

6. Black Faith Reexamined

1. W. E. B. Du Bois, *The Souls of Black Folk,* with an introduction by Arnold Rampersad (New York: Alfred A. Knopf, 1976; first published 1903), 160.

2. This discussion of core theological themes within the black faith tradition and the discussion to follow on contingent claims draws on an article I coauthored with Ronald E. Hopson, "Understanding the Black Church: The Dynamics of Change," *Journal of Religious Thought* 56, no. 2; and 57, no. 1 (2000-2001): 95-113.

3. James H. Cone, "Calling the Oppressors to Account: Justice, Love and Hope in Black Religion," in *The Courage to Hope: From Black Suffering to Human Redemption,* ed. Quinton Hosford Dixie and Cornel West (Boston: Beacon Press, 1999), 75.

4. Reprinted in *Call and Response: The Riverside Anthology of the African American Literary Tradition,* general editor Patricia Liggins Hall (Boston: Houghton Mifflin, 1998), 47.

5. See Karl Barth, *Church Dogmatics,* ed. G. W. Bromiley and T. F. Torrance (Edinburgh: T & T Clark, 1975); vol. 1, part 1, 2nd ed., pp. 6ff.

6. See my comprehensive discussion of this in *Sexuality and the Black Church: A Womanist Perspective* (Maryknoll, N.Y.: Orbis Books, 1999).

7. "Is Gay Rights a Civil Rights Issue: Leaders Debate Same-Sex Marriages and Gay and Lesbian Rights," *Ebony Magazine,* July 2004, 144.

8. Ibid., 144 and 146.

9. Quoted by Keith Boykin in "Why the Black Church Opposes Gay Marriage: Whose Dream?" *The Villiage Voice Features,* May 24, 2004, http://www.Villagevoice.com/news/0421,boykin,5375.

10. See, e.g., Naomi Zack "The American Sexualization of Race," in

Race/Sex: Their Sameness, Difference, and Interplay, ed. Naomi Zack (New York: Routledge, 1997).

11. "Is Gay Rights a Civil Rights Issue," 144.

12. See, e.g., Frederick Douglass's critique of white Christianity in "Slaveholding Religion and the Christianity of Christ," in *Afro-American Religious History,* ed. Milton Sernett (Durham, N.C.: Duke University Press, 1985), 100-109.

13. W. E. B. Du Bois, "Religion in the South," in *Du Bois on Religion,* ed. Phil Zuckerman (Walnut Creek, Calif.: Alta Mira, 2000), 85.

A Womanist's Postscript: How Can I Be a Christian?

1. Kelly Brown Douglas, *The Black Christ,* Bishop Henry McNeal Turner/Sojourner Truth Series in Black Religion (Maryknoll, N.Y.: Orbis Books, 1994), 117.

Index

250   INDEX

Kant, Immanuel
    and motto of Enlightenment,
        115
    on religion, 120

Locke, John
    on reason and Christianity, 120-
        21, 141
    on reason as authority, 116
    on slavery, 235n. 27
lynching, 4-6
    Christianity's complicity in, xvi,
        4-5, 9, 109-10
    cross and, 61-70
    and fundamentalist religion of
        South, 65-66
    as historical-cultural paradigm,
        xv
    as human sacrifice, 72
    of John Henry Williams, 71-73
    of Richard Coleman, 3
    of Sam Hose, 4-5, 71-74
    as saving white souls, 147
    and sexuality, 67

Martin, William: on Great Revival,
    135
Marty, Martin
    on Christianity and reason, 121
    on evangelical conversion, 140
Mather, Cotton, 138, 144
McKay, Claude: on lynching, 63
Mills, Charles W.: racial contract
    of, 234n. 22
monotheism
    closed, xv, 10-16; Christianity
        as, 104; and dualism, 21;
        and oppression, 46; and
        power, 42-50; rejecting
        other gods and religions, 21
    and evil, 224n. 20

Nicaea, Council of, 17, 79-80
Nicene Creed, 44, 53-54, 80
Nott, Josiah, 125

Pagels, Elaine
    on monotheism, 14-15
    on Paul's celibacy, 33
paradox
    christological, 16-21
    existential, 82; of Jesus, 83;
        Jesus as, 88
    ontological, 84
    versus dualism, 19-21
Paris, Peter: on African theological
    heritage, 157, 160-61
patriarchy: and sexualization of vic-
    tims, 187-88
Patterson, Orlando
    on fundamentalist religion of
        South, 65-66
    on lynching, 147
    on Pauline Christianity, 6
Paul
    influence of, on Augustine, 35
    influence of Hellenistic culture
        on, 24
    and platonized Christian tradi-
        tion, 30-38, 141-42
    teachings of, concerning sexual-
        ity, 30-38
Payne, Buckner [Ariel]: on black
    people as beasts, 129-30
perichoresis, 77-78
Philo, 23-24
philosophy
    Greek, 23-38
    Stoic, 23-24; influence of, on
        Christianity, 25-29
    See also Platonic tradition